A
BIBLIOGRAPHY
OF
VOCATIONAL
EDUCATION

A
BIBLIOGRAPHY
OF
VOCATIONAL
EDUCATION

An Annotated Guide

by

FRANCESCO CORDASCO
Montclair State College

AMS Press
New York

All rights reserved. Published in the United States by AMS Press, Inc.,
56 East 13th Street, New York, New York 10003

Library of Congress Cataloging in Publication Data

Cordasco, Francesco, 1920-
   A bibliography of vocational education.

   Includes indexes.
   1. Vocational education – Bibliography. 2. Technical
education – Bibliography. I. Title.
Z5814.T4C63 [LC1043] Q16.37011'3   76-5961
ISBN 0-404-10125-9

Manufactured in the United States of America

TABLE OF CONTENTS

INTRODUCTION

There can be little doubt that vocational education is a major concern in American educational policy: the history of the concern with the vocational education of American youths extends far back into the nineteenth century. The very relationship between vocational education and the broad range of political issues which impinged on the development of an American educational system made inevitable the confrontation of a number of policy issues which American educational theorists faced.[1]

A decade ago, with the Johnsonian war on poverty launched, vocational education was envisaged as the broad base of educational change: in the rhetoric which characterized the heady enthusiasm of the period, I was not alone in anticipating dramatic developments. At that point in time the issues were, for me and my confrères, pellucidly clear:

---

1 See, for historical overview, Henry J. Perkinson, *The Imperfect Panacea: American Faith in Education, 1865-1965* (New York: Random House, 1968), particularly, Chapter IV: "Economic Opportunity and the Schools," pp. 103-159; also [James S. Coleman, Chairman] *Youth Transition to Adulthood: Report of the Panel on Youth of the President's Science Advisory Committee* (Washington: U.S. Government Printing Office, 1973). "Beginning with the Report of the Committee of Ten in the 1890s, running through the Cardinal Principles of Secondary Education of 1918, and continuing up to the present, a prolonged debate has taken place concerning the purpose and content of high school education. Advocates of education for 'social efficiency' have contended with spokesmen for vocational education, intellectual education, and life adjustment education. Behind the debate lies the explosion of the high school population, which put insupportable stress on older and more academic notions of secondary education, and the reality that teen-agers have lost many of their economic functions in our society, so that new goals and roles must be defined for them. Out of the debate has come the comprehensive high school which, with characteristic American ingenuity, has resolved the issues in favor of all parties by providing something for everyone." (*loc. cit.*, p. 27)

Vocational education will become the broad base of educational change, and it alone can afford the meaningful catalyst for this change; but vocational education in this sense must be understood to mean the preparation of our youngsters for all measures of true identity in American society. This means not only the technical skills and basic proficiencies, but all skills which have been dramatized in home economics education; expanding opportunity for women; family life education; cultivation in our young of a new sense of the dignity of work and achievement; a tremendous awareness of the needs of the community and of youth. It suggests a better guidance and counseling for our youngsters, and stipulates a dynamic relationship of what we do in the school with what we do in the community. Fundamentally, it must recognize that eighty percent of our youth will not go on to college, as colleges are presently structured, and I sincerely trust that, in this connection, those of us in higher education will energetically reform our own temple, and activate a community college concept which is basically attuned to the broad occupational orientation which will have dramatically begun under the public schools. I am not talking of social or educational utopias. It is a sociological truism that change takes place slowly, relentlessly with reference to needs; no institution can survive social unrelatedness: and the American school is no exception. Vast educational change is taking place in this country, and it is following the patterns already sketched. I call attention to the programs in Flint, Mich., or to those in New Haven, Conn. (among many), which clearly point up the adequacy of American educational leadership when it is joined with total community commitment. Basic to the innovative program is the meaningful occupational orientation that vocational education is affording. [2]

In the hindsight that a decade affords, sanguine optimism has been replaced by more cautious assessment. It is not that vocational education has become less important, or that the educational needs of American youth have been perceived as lying in other domains: on the contrary, education reform has been even more vigorously pursued; and vocational education has been strengthened and generously funded by the Congress. [3] The problems have lain elsewhere. In 1968 Professor Elizabeth M. Ray (in speaking to the future prospects for vocational education) circumspectly observed:

[2] F. Cordasco, "The Federal Challenge and Peril to the American School." *School & Society*, vol. 94 (Summer, 1966), pp. 264-265.

[3] See, generally, Rupert N. Evans, et al., *Education for Employment: The Background and Potential of the 1968 Vocational Education Amendments* (Ann Arbor: University of Michigan, Institute of Labor and Industrial Relations, 1969); and for the texts of the Vocational Education acts (1963; and 1968 amendments), see *A Compilation of Federal Education Laws As Amended Through December 31, 1974* (Washington: U.S. Government Printing Office, 1975, pp. 481-525.) S. 2657 (94th Congress 1st Session) which extends and further amends the Vocational Act of 1963 was introduced by Senator Claiborne Pell on November 12, 1975, *q.v.*

Despite the impression that the foundations of vocational education are firmer than at any time in its history, the Advisory Council on Vocational Education (1968) did not find much empirical evidence that programs had made significant gains since 1965 when provisions of the Vocational Education Act of 1963 went into effect. Although they were critical of leadership and administrative inadequacies during the period, they tended to be optimistic about the future and make recommendations which are seemingly designed to emphasize the need to deal aggressively with certain persistent problems. To this reviewer, the future status of vocational education appears to be contingent on at least two major considerations. First, the field of vocational education must itself respond to the demand for a quality product. The concept of an expanded role for vocational or occupational oriented objectives must be implemented. The initial phase of this new thrust must await the development of a viable model for the program and a marketable general and technical curriculum base. Degree of success will be related to the model curriculum's capacity to extend the teacher's role through utilization of technological resources and by strategic use of industry and the marketplace as the laboratory for vocational education. Particular attention must be given to the fact that when vocational programs expand, some other facet of the educational program must accommodate the expansion. Innovative proposals originating from well documented premises which have been fully supported by individuals in administrative and leadership positions must be sold to communities and schools. The second consideration is related to the observation that the framework for vocational education has tended to be, and is presently, more responsive to political and economic factors than to philosophical positions. If there is validity to the argument that vocational education belongs in the mainstream of education, then the justifications are social, psychological, and cultural. Vocational education for all can be affirmed by educational leaders at the national level as the look of the future. Thus one can propose that an educationally sound program of studies should include opportunities for every student, regardless of his ability or his educational aspirations, to develop a marketable skill of his choice before completing the twelfth grade.[4]

In the revisionist canons which have dominated American educational historiography in recent years, Professors Marvin Lazerson and W. Norton Grubb (in a prolegomenon to their centennial [1870-1970] documentary history, *American Education and Vocationalism*) have articulated the framework and defined the perspectives in which vocational education is to be understood:

---

[4] Elizabeth M. Ray, "Social and Philosophical Framework" [of Vocational, Technical, and Practical Arts Education], *Review of Educational Research*, vol. 38 (October 1968), 321-322.

In the four decades surrounding 1900, American's schools were thoroughly transformed. Fears for the socialization of the young led to a focus on family life and to new programs in early childhood education. Challenged to run their schools more efficiently and economically, schoolmen adopted business models of administration. The belief that schooling was necessary for proper moral development and economic growth accelerated the compulsory attendance movement and calls for more practical education. A society threatened by heterogeneity turned to schools for citizenship training and enlarged their social responsibilities. None of these developments were new; many simply extended, intensified, or moderately revised previous trends. Taken together, however, they radically changed the workings and functions of the educational system.

No development was more crucial to this reconstruction than vocational education. Vocationalism raised more explicitly than ever before questions about the purposes of schooling and the utility of various kinds of knowledge. It demanded that the school be closely integrated with economy, and that the school be the primary selecting agency for the occupational structure. Questions about the criteria of selection — who should be chosen to do what — made guidance and testing fundamental to the way schools functioned. In all this, vocationalism led to a reassessment of the meaning of democracy in education.

Issues such as these lie at the heart of this book. We do not answer all the questions raised. Nor do we cover all aspects of the vocational education movement — commercial education, home economics, and agricultural education are slighted. While we mention the ramifications of vocational education — vocational guidance, educational testing, the junior high school — they are not emphasized. Instead we have chosen to focus on the development of industrial and trade education, since this aspect of vocationalism in education proved to be the primary concern of the vocational education movement during its most important phase, the years from 1900 to 1917. In the period before 1900, many of the arguments for vocationalism were developed as part of the manual training movement, and we have viewed that movement both as an entity unto itself and as a transition to vocational education. And while vocationalism has changed since 1917, most of what has happened can be best understood as a reworking and consolidation of themes and practices established during the earlier periods.[5]

Although some modifications of the statements might be proposed (and serious objection registered to a set of paragraphs in which their conclusions

---

[5] Marvin Lazerson and W. Norton Grubb, eds., *American Education and Vocationalism: A Documentary History, 1870-1970* (New York: Teachers College Press, Columbia University, 1974), pp. 1-2.

are embodied),[6] the Lazerson/Grubb theme (*i.e.*, "And while vocationalism was changed since 1917, most of what has happened can be best understood as a working and consolidation of themes and practices established during the earlier period") remains unchallenged. The "reworking and consolidation of themes and practices established during the earlier period" are predicated on the availability of a convenient register of the enormous literature on vocational, industrial, manual, trade, and (if to a lesser extent) career education, generated since 1900: it is this need for a bibliographical apparatus and register that this book addresses.

A Bibliography of Vocational Education is intended as a dimensionally comprehensive guide to the literature on vocational, industrial, manual, trade, and career education. It covers the period from the early twentieth century to the close of 1975. Of course, the *Bibliography* is not a definitively complete register of all titles published in the period covered; not only would inclusive coverage prove impracticable, there remains a serious question as to the value of an inclusively complete register of titles. The *Bibliography* has, as its base, the consolidated lists represented in three invaluable registers issued by the United States Office of Education:

[United States Bureau of Education] Bulletin, 1913, No. 22. *Bibliography of Industrial, Vocational, and Trade Education.* Washington: Government Printing Office, 1913.

[United States Office of Education] *Vocational Education: An Annotated Bibliography of Selected References, 1917-1966.* Washington: Government Printing Office, 1967.

[United States Office of Education] *Vocational Education: Secondary and Post Secondary, 1967-1972: An Annotated Bibliography.* Washington: Government Printing Office, 1973.

---

6   "The continuity of the debates and the uncertainty over the impact of vocational education should not obscure the momentous impact vocationalism has had on America's schools. While its actual place in the curriculum has always been less than its advocates desired, and while it has invariably been accorded second class citizenship and has never enrolled more than a small percentage of the total school age population, vocational education has been a major force in the reconstruction of the American school. The nineteenth-century expansion of educational opportunity had been predicated on notions of commonality, the inculcation of moral values, and the expectation that knowledge broadly applied would enhance the industrial progress. At the turn of the century, however, an ideology emerged that demanded explicit ties between schooling and the occupational structure. The traditional emphasis on industriousness, thrift, and sobriety was supplemented by a commitment to instruction in job skills and to the categorization of youth by their future occupational roles. The trend was revealed by Helen and Robert Lynd in their study of Muncie, Indiana, during the mid-1920's: 'specific tool and skill activities in factory, home, and office' had become the most prominent feature of the city's high school. The president of Muncie's Board of Education congently summarized the importance of vocationalism when he declared: 'For a long time all boys were trained to be Pres-

Other references have served to expand the base that the consolidation of these *grundriss* compendia afforded, and these have been used freely to expand coverage through 1975.[7] The consolidation, expansion, and updating of the three federal registers provide the most comprehensive, currently available, guide to literature on vocational, industrial, manual, trade, and (as noted above, to a lesser extent) career education. In this sense, the *Bibliography* serves a

---

ident. Then for a while we trained them all to be professional men. Now we are training boys to get jobs.' The transformation in goals was accompanied by radical changes in the methodology of public education. Once the principle of preparation for economic roles was accepted, curricula and students had to be differentiated. Schools were now required to proivide a variety of 'relevant' courses and students had to be chosen for their particular roles. The former intensified pressure on the schools to respond to almost any real or fancied social need. The latter raised the serious question of who was to be chosen for which curriculum and how they were to be chosen. These issues gave powerful force to the evolving educational testing, guidance, and junior high school movements, all of which seemed to provide more opportunities for choice, greater objectivity in selection, and more individualized *and* more efficient methods of running the schools. Seeking to resolve the problem of how to absorb the 'children of the plain people' flooding secondary education after 1890, vocationalism and its spinoffs established a new definition of equality of educational opportunity which focused on the 'evident and probable destinies' of youth, and which furnished the justification for mechanisms tending to segregate pupils by class. The impact of vocationalism also revealed the extent to which American education had accepted the ethics of the merging corporate order. Vocational education was part of a braoder rationalization of the schools, which included specialization of function, cost accounting, research and testing departments, and development of a science of administration. The ideal school system had come to be modeled after the modern corporation, both in its hierarchical and bureaucratic organization and in its purpose; students were raw materials to be processed in an efficiently run plant, and the criterion of success was the price the finished product could bring in the market place. Hence the enthusiastic acceptance of vocational education into the public schools, despite its contradiction of earlier ideals, paralleled the enthusiastic acceptance by educators of the industrial order. With the vocational education movement, educators saw their role as serving the industrial order and adapting students to its requirements. Economic criteria had become a primary force in educational decision-making." (Lazerson and Grubb, pp. 48-50)

7   Other sources used include *Abstracts of Research and Related Material in Vocational and Technical Education* [ARM]. No. 1, 1967 — (Columbus: ERIC Clearinghouse, Center for Vocational and Technical Education; Ohio State University. Quarterly); *Abstracts of Instructional Materials in Vocational and Technical Education* (1967 —); "Vocational, Technical, and Practical Arts Education," *Review of Educational Research,* vol. 38 (October 1968), pp. 305-442; also *Ibid.,* vol. 32 (October 1962), and *Ibid.,* vol. 26 (October 1956); Edwin G. York, *A Compilation of Resource Lists for Vocational Education: An Annotated Bibliography of Bibliographies in Vocational Education, 1960-1969* Trenton, N. J. :Bureau of Occupational Research Development, Department of Education, 1969); and Francesco Cordasco and William W. Brickman, eds., *A Bibliography of American Educational History* (New York: AMS Press, 1975).

clear need at a time when vocational education (and its related components) have assumed a critical and compelling importance; in all, some 2,500 entries are included, with fully articulated subject and name/author indexes. The annotations for the entries in each of these three basic lists have been retained as they were originally written. Despite the awkwardness of some of the language (and its patent incongruity with contemporary usage), to have rewritten the annotations would have violated the historical value of the annotations which afford insights into the assessments which particular time periods have made; and this is particularly apparent in the annotations for the 1913 compilation.

The emergence of a new public policy for work and education is nowhere more clear than in the recently published *The Boundless Resource: A Prospectus for an Education-Work Policy* by former Secretary of Labor Willard Wirtz and the National Manpower Institute. This comprehensive two-year study of the gap between education and work and on the need to integrate both provides a sharp challenge to the traditional scenario of education, work and then retirement, and offers concrete proposals for establishing "a lifetime continuum of education and work opportunity" in America. The challenge is eloquently addressed in *The Boundless Resource:*

> To look hopefully but hard beyond the next five years in the development of an education-work policy for America is to recognize that its future depends on a broader course of events. At the same time, what we do during the next five years can be a key element in the shaping of that future. Everything in this prospectus for such a policy has been shaped to what appear to be the four critical elements in a return in this country to a Politics of Idealism.
>
> First, the American people today are deeply skeptical about any grandiose representation. They have been oversold for too many years on too many grand initiatives. They have become incredulous about everything they are told and everybody who makes any new promise or proposal. The first demand on policy today is that it be totally *credible.*
>
> This education-work policy — identified deliberately in a bland phrase, no acronym possible — has been set out, accordingly, in spare and disciplined terms of particulars that are clearly do-able, assuming only the most reasonable diligence.
>
> Second, people are willing to consider only what they can be shown the results of and what they are satisfied they can pay for. The second demand on policy today is *fiscal responsibility.* This is the reason for emphasizing so strongly here the mundane and undramatic subject of measurements and evaluation. It is the reason, too, for identifying the importance of contributing through the fuller development and use of the human resource — which is what the coordination of education and work is all about — to the revitalization of the idea of growth unlimited for the nation.

Third, people in this country today want very much to start thinking again in terms of human values rather than just about a Gross National Product. The third demand on policy today is that we speak to the *quality of life*. An education-work policy *will* improve the prosspect of a higher and better use of the life experience at the stage called youth but equally across its broader course. There *is* a human desire to break out of the time traps of youth for learning, midlife for earning, older age for obsolescence. Education and work *are* human values.

Finally, today, people in every American community and every walk of life feel left out— that they don't count. They want back into their own affairs. Representation, at least through the established channels, isn't enough. The fourth demand on policy today is that it provide the opportunity for *participation*.

This is the reason for pressing so strongly here for the development of citizens involvement processes, particularly at the local community level. An education-work policy offers superior opportunity to return to a Politics of Idealism in America.[8]

It is hoped that the *Bibliography* will serve as a compendious resource for sharpening the perspectives' in which these contemporary educational needs and challenges will have to assessed. — **Francesco Cordasco**

8 Willard Wirtz, *The Boundless Resource: A Prospectus for An Education-Work Policy* (Washington; New Republic Book Company, 1975), pp. 184-185.

A
BIBLIOGRAPHY
OF
VOCATIONAL
EDUCATION

I. BOOKS, MONOGRAPHS, AND MISCELLANEA

Abramov, I. V. *Les Ecoles du Dimanche en Russie* . . . Paris, O. Delagrave [1900?]. 44 pp.

Abstracts of Research and Related Materials in Vocational and Technical Education (ARM). No. 1 --, 1967 --. Columbus: ERIC Clearinghouse, Center for Vocational and Technical Education, Ohio State University.
Quarterly. Complete bibliographical information and abstracts of each document (200 words or less). Yearly cumulation. See also, *Abstracts of Instructional Materials in Vocational and Technical Education* (1967 --).

Adams, Thomas S. and Helen L. Sumner. *Labor Problems.* New York, Macmillan Company, 1905. xv, 579 pp.
Bibliography: p. 15-15. Industrial education is treated in Chapter XI. Author notes the decline of the apprenticeship system, its causes, and present status. Also discusses the provisions for trade, technical and art schools and the problems involved.

Addams, Jane. *Democracy and Social Ethics.* New York, Macmillan Company, 1905. 281 pp.
Chapter VI (Educational methods) discusses the educational needs of an industrial democracy. Notes the failure of the present schools to prepare for industrial life. Author says that they are largely ruled by the traditions of class and commercial education.

Aerospace Education Foundation. *Vocational Instruction Systems of the Air Force Applied to Civilian Education.* New York, Praeger, 1971. 128 pp.
Experimental methods of vocational education used in Utah schools.

Alexander, Magnus W. *The Training of Men—a Necessary Part of a Modern Factory System.* [New York, 1910] pp. [33]-49.
Reprint from the *Journal of the American Society of Mechanical Engineers* [January 1910].

American Academy of Political and Social Science, Philadelphia. *Industrial Education*. Philadelphia, American Academy of Political and Social Science, 1909. iii, 224 pp. (The Annals of the American Academy of Political and Social Science. vol. xxxiii, no. 1)

Contents. — Relation of industrial education to national progress [by] B. T. Washington. — The work of the National society for the promotion of industrial education [by] C. D. Wright. — Vocational training and trade teaching in the public schools [by] J. P. Haney. — Elementary trade teaching [by] C. H. Morse. — The secondary industrial school of Columbus, Georgia [by] C. B. Gibson. — Partial time trade schools [by] H. Schneider. — Public evening schools of trades [by] C. F. Warner. — The short course trade school [by] J. E. G. Yalden. — The Milwaukee school of trades [by] C. F. Perry. — The Philadelphia trades school [by] W. C. Ash. — The Manila trade school [by] J. J. Eaton. — Technical education at the Polytechnic institute, Brooklyn [by] F. W. Atkinson. — The work of the Pennsylvania museum and school of industrial art [by] L. W. Miller. — The Berean school of Philadelphia and the industrial efficiency of the negro [by] M. Anderson. — The industrial training of women [by] Florence M. Marshall. — The relative value and cost of various trades in a girls' trade school [by] Mary S. Woolman. — The apprenticeship system of the General Electric Company at West Lynn, Massachusetts [by] M. W. Alexander. — The John Wanamaker commercial institute — a store school [by] J. Wanamaker. — Trade teaching in the boot and shoe industry [by] A. D. Dean. — The apprentice system on the New York Central Lines [by] C. W. Cross. — Apprenticeship system at the Baldwin locomotive works, Philadelphia [by] N. W. Sample. — Trade teaching under the auspices of the Typographical union [by] W. B. Prescott. — The position of labor unions regarding industrial education [by] J. Golden. — Book Department.

American Association of School Administrators. *Educational Administration in a Changing Community. Thirty-seventh Yearbook*. Washington, The Association, a Department of the National Education Association, 1959. 221 pp.

A summary of the research on community structures and techniques. A guide for studying the community as a preface to planning and operating effective educational programs, including an effective vocational education program.

American Enterprise Institute. *Legislative Analysis: the Youth Employment Bill, S. 1, H. R. 1890*. Washington, 1963. 21 pp. (88th Cong., 1st sess., AEI report, No. 2, Mar. 14, 1963.)

An analysis of the historical background of this proposal. A summary of the bill's provisions and the importance of the issues concerning unemployed youth.

American Federation of Labor. *Industrial Education. Consisting of an Investigation and Report by a Competent Special Committee; Reports of Officers and Committees; Action of A. F. of L. Convention; the Attitude of Organized Labor and Others toward the Problem; a Glossary of Definitions, etc.; Labor's Bill for Congressional Enactment.* 1st ed. Washington, American Federation òf Làbor, 1910. 69 pp.

A brief summary of the entire field of industrial education, with particular emphasis on the attitude of organized labor toward the problem, in foreign countries and in the United States. Describes apprenticeship schools, legislation, etc.

Report warns against the exploitation of boys who desire to become skilled craftsmen.

"A proper apprenticeship system which will guarantee to the youth the opportunity of learning his trade as a whole is very much desired.

"One of the disadvantages of many apprenticeship systems is that establishments have become so large and with so many departments with their divisions and subdivisions and processes that the time of the boy is fully employed in mastering details of one department to the exclusion of all other departments. Public industrial schools or schools for trade training should never become so narrow in their scope as to prevent an all-round shop training."

American Federation of Labor. *Industrial Education. Report of Committee on Industrial Education; Compiled and Edited by Charles H. Winslow.* Washington, [Government Printing Office] 1912. 114 pp. (62d Congress, 2d sess. Senate. Document no. 936)

Presents the authoritative, official statement of the attitude of the American Federation of Labor toward vocational education. Gives the conclusions and recommendations of the committee, based on a careful study of the situation. Various schools already established are described.

American Foundrymen's Association. Committee on Industrial Education. *Report . . . Toronto Convention, June 8-12, 1908 . . .* [n. p.] 1908. 7 pp.

P. Kreuzpointner, chairman.

Summarizes the conclusions of the Committee under eight heads. Says: ". . . Industrial education and trade training must not only consider the mechanical and technical necessities of the mechanic, but also the culture and moral aesthetic side of life of the man and citizen.

"That manual training, as now conducted, is too exclusively devoted to the acquisition of manual dexterity, but if broadened and deepened and made more technical by the addition of suitable subjects, it can be made an excellent foundation for industrial education, and become a preparation for trade training." Recommends a system of specific trade schools, the burden of conducting them being equally divided between the community and the state."

American Foundrymen's Association. Committee on Industrial Education. *Report . . . Cincinnati Convention, 1909.* [n. p. 1909] 12 pp.

P. Kreuzpointner, chairman.

Sums up opinions of other organizations. Discusses industrial education as a social force, etc.

American Foundrymen's Association. Committee on Industrial Education. *Report . . . 1911*. [n. p. 1911] 11 pp.
P. Kreuzpointner, chairman.
Discusses the value of continuation schools upon the Cincinnati and Boston plan. Declares that for the present at least such schools are preferable to the more expensive trade schools.

American Foundrymen's Association. Committee on Industrial Education. *Report . . . 1912*. [n. p. 1912] 13 pp.
P. Kreuzpointner, chairman.
Reports a growing demand "for shop apprenticeship schools, continuation schools, and for a system of state or nationally subsidized industrial schools, leaving to local effort the adjustment of these schools to local conditions." Discusses the Cincinnati continuation schools, etc.

Anderson, Lewis F. *History of Manual and Industrial School Education*. New York, Appleton, 1926.
Includes notices of developments in Europe and their influence on American schools.

Anlyan, William G., et al. *The Future of Medical Education*. Durham, Duke University Press, 1973.

Apprenticeship and Skilled Employment Association. *Trades for London Boys and How to Enter Them*. London, New York, Longmans, Green and Co., 1908. 170 pp.
A very detailed consideration of the advantages of different trades and of the schools which offer courses preparing pupils for these trades.

Arnold, Walter, M. *Vocational, Technical and Continuing Education in Pennsylvania; a Systems Approach to State-local Program Planning*. Harrisburg, Pennsylvania Department of Public Instruction, 1969. 493 pp.
This analysis of Pennsylvania's vocational, technical and continuing education program covers the years 1964 through 1968. This study was not intended or planned as a basic research project to analyze philosophical issues in vocational education" but with a vew of "determining its achievements, deficiencies and direction in the light of priority needs of the people and employers."

Ashby, Eric. *Adapting Universities to a Technological Society*. San Francisco, Jossey-Bass, 1974.

Astier, P. and I. Cuminal. *L'Enseignement Technique, Industriel et Commercial en France et à l'Étranger*. Paris, 1909.

Astin, A. W. and R. J. Panos. *The Educational and Vocational Development of College Students*. Washington, American Council on Education, 1969.
Focus on educational attainment and the determinants of career plans and aspirations.

Austin, John J. and D. A. Sommerfield. *An Evaluation of Vocational Education for Disadvantaged Youth.* Muskegon, Michigan, Muskegon Public Schools, 1967. 189 pp.

The results of a study of two main groups of youth-trainees and non-trainees of the Muskegon Area Skill Training Center for disadvantaged youth. The authors seek to provide a model for measuring the effects of a program, geared to train disadvantaged youth for employment.

Bailey, Henry Turner. *Instruction in the Fine and Manual Arts in the United States.* Washington, Government Printing Office, 1909. 184 pp. (U. S. Bureau of Education. Bulletin no. 6, 1909.

References: p. 182.

Discusses instruction in fine arts and in the applications of art to handicraft in this country. Mainly statistical.

Baldwin, William Alpheus. and others. *Industrial-social Education.* Springfield (Mass.), Milton Bradley Company, 1907. 147 pp. illus.

The work of the Hyannis normal school in the industrial training of the grade children, Hyannis public school

Baltimore. Board of School Commissioners. *Report on Vocational Classes.* [Baltimore, 1909.] [4] pp. Caption title.

Banes, Charles E. *Manual. Training and Apprenticeship Schools in 1890.* Philadelphia, George H. Buchanan and Co., 1890.

An overview of late 19th century practice, with some notices of historical backgrounds.

Barger, Florence E. *Continuation School Work in the Grand Duchy of Baden and in Canton Zurich.* London, Wyman & Sons [1907?.] 35pp. ([Great Britain] Board of Education. Educational pamphlets, no. 6)

Barlow, Melvin L. *History of Industrial Education in the United States.* Peoria, Illinois, Chas. A. Bennett Co., 1967.

The heritage of industrial education from its beginnings to the present.

Barlow, Melvin L. *Principles of Trade and Industrial Education.* Austin, The University of Texas Press, 1963. 150 pp.

A review of the philosophical basis of industrial education and a historical account of such training during the 1906-17 period.

Barlow, Melvin L., ed. *Vocational Education.* (National Society for the Study of Education, 64th Yearbook, Part I). Chicago, University of Chicago Press, 1965.

Largely, a commentary on vocational education and the Vocational Education Act of 1963, with examination of different phases of vocational education.

Bawden, William T. *Leaders in Industrial Education.* Milwaukee, Wis., Bruce Publishing Co., 1950. 196. pp.

Chapters are devoted to the work of C. M. Woodward, C. R. Russell, F. G. Bonser, I. S. Griffith, J. D. Runkle, L. D. Harvey, J. H. Stout, W. E. Roberts, and F. T. Struck. A bibliography is included.

Becker, Joseph M. *In Aid of the Unemployed.* Baltimore, John Hopkins Press, 1965. 317 pp.

A history and current evaluation of programs to aid the unemployed in the United States. In chapter 2 (pp. 227-250), Gerald Somers reviews public training programs and assesses government and private retraining of the unemployed.

Beckwith, Holmes. *German Industrial Education and Its Lessons for the United States.* Washington, Government Printing Office, 1913. (U. S.) Bureau of Education. Bulletin no. 19).

Belgium. Ministeɽe de L'industrie et du Travail. *Rapport Général sur la Situation de l'Enseignement Technique en Belgique . . . 1902-1910.* Bruxelles, Office de Publicité, J. Lebègue et Cie. [etc], 1912. 2 v.

Volume I contains a resume of industrial, commercial, and domestic education in Belgium, followed by elaborate presentations of each subject. Volume II gives statistical details regarding courses in commerce and languages; industrial arts schools; apprenticeship, etc.

Belgium, Ministère de l'Industrie et du Travail. *Rapport sur la Situation de l'Enseignement Technique en Belgique, 1897-1901.* Bruxelles, Lebègue Cie. (etc.), 1909. 2v.

Belitsky, A. Harvey. *Private Vocational Schools and their Students: Limited Objectives, Unlimited Opportunities.* Cambridge, Mass., Schenkman Pub. Co., 1969. 186 pp.

This book has a two-fold purpose: 1) to show the workings of private vocational schools in regard to their diversity, operation and organization; 2) how private vocational schools may be more widely utilized to train disadvantaged persons. A summary of major recommendations is included. The author is a staff member of the W. E. Upjohn Institute for Employment Research.

Bennett, Charles A. *History of Manual and Industrial Education 1870-1917.* Peoria, Ill. Manual Arts Press, 1937.

A continuation of the author's earlier volume. The last five chapters (pp. 310-552) are devoted to education in the United States, with emphasis on the development of shopwork training and manual training in the elementary and secondary school, teacher training, and the vocational education movement.

Bennett, Charles A. *History of Manual and Industrial Education up to 1870.* Peoria, Ill., Manual Arts Press, 1926. 461 pp.

General historical development of labor and learning, beginning with the Greeks and their attitudes toward the mechanical arts. Covers the development of industrial education and schools in Europe and the transfer of these ideas and movements to America. Includes reprints of source material in this field.

Bennett, Guy. *Vocational Education of Junior College Grade*. Baltimore, Warwick and York, 1928. 244 pp.

The status of vocational training in the junior college in the early 1920's. Useful as a source of statistics (taken from the 1920 census) on occupations pursued by junior college students in each State and the types of training furnished by the institutions surveyed.

Berry, Thomas W. *The Pedagogy of Educational Handicraft*. London, Glasgow (etc.), Blackie & Son, Limited, 1909. 100 pp.

Bibliography: pp. 97-100.

"Makes no pretence to originality, but gives in a small compass the utterances of eminent educationists on the subject and other practical information not easily accessible. Thus we have an estimate of the cost of materials and fittings for a workshop, examination questions for teacher's diploma, and a bibliography." *Journal of Education* (London) April 1910, p. 256.

Bhabha, H. J. *Special Report on Manual Training in Schools of General Education*. Bangalore, Government Press, 1909. 145 pp. illus.

Binns, Charles L. and Rufus E. Marsden. *Principles of Educational Woodwork, a Handbook for Teachers and Others Interested in Education*. London, J. M. Dent & Co.; New York, E. P. Dutton & Co. [1909] viii, 310 pp.

"The teacher and his reading": pp. 61-71.

Suggestions for teaching woodwork, with emphasis on the need that manual training teachers be as well equipped on the pedagogical side as teachers of other subjects.

Birchill, George W. *Work Study Programs for Alienated Youth*. Chicago, Science Research Associates, Inc., 1962. 265 pp.

A casebook describing nine work study programs for secondary students provided by eight public school systems and one private group.

Blondel, Georges. *l'Education Economique du Peuple Allemand*. 2. ed. augm. Paris, L. Larose et L. Tenin, 1909. xxiv, 156 pp.

Contents. — 1. Évolution des idées en matière d'enseignement. 2. Les écoles industrielles. 3. Les écoles commerciales. — Les ecoles de perfectionnement. 4. Les créations auxillares des écoles.

Bloomfield, Meyer. *The Vocational Guidance of Youth*. Boston, Houghton Mifflin, 1911.

Bloomfield was the most important writer on vocational guidance in the period before World War I. See also the author's *Youth, School, and Vocation* (Boston, Houghton Mifflin, 1915); and *Readings in Vocational Guidance* (Boston, Ginn, 1915).

Bolen, George L. *Getting a Living.* New York, Macmillan, 1903. 769 pp.
Discusses (Chapter XI) the function of shop schools, manual training, and trade schools. Attitude of organized labor toward trade schools.

Bolino, August C. *Career Education: Contributions to Economic Growth.* New York, Praeger, 1973.

Borrow, Henry, ed. *Man in a World at Work.* New York, Houghton Mifflin, 1964. 606 pp.
The 50th anniversary of the National Vocational Guidance Association was marked by the publication of this volume. It represents "the profession's best thinking on the nature of vocational guidance, the meaning of the human work experience, the relationship of the individual to the labor force, and research and practice in vocational guidance." Contains papers of 24 contributors in the field.

Boston. *Report of the Mechanic Arts High School . . .* Boston, Muncipal Printing Office, 1901. 53 pp. illus. plates.
Describes equipment, etc.

Boston. Committee on Drawing. *Special Report on the Evening Drawing Schools.* Boston, Muncipal Printing Office,˙1905. 110 pp. illus. figs. charts. (School doc. no. 3-1905)
Chairman, James A. Macdonald.
Occupations of graduates from grammar and high schools, pp. 66-67.

Boston. Superintendent of Public Schools. *Boston Public Schools. Annual Report of the Superintendent.* Boston, Printing Department, 1910..157 pp. plates. (School document no. 10, 1910)
Exhibiting especially situation with regard to vocational education and vocational direction.

Boston. Superintendent of Public Schools. "[Work] in Elementary School Industrial Classes." In his *Annual Report, July 1910.* pp. 56-78. (School document no. 10, 1910)

Boston, Mass. Business Men's Advisory Committee. *Reports Regarding the Boston School of Commerce, 1909, 1910.*
F. P. Fish, chairman.
Traveling scholarships to South America and Central America, Germany and Belgium.

Brandon, Edgar Ewing. "Industrial Education [in Latin America]." In his *Latin-American Universities and Special Schools.* Washington, Government Printing Office, 1913. pp. 115-25. (U. S. Bureau of Education. Bulletin no. 30, 1912)

Brandon, George. "Vocational and Technical Education." In *Encyclopedia of Educational Research, a Project of the American Educational Research*

Association. Edited by Robert L. Ebel. (London, Collier-MacMillan Ltd. 1969.) pp. 1506-1522.

Brief survey of the status of vocational education in the U.S. Topics covered in article: "Changing Nature and Role of Vocational and Technical Education," "Transfiguration and a New Challenge," "Current Nature and Support of Research" (includes the Federal role)

Bray, Reginald Arthur. *Boy Labour and Apprenticeship.* London, Constable & Co., Ltd., 1911. xi, 248 pp.

List of authorities: pp. 241-44.

Deplores the conditions in England.

"The object of this volume is altogether practical — to show what reforms are necessary to prevent the growth of the evil by laying the foundation of a new and true apprenticeship system."

Brewer, John M. *A History of Vocational Guidance: Origins and Early Development.* New York, Harper, 1942.

The most comprehensive history for the period it covers; see also the author's *The Vocational Guidance Movement* (New York: Macmillan, 1918).

Brickman, William W., ed. *Automation, Education, and Human Values,* edited by William W. Brickman and Stanley Lehrer. New York, School and Society, 1966. 419 pp.

This work consists of essays by eminent educators and others on the effects of technological change on the home, training received in school, government, the American economy, employment, and use of leisure time.

Bristow, Adrian. *The American Experience; a Report on Vocational Education for Young Women Aged 15-20 in the United States.* Chester, England, Chester College of Further Education, 1969. 90 leaves.

A survey of vocational education programs for women, made by the Principal of Chester College of Further Education, Chester England, on a two months visit made in the autumn of 1968. This survey includes a summary of women in the labor market, education in general in the U.S., the vocational aspects of American education and the career courses provided for American women in senior high schools, vocational schools, technical institutes and junior and community colleges.

Broach, Howell H. and Julia O'Connor Parker. "The Experience of Labor with Trade and Industrial Education." Appendix A. In *Vocational Education* by John Dale Russell and Associates. Staff Study no. 8. Prepared for the Advisory Committee on Education. (Washington, U.S. Government Printing Office, 1938.) pp. 241-289.

A special report prepared for the Advisory Committee on Education. Contents: History of labor's attitude up to the passage of the Smith-Hughes Act, changes in attitudes, reasons for dissatisfaction; general criticism by organized labor of vocational education in secondary schools and in industrial plants, labor representation on advisory boards of vocational educational institutions; recommendations; and summary.

Brookover, Wilbur S. and Sigmund Nosow. "A Sociological Analysis of Vocational Education in the United States." In *Education for a Changing World of Work*. Report of the Panel of Consultants on Vocational Education. Appendix III. (Washington, U.S. Government Printing Office, 1963). pp. 21-52.

A discussion of the relationships between vocational education and social institutions. Topics covered: The social setting of vocational education; contemporary vocational education in the United States; and a conceptual approach to the sociological analysis of vocational education.

Bruere, Henry. *An Investigation of Trade and Industrial Schools.* Chicago, The International Harvester Co.. 1904. 50 pp. (Out of print)

Part I of report deals with industrial trade schools of the South, and Part II with Northern industrial and trade schools and technical institutes. Schools of technology not included. The article on factory education is reprinted in *The Commons* [now *The Survey*] 9:235-38, June 1904.

Brunot, H. P. "Technical Education in France." In *U. S. Department of Commerce and Labor. Daily Consular Reports, no. 2178, February 8, 1905*. Washington, Government Printing Office, 1905. 8 pp.

Reviews the vocational and trade schools of France. Gives curricula, sources of income, administrative methods, types of teachers, etc.

Bryam, Harold M. and Ralph C. Wenrich. *Vocational Education and Practical Arts in the Community School.* New York, Macmillan, 1956. 512 pp.

Written primarily as a college text, this book gives emphasis to the role of the community in introducing and maintaining vocational education programs in its schools. Attention is given to the Federal and State laws which enable vocational programs to exist and the means to develop these aids in the community.

Burkett, Lowell A. "Marriage of Vital Skills: Vocational Education and Manpower Training." In *The Courage to Change; New Directions for Career Education*. Edited by Roman C. Pucinski and Sharlene P. Hirsch. (Englewood Cliffs, N. J., Prentice-Hall, Inc., 1971) pp. 150-159.

In this chapter the author states that "vocational education and manpower training are used as two distinct, unrelated segments of national and state manpower efforts." He then proceeds to explain why "vocational education is manpower training and development in its most comprehensive sense."

Burnham, Frederic L. *Supervision and the Teaching of the Manual Arts in the High School.* (Boston, Wright & Potter Printing Company, 1909.) 30 pp.

Reprinted from the 72d report of the Massachusetts Board of Education.

Burt, Samuel M. *Industry and Community Leaders in Education; the State Advisory Councils on Vocational Education.* Kalamazoo, Michigan, W. E. Upjohn Institute for Employment Research, 1969. 54 pp.

A paper prepared to assist the State Advisory Councils on Vocational Education for a greater utilization of their volunteer representatives of industry, education and the general public. It analyses the role, functions, management and organization of these Councils, and gives practical suggestions in dealing with State boards of vocational education and local advisory committees.

Burt, Samuel M. *Industry and Vocational-technical Education; a Study of Industry-advisory Committees.* New York, McGraw-Hill, 1967. 520 pp.
The results of a study ranging over a 16-month period, of industry participation and involvement in vocational and technical education programs.

Bustico, Guido. *l'Educazione Vocazionale e la Scuola.* Desenzano, F. Legati e. c., 1909. 16 pp.

Calhoun Colored School, Calhoun, Ala. *Nineteenth Annual Report of the Principal . . . 1910-11.* Boston, Geo. H. Ellis Co., Printers (etc.) 1911. 65 pp. illus.
Presentation of industrial training of boys and girls. Boys taught agriculture, blacksmithing, carpentry, cobbling, manual training, and wheelwrighting.

Carlton, Frank T. *Economic Influences upon Educational Progress in the United States, 1820-1850.* Madison, University of Wisconsin, 1908.
Important materials for vocational and practical arts education. See also, Carlton's *Education and Industrial Evolution* (1908).

Carlton, Frank Tracy. *Education and Industrial Evolution.* New York, The Macmillan Company, 1908. xiv, 320 pp. (The citizen's library of economics, politics, and sociology, ed. by R. T. Ely . . .)
A thoroughgoing study of the problem of education in the industrial state of civilization. The point of view that of pragmatism." — *American Journal of Sociology,* November 1908, pp. 414.
A resume of what has already been done in public education to promote social efficiency and of the present tendencies.

(Carnegie Commission on Higher Education). *Toward a Learning Society: Alternative Channels to Life, Work, and Service.* New York, McGraw-Hill, 1973.
Considers the totality of postsecondary education and the patterns of education and training for work.

Carton de Wiart, Henry. *l'Enseignement pour la Vie et l'Introduction d'un Quatrième Degré d'Etudes dans l'Instruction Primaire. Conférence Donnée à l'Ecole Supérieure Commerciale et Consulaire à Mons le 15 Mai 1911.* Bruxelles, Impr. "La Rapide," 1911. 22 pp.

Cartwright, Morse Adams, ed. *Unemployment and Adult Education, a Symposium on Certain Problems of Re-education Arising from "permanent* layoff"—the Displacement of Men and Women in Industry through the Introduction of Machinery and Other Laborsaving Devices Sometimes Known as Technological Unemployment . . . New York, American Association for Adult Education, 1931. 63 pp.

Papers and excerpts from the proceedings of this symposium held under the auspices of the American Association for Adult Education in New York, December 18, 1930.

Center for Studies in Vocational and Technical Education. *Annual Report, 1969.* Madison, Wisconsin, University of Wisconsin, Industrial Relations Research Institute, 1969. 75 pp.

Summaries of research in progress and that already completed for the years 1965-1969. Brief information on three conferences sponsored by the Center is also included.

Chamberlain, Arthur Henry. *Bibliography of the Manual Arts.* Chicago, New York, A. Flanagan Company (1902). 100 pp.

Chamberlain, Arthur Henry. *Standards in Education, with Some Consideration of Their Relation to Industrial Training.* New York, Cincinnati [etc.], American Book Company (°1908). 365 pp.

Bibliography: p. 99-101.

Industrial training: Its aim and scope,'p. 68-101.

Cheit, Earl F. *The Useful Arts and the Liberal Tradition.* New York, McGraw-Hill, 1975. 166 pp.

The newer professional schools in the context of American education, focusing on agriculture, engineering, business administration, and forestry.

Citizens' Trade School Convention. *Proceedings and Addresses Given at Indianapolis, June 10-12, 1907.* [Indianapolis, Winona Technical Institute.] 53 pp.

Addresses by Frank Gunsaulus, J. A. Emery, P. M. Kling, Walter H. Page, J. W. Van Cleave, Anthony Ittner, Arthur D. Dean.

City Club of Chicago. *Report on Vocational Training in Chicago and in Other Cities. By a Sub-committee of the Committee on Public Education, 1910-11.* Chicago, Published by the City Club of Chicago, 1912. xiii, 315 pp.

Committee consisted of G. H. Mead, E. A. Wreidt, and W. J. Bogan. Report in four sections. The first section contains the recommendations of the committee; the second presents considerable information about schools; the third gives facts concerning business colleges and commercial schools; the fourth discusses the results of tests made on boys who left school to go to work as soon as the law allowed, regardless of their advancement in the grades. Boys were examined with regard to their ability in simple arithmetic, civics, history, and English composition. Tests showed that the boys were very deficient in these studies.

The Committee recommends "a plan worked out in some detail, of a type of school in which half of the time in the seventh and eighth grades may be given to vocational work, while during the other half of the school time we are confident that as much can be accomplished in the academic studies as is accomplished to-day. We recommend for these vocational grades a school day of six hours instead of the present five hours and a rearrangement of the time given to different subjects.

"Our great contention is that vocational training be introduced into our school system as an essential part of its education — in no illiberal sense and with no intention of separating out a class of workingmen's children who are to receive trade training at the expense of academic training."

In commenting on this report, the *Elementary School Teacher* for January, 1913, says (p. 249): "The conclusions to which this committee comes are diametrically opposed to those which underlie the Massachusetts plan and to those which Mr. Cooley presents in his report to the Commercial Club of Chicago. The position defended in the present report is, however, so typically American, so clearly feasible as a school program, and so simple to put into operation as contrasted with the plan of special and separate schools, that it is certainly worthy of careful consideration before any other course is adopted."

Clark, Harold F. "The Economic and Social Background of Vocational Education in the United States." In *Education for a Changing World of Work*. Report of the Panel of Consultants on Vocational Education. Appendix III. (Washington, U. S. Government Printing Office, 1963.) pp. 1-17.

Generalizations on various aspects of vocational training as it exists today in the United States. Partial contents: Vocational training by schools, business and industry, the military, and by various agencies and vocational education and training needed by various parts of the population. Six recommendations are given by the author.

Clark, Harold F. and Harold S. Sloan. *Classrooms in the Factories: An Account of the Educational Activities Conducted by American Industry.* Rutherford, N. J., Institute of Research, Fairleigh Dickinson University, 1958.

Descriptions of some 300 programs offered by American industry, largely technical and business.

Clark, Harold F. and Harold S. Sloan. *Classrooms on Main Street: An Account of Specialty Schools in the United States That Train for Work and Leisure.* New York, Teachers College, Columbia University, 1966.

Non-traditional programs preparing students for business and industrial employment.

Clarke, Isaac E. *Art and Education.* (46th Congress, 2nd Session, U. S. Senate, Executive Documents, 1897), VII, No. 209, pts. 1-4.

A comprehensive discussion of "practical" education containing considerable primary source material on manual arts education.

Cleveland, O. Board of Education. *Elementary Industrial School. Report of Plans, Course of Study and a Brief Summary of Results.* Cleveland, Board of Education, 1910. 14 pp.

Report on school made by William N. Hailmann.

Coates, Charles P. *History of the Manual Training School of Washington University* (St. Louis Manual Training School). U. S. Bureau of Education. Bulletin no. 3 (193).
The first major manual training high school in the United States.

Cochran, Leslie H. *Innovative Programs in Industrial Education.* Bloomington, McKnight and McKnight Pub. Co., 1970. 114 pp.
An informative book designed mainly for the instructor of industrial education, but containing chapters of general interest to all interested in vocational education. Of note are the chapters "Contemporary influences in industrial education", "Interpretation of industry programs" and "A comparison of seven contemporary programs".

Colorado Department of Education. *Southwestern States Developmental Project Relating to Educational Needs of Adult Agricultural Migrants.* Calvin Raymond Orr, Project Director. Denver, 1965. 83 pp. (Cooperative research report No. K-005)
A description of the developmental project to assist the adult migrant worker. It was conducted through the cooperation of the chief State school officers of Arizona, Colorado, New Mexico, and Texas and the colleges of education of Arizona State University, University of New Mexico, University of Texas, and Adams State College.

Columbia University. Teachers College. School of Industrial Arts. *Annotated List of Books Relating to Industrial Arts and Industrial Education.* New York City, Teachers College, Columbia University, 1911. 50 pp. (Technical education bulletin, no. 6)

Columbia University. Teachers College. School of Industrial Arts. *Requirements and Course of Study Leading to a Certificate for Teaching in Industrial and Trade Schools.* 12 pp. (Second series, no. 12, February 11, 1911)

Commercial Club of Chicago and others. *Tentative Draft of Proposed Law for Establishing a System of Vocational Schools for Illinois.* Chicago, 1912. 10 pp.

(Commission on Industrial Education). *Report of the Commission on Industrial Education Made to the Legislature of Pennsylvania.* Harrisburg, Edwin K. Meyers, State Printer, 1889.
Influential state report.

(Commissioner of Labor). *Industrial Education in the United States.* Twenty-Fifth Annual Report of the Commissioner of Labor. Washington, Government Printing Office. 1911.
A massive repository of information on industrial America and its impact on the schools.

(Commissioner of Labor). *Trade and Technical Education.* Seventeenth Annual Report of the Commissioner of Labor. Washington, Government Printing Office, 1902.

Valuable source on 19th century programs.

Committee for Economic Development. *Raising Low Incomes Through Improved Education; a Statement on National Policy by the Research and Policy Committee of the Committee for Economic Development.* New York, 1965. 51 pp.

A description of some of the improvements and extensions of educational programs to raise the level of productivity and the incomes of many Americans.

Committee for Economic Development. Research and Policy Committee. *Training and Jobs for the Urban Poor.* New York, 1970. 78 pp.

A statement on national policy regarding "long-term solutions to the problem of urban poverty." Vocational education and job training are discussed in Chapter 4: "Recommended Directions for Manpower Policy".

Conference on the Education and Training of Racial Minorities. University of Wisconsin, 1967. *The Education and Training of Racial Minorities;* Proceedings edited by Betty Shaw and Karen Krueger. Prepared by the Center for Studies in Vocational and Technical Education. Madison, University of Wisconsin, 1968. 211 pp.

Papers given at the Conference were by government officials and educators from vocational schools and other institutions. Topics under consideration included: "Public Education's Role for Manpower Development" and "Providing Mobility for America's Immobile Population."

Conference on Research in Vocational and Technical Education. University of Wisconsin, 1966. *Research in Vocational and Technical Education; Proceedings* Edited by Cathleen Quirk and Carol Sheehan. Madison, University of Wisconsin, Center for Studies in Vocational and Technical Education, 1967. 285 pp.

"This conference concentrated upon reports and critical discussion of research and experimentation recently completed or near completion." Topics for discussion included these subjects: "Vocational education and the disadvantaged"; "Job clusters and general vocational skills"; "Curriculum developments in Vocational Education Programs".

Conference on Unemployed Out-of-school Youth in Urban Areas. *Social Dynamite.* (Washington) National Committee for Children and Youth, 1961. 265 pp.

This report includes a listing of the services, programs, and projects in effect that deal with the problems of unemployed youth and a bibliography of references.

Congrès International d'Enseignement Menager. *1st Fribourg, 1908 . . . Fribourg, les 29 et 30 septembre 1908.* Fribourg, Suisse, 1908-1909. 2 v.
    Contents. — I. Rapports avant le Congrès. 1908. — III. Compte rendu des seances. 1909.

Connecticut. Commission on Trade Schools. Appointed, 1903. *Report . . . Concerning Trade Schools.* Hartford, Hartford Press, 1907. 10 pp.

Consumers' League of Connecticut. *A Glance at Some European and American Vocational Schools for Children from Twelve to Sixteen Years of Age.* Hartford, The Consumers' League, 1911. 64 pp. front., pl.

Contemporary Concepts in Vocational Education; the First Yearbook of the American Vocational Association. Edited by Gordon F. Law. Washington, D. C., American Vocational Association, 1971. 435 pp.
    A compilation of writings dealing with various contemporary aspects of vocational education. Topics are divided into ten groups. Partial list: "Philosophical Aspects of Vocational Education"; Equipping All Persons for a Productive Life"; "Schools, Programs and Systems: The Delivery of Vocational Education"; "The Economic Role of Vocational Education"; "Evaluation, Accreditation and Accountability in Education."

Cooke, Morris L. *Academic and Industrial Efficiency; a Report to the Carnegie Foundation for the Advancement of Teaching.* New York [1910]. 134 pp. (Carnegie Foundation. Bulletin no. 5; .

Cooley, Anna M. *Domestic Art in Woman's Education, for the Use of Those Studying the Method of Teaching Domestic Art and Its Place in the School Curriculum.* New York, C. Scribner's Sons, 1911. xi, 274 pp. tables.
    "References for study" at the end of most of the chapters.
    "A selected bibliography of books helpful in the study of the various phases of domestic art": pp. 269-74.

Cooley, Edwin G. *Vocational Education in Europe. Report to the Chicago Commercial Club.* Chicago, R. R. Donnelley & Sons Co., 1912. 347 pp. illus.
    "This report undertakes to describe some of the typical vocational schools observed by the author during his year in Europe. The major part of the report is devoted to the educational institutions of Germany. Some special institutions in Austria and Switzerland are described on account of their relations to the general problem of vocational education."

Council of Supervisors of Manual Arts. *Year-book, 1907. Seventh Annual Meeting, New York, 7-8, February 1908.* 168 pp.
    Contains: 1. Mable B. Soper—Constructive work in town schools without special equipment, p. 13-19. 2. C. L. Boone—Centers of interest in handwork, p. 20-26. 3. C. A. Bennett—The relationship between drawing and the other manual arts, p. 27-31. 4. W. B. Anthony—The development of school handicraft, p. 32-42. 5. Walter Sargent—The relation of public

schools to museums of fine arts, p. 43-50. 6. M. W. Murray — Woodworking for country schools, p. 51-56. 7. J. P. Haney — The adaptation of pattern to material, p. 57-76. 8. F. E. Mathewson — A shop problem in design, p. 77-80. 9. T. M. Dillaway — Creating ideas in furniture design, p. 81-87. 10. A. W. Garritt — Toy-making as a form of constructive work, p. 88-96. 11. Julia C. Cremins — Some phases of bookbinding in the elementary schools, p. 97-132. 12. Amy R. Whittier — The intermediate grades. p. 133-38.

Crane, Richard T̃. *The Futility of Technical, Industrial, Vocational, and Continuation Schools.* Chicago, 1911. 13 pp.
  States that the immense prosperity of the United States "has been accomplished without any of the German ideas regarding the class of schools above mentioned." Claims that Germany's industrial advancement is "due simply to its freedom from trade unions and to the low wages which prevail there, and is not the result of technical schools, trade schools, or any other kind of education. . . . Germany simply has been copying England, even in such lines as chemistry, the production of coloring dyes and enameling." Says that England has attained its high position in the industrial world, "without anything in the way of continuation, vocational, industrial or technical schools."

Crawshaw, F. D. *Manual Arts: Public School Manual Arts, an Agency for Vocational Education.* Madison, Published by the Board, 1912. 17 pp. (Wisconsin. State board of industrial education. Bulletin no. 6)
  Suggested possibilities for grammar grade adjustment. Specialization in the high school, etc. Says: "Put the special work followed by the pupil in his senior year under the supervision of the leaders in the industry represented." But the executive heads in the school system must remain in general control.

Creasey, Clarence Hamilton. *Technical Education in Evening Schools . . .* London, S. Sonnenschein & Co., 1905. 309 pp. diagr.
  A comprehensive study of evening technical education, the German and English point of view; subjects and methods of instruction.

Cremin, Lawrence A. *The Transformation of the School: Progressivism in American Education, 1876-1957.* New York, Knopf, 1961.
  Particularly Chapter 2 ("Education and Industry") on the history of the manual training and vocational education movement.

Cross, K. Patricia, et al. *Planning Non-Traditional Programs.* San Francisco, Jossey-Bass, 1974.

Damm, Paul Friedrich. *Die technischen Hochschulen Preussens.* Berlin, E. S. Mittler und Sohn, 1909. viii. 324 pp.

Davenport, Eugene. *Education for Efficiency; a Discussion of Certain Phases of the Problem of Universal Education with Special Reference to Academic Ideals and Methods.* Boston, D. C. Heath & Co., 1909. v, 184 pp.

Contents. Introduction, pp. 1-7. 1. Education for efficiency, pp. 11-36. 2. Industrial education with special reference to the high school, pp. 37-59. 3. Industrial education a phase of the problem of universal education, pp. 60-77. 4. The educative value of labor, pp. 78-89. 5. The culture aim in education, pp. 90-99. 6. Unity in education, pp. 100-21. 7. Agriculture in the high schools, pp. 124-35. 8. Agriculture in the elementary school, pp. 136-43. 9. Agriculture in the normal schools, pp. 144-46. 10. The development of American agriculture, etc., pp. 147-84.

In the introduction the author lays down certain fundamentals which he says "must soon be clearly recognized and brought into and made a part of our educational ideals, policies, and methods." If we are to have universal education, it must contain a large element of the vocational. He writes: "We must agree that in a system of universal education the best results will always follow when as many subjects as possible and as many vocations as may be are taught together in the same school, under the same management, and to the same body of men."

Declares it to be a blunder to transport the European trade school and transplant it into the soil of America.

Davenport, Eugene. *Industrial Education with Special Reference to the High School; an Address.* Urbana, Ill. (1908). 20 pp.

This address was read at the high school conference, University of Illinois, November 20, 1908.

Dean, Arthur D. *Industrial Education and a State Policy; an Address before the National Society for the Promotion of Industrial Education, Milwaukee, December 3, 1908 . . .* Albany, New York (State) Education Department, 1910. 16 pp.

Dean, Arthur D. *Industrial Education in Its Relation to the High School Problem.* Syracuse, N. Y., C. W. Bardeen, 1910. 34 pp.

Dean, Arthur D. *Vocational Education: a Reprint from the Annual Report of the Education Department, Submitted January 1910.* Albany, New York (State) Education department, 1910. 26 pp.

Dean, Arthur D. *Vocational Schools.* Albany, N. Y., 1912. 29 pp.

Technical education, domestic economy and agricultural education in the state of New York. Reprinted from New York (State) Education department. 8th annual report.

Dean, Arthur D. *The Worker and the State, a Study of Education for Industrial Workers;* with an introduction by Andrew S. Draper, Commissioner of Education of the State of New York. New York, The Century Co., 1910. xix, 355 pp.

Bibliography: pp. 345-55.

One of the most useful books that has appeared on the subject of industrial education. Describes the movement for vocational instruction as a popular one, as evolution and not revolution. Treats of the educational significant of modern industry; trade schools at sixteen; trade unions and trade schools; schools in the factory; supplemental education in its relation to industry, etc.

In discussing the public and private control of trade schools, the author says: "Undoubtedly if the trade school movement in America is to make appreciable headway it must have the sympathy and aid of labor organizations. This is perhaps the strongest reason for urging that these schools become a part of the public school system." Industrial education "to command respect must be in the hands of real artisans and not theorists who are indifferent mechanics."

Dearborn, Ned H. *Once in a Lifetime; a Guide to the CCC Camp.* New York, Charles E. Merrill Co., 1936. 308 pp.

Prepared for the CCC camp enrollee, this guidebook offers a detailed account of the organization of the camps, courses offered, and the approach used in motivating the students to greater achievements.

DeCarlo, Charles R. *Education in Business and Industry.* New York, Center for Applied Research in Education, 1966.

A discussion of the role of industry and business in education, with historical backgrounds.

Development of Vocational Education Programs for American Indians. Conference Proceedings. Edited by Everett D. Edington and Philip Hocker. Las Cruces, New Mexico, Clearinghouse on Rural Education and Small Schools, New Mexico State University, Oct. 1969. 50 pp.

Participants in the Conference included educators, Indian leaders, employment personnel and representatives of industry. Out of many, one conclusion reached was that vocational education programs for Indians should be developed at local levels, instead of on a national basis.

Dickinson, William B., Jr. *Retraining for New Jobs.* Washington, Editorial Research Reports, 1962. 775-792 pp. (Editorial research reports, 1962, v. 2, No. 16, Oct. 31, 1962)

Contents: Need to retrain displaced workers; State and Federal retraining plans; retraining provisions of trade expansion act; obstacles to effective training; and foreign experience with retraining.

Diggs, Annie L. *Bedrock. Education and Employment, the Foundation of the Republic.* Detroit, Mich., Social Center Publishing Co., [1912]. x., 70 pp.

Based on the proposition that a bureau of employment should be established in connection with each and every educational institution throughout this country.

Dodge, Harriet Hazen. *Survey of Occupations Open to the Girl of 14 to 16 Years.* Boston, Mass., Girls Trade Education League, 1912. 39 pp.

"This survey is designed especially to meet the numerous inquiries of teachers, vocational counselors, and social workers as to what the girl can do who seeks wage earning in the earliest years in which the law allows her to engage in it." — Pref.

Dopp, Katherine Elizabeth. *The Place of Industries in Elementary Education*. rev. ed. Chicago, [University of Chicago Press], 1909. 270 pp.

Contains discussions regarding the significance of industrial epochs; the origins of attitudes that underlie industry; and practical applications. Philosophical in character.

Douglas, Paul H. *American Apprenticeship Industrial and Education* (Columbia University Studies in Economics, History, and Law, XCV, No. 2). New York, Longmans, Green, 1921.

An important history with an excellent summary of the many surveys of the adequacy of traditional schooling, and a major critique of the vocational education movement. See also, George S. Counts, *The Selective Character of American Secondary Education* (1922) for the impact of vocationalism; and Counts, *School and Society in Chicago* (1928) for the controversy which surrounded vocational education; also, for the impact of vocational education on schooling, see Robert and Helen Lynd, *Middletown* (1929).

Downer, Harry E. *The Boy and His Job*. Davenport, Iowa. The Contemporary Club, 1911. 32 pp.

Draper, Andrew S. *The Adaptation of the Schools to Industry and Efficiency*. Albany, N. Y. [1908] 19 pp. (New York State) Education department)

Read before the National Education Association of the United States, June 29, 1908.

The author contends that the new industrial schools "can not displace, nor half displace, the common elementary school. They will have to follow and supplement it. . . . They ought to be wholly apart from manual training schools. They are not to train mechanical or electrical engineers. . . . They are to train workmen to do better work that they may earn more bread and butter."

Draper, Andrew Sloan, *Our Children, Our Schools, and Our Industries; Commissioner's Special Theme, Annual Report 1908*. Albany, N. Y., [1907]. 48 pp.

Also in New York State Teachers' Association. *Proceedings, 1907*. Albany, University of the state of New York, 1908. pp. 32-78. (Education department. Bulletin no. 424, May 1908)

Du Bois, W. E. Burghardt, ed. *The Negro Artisan. A Social Study Made under the Direction of Atlanta University* . . . Atlanta, Ga., Atlanta University Press, 1902. viii, 192 pp. (Atlanta university publications, no. 7) Cover title.

Bibliography: pp. v-vii.

Discusses among other topics the ante-bellum artisan; economics of emancipation; the evolution of the southern industrial school for negroes; manual training; distribution of negro artisans, etc. Contains also the proceedings of the Seventh conference for the study of the negro problems, Atlanta university, May 27, 1902.

Duffy, Frank. *Industrial Education and the Labor Unions.* New York, Teachers College, Columbia University, [1912]. 14 pp. (Teachers college. Technical education bulletin no. 15. 3d series, no. 18)

Address given at Teachers college, February 15, 1912. Voices the op- position of labor unions to the private trade schools. Tells about the unions giving industrial education to their members. Thinks industrial education should be part of the public school system.

Dunlop, O. Jocelyn. *English Apprenticeship and Child Labour . . . with a Supplementary Section on the Modern Problem of Juvenile Labor . . .* London, T. Fisher Unwin, 1912. 390 pp.

Bibliography: pp. 355-63.

The history of apprenticeship is traced from medieval until modern times. Contains chapters on technical training in 1550; national system of in- dustrial training and the difficulties of its administration; the dissolution of the apprenticeship system; cost of technical education; the development of the twentieth century problems of child labor, etc.

Dymond, T. S. *Suggestions on Rural Education . . .* London, Eyre and Spot- tiswoode, 1908. 54 pp.

Rural "evening" schools, pp. 15-20.

Eastern Art and Manual Training Teachers' Association. *Proceedings. First Annual Convention, Boston, May 4-7, 1910. Second Annual Convention, Philadelphia, May 11-13, 1911.* [Newark, N. J., Press of Baker Printing Co., 1912]. 213 pp.

Eastern Manual Training Association. *Proceedings, Fifteenth Annual Con- vention, Washington, D.C., April 13-15, 1908.* [Springfield, Mass., The F. A. Bassette Company], 1908. 122 pp.

Contains 1. J.'C. Park: Fundamental Principles of Manual Training, pp. 15-18. Discussion, pp. 19-21. 2. W. J. De Catur: The Content of the Course of Study for the Grades and High School, pp. 22-25. 3. G. E. Myers: Correlation Based on Social and Individual Needs, pp. 26-31. Discussion, pp. 32-34. 4. A. E. Dodd: Hand Work Training for the Normal Student, pp. 42- 48. 5. T. D. Sensor: The Needs of Rural Schools, pp. 55-61. 6. Mrs. Ada Williams: The Social Value of Domestic Science Training, pp. 77-80. 7. Sarah E. Bowers: Aims of Domestic Science in the Elementary Schools, pp. 81-86.

Eaton, J. Shirley. *Education for Efficiency in Railroad Service.* Washington, Government Printing Office, 1909. 159 pp. (U. S. Bureau of Education. Bulletin no. 10, 1909)

Discusses the apprenticeship system; vocational railroad schools; higher education for railroad careers, etc. Appendices contain statistics of railway apprenticeship; and the educational and welfare work on European railroads.

Eaton, Joseph J. "A Corporation School. In *National Society for the Promotion of Industrial Education. Proceedings of the Third Annual Meeting, 1909.* (Its Bulletin No. 10)
  Discussion: pp. 106-12.
  Describes the Ludlow, Mass., Textile School.

"Education and Industry." In *The Transformation of the School* by Lawrence A. Cremin. (New York, Alfred Knopf, 1961.) pp. 23-57.
  The historical movement in vocational education is described up to and including the passage of the Smith-Hughes Act of 1917.

Education and Training. A Chance to Advance. 7th Annual Report of the Secretary of the Department of Health, Education and Welfare to the Congress on Training Activities under the Manpower Development and Training Act. Washington, U.S. Govt. Print. Off., 1969. 102 pp.
  Partial contents: Manpower Training Skills Center; National Programs and Services; Innovations, experiments and special programs; Evaluation.

Education and Training: Doorway to the Seventies. 8th Annual Report of the Secretary of the Department of Health, Education and Welfare to the Congress on Training Activities under the Manpower Development and Training Act. Wash., U.S. Govt. Print. Off., 1970. 88 pp.
  Entire report devoted to MDTA* Institutional Training-Program Responsibility and Cost. This report also contains information on: training given in classroom shop and skills centers, staff development, curriculum materials and training equipment, evaluation of institutional training.

Education and Training: Expanding the Choices. 5th Annual Report of the Secretary of the Department of Health, Education and Welfare to the Congress on Training Activities under the Manpower Development and Training Act. Washington, U.S. Govt. Print. Off., 1967. 107pp.
  Partial contents: Changing Directions; The Training Programs; Teachers, Curricula, Methods and Materials; Innovation and Improved Training Methods.

Education and Training. Learning for Jobs. 6th Annual Report of the Secretary of the Department of Health, Education and Welfare to the Congress on Training Activities under the Manpower Development and Training Act. Washington, U.S. Govt. Print. Off., 1968. 96pp.
  Partial contents: Adapting to Economic Change; The Range of Training; National Programs and Services; Innovations and Experiments; Evaluating Training.

Education and Training: Opportunity through Learning. 9th Annual Report of the Department of Health, Education and Welfare to the Congress on Institutional Training under the Manpower Development and Training Act in 1970. Washington, U.S. Govt. Print. Off., 1971. 72pp.
  Contents: Preparing People for Progress; Program Developments and Innovations; Evaluating Institutional Training. Appendices. Manpower Training Skills Centers; Area Manpower Institutes for the Development of Staff; Statistical Tables.

Education for the Urban Disadvantaged: from Preschool to Employment. A Statement on National Policy by the Research and Policy Committee of the Committee for Economic Development, March 1971. New York, Committee for Economic Development, 1971. 86pp.

"A comprehensive review of the current state of education for disadvantaged minorities; sets forth philosophic and operational principles which are imperative if the mission of the urban schools is to be accomplished successfully";

Educational Activities for Boys . . . New York, Young Men's Christian Association Press, 1907, 52 pp. illus.

Reprinted from *Association Boys.*

Contains papers by different writers on vocational training, manual training, etc.

Educational Policies Commission. *Manpower and Education.* Washington, National Education Association, 1956. 128 pp.

This report is devoted to facts concerning the Nation's manpower situation and recommendations for education concerning shortages and underused potentials in American manpower.

Educationally Deficient Adults: Their Education and Training Needs. Washington, Government Printing Office, 1965.

The needs of unskilled and deskilled adults with discussion of vocational education programs to meet the needs.

Eells, Walter C. *Present Status of Junior College Terminal Education.* Washington, American Association of Junior Colleges, 1941. 340 pp. (Terminal Education Monograph No. 2)

A report prepared for the Commission on Junior College Terminal Education of the American Association of Junior Colleges. This book describes the eight parts of the vocational curricula predominant in the 610 junior colleges under examination and methods used in creating training.

Elliott, Edward C. *Industrial Education; Summary of Legislation Concerning Industrial Education in Public Elementary and Secondary Schools.* [Madison, Wis., American Association for Labor Legislation], 1909. 16 pp.

Elliott, Edward C. *Industrial Education. Summary of Legislation Concerning Industrial Education in Public Elementary and Secondary Schools* [in the United States]. [New York, 1910]. 16 pp. tables. (American Association for Labor Legislation. *Legislative Review,* no. 2)

Elliott, Edward C. and C. A. Prosser. *Legislation upon Industrial Education in the United States; Prepared for the American Association of Labor Legislation and the National Society for the Promotion of Industrial Education . . .* New York City, National Society for the promotion of Industrial Education, 1910. 76 pp. table. (National Society for the Promotion of Industrial Education. Bulletin no. 12.)

The Emerging Role of State Education Departments with Specific Implications for Divisions of Vocational-technical Education. Report of a National Conference on State Department Leadership in Vocational Education (Feb. 27-Mar. 2, 1967). Edited by Dick C. Rice and Powell E. Toth. Columbus, Ohio, Ohio State University, Center for Vocational and Technical Education. 1967. 407 pp.

Twelve papers presented at the Conference. The "emerging role" of the state education departments is defined as an effort to coordinate existing programs, evaluate and maintain standards, initiate new programs.

Emerson, Lynn A. "Technical Training in the United States." In *Education for a Changing World of Work: Report of the Panel of Consultants on Vocational Education.* Appendix I. (Washington, U. S. Government Printing Office, 1963.) 170 pp.

This report is devoted to technical education on semiprofessional levels and its role in providing trained workers for industry, including methods in which workers are prepared to fill jobs available. A survey of the current needs for technicians is given, how these needs are being met, and recommendations for meeting future needs.

Eninger, Max U. *The Process and Product of Technical and Industrial High School Level Vocational Education in the U. S.* Pittsburgh, American Institute for Research. Published in two parts: Pt. I: The Product (1965) 445 pp.; Pt. II: The Process (1968) 635 pp.

A follow-up study of the impact of vocational education on male graduates of 100 high schools. The students, having graduated in 1953, 1958, 1963, were all formerly enrolled in a trade and industrial curriculum. Study also includes such data as students' attitudes toward teachers and the physical plants where the training took place.

Essex, Martin, et al. *Notes and Working Papers Concerning the Administration of Programs Authorized under the Vocational Education Act of 1963, Public Law 88-210, As Amended.* Washington, U. S. Government Printing Office, 1968.

A report by the National Advisory Council on Vocational Education reviewing the administration and status of vocational education programs.

Evans, Charles S. *Technical Training in the Berkeley High School.* Berkeley, Cal., 1910. [22] pp. illus. ([Berkeley, Cal. Board of Education] Pamphet no. 4)

Evans, Luther H. and George E. Arnstein, eds. *Automation and the Challenge to Education.* Washington, National Education Association, 1962. 190 pp.

Proceedings of a symposium held in Washington, D. C., January 17-19, 1962, sponsored by the Project on the Educational Implications of Automation of the National Education Association. Twelve representatives of education, economics, political science, labor, and management submitted papers on how education can best answer the challenge of automation.

Evans, Rupert N. and others. *Education for Employment: the Background and Potential of the 1968 Vocational Education Amendments.* Ann Arbor, Michigan, University of Michigan, Institute of Labor and Industrial Relations, 1969. 120 pp.

How the Amendments of 1968 expanded the definition of vocational education, freed it from many strictures, demanded comprehensive planning of programs from the States and strengthened the role of the federal government in implementing plans. The administrative shortcomings of VEA of 1963 are also discussed.

Fee, Edward M. *The Origin and Growth of Vocational Industrial Education in Philadelphia to 1917.* Philadelphia, Westbrook Publishing Co., 1938.

A University of Pennsylvania doctoral dissertation which chronicles development of vocational education programs in late 19th and early 20th century urban America.

Feinberg, Walter and Henry Rosemont, eds. *Work Technology and Education: Dissenting Essays in the Intellectual Foundations of American Education.* Urbana, University of Illinois Press, 1975. 222 pp.

Essays on the theme that American education has too successfully served the interests of industrial capitalism.

Feldman, Marvin J. *Making Education Relevant.* New York, Ford Foundation, 1966.

A redefinition of vocational education "at least in part as that aspect of an educational experience which helps a person discover, define, and refine his talents and to use them in working toward a career."

Fern, George H. *What is Vocational Education? A Series of Discourses on Various Aspects ,of Vocational Education.* Chicago, American Technical Society, 1944. 159 pp.

Written mainly for the "general educator" to show how vocational education fits into the general curriculum, its purposes, and philosophy.

Ferrin, Richard I. and Solomon Arbeiter. *Bridging the Gap: A Study of Education-to-Work Linkages.* Princeton, College Board Publications, 1975.

Includes A Selection of Education-to-Work Linkages and A Summary. These reports delineate a year-long study which analyzes some 100 education to-work linkages, offers proposals for improvement, and makes recommendations to the National Institute of Education.

Fisher, Berenice. *Industrial Education: American Ideals and Institutions.* Madison, University of Wisconsin Press, 1967.

An overview of the controversy surrounding vocational training in the first decades of the 20th century, and related developments.

Flicker, Bernard. *A School and Work Program in an Adult Manpower Setting for Potential Dropouts Needing Educational Redirection.* New York, Center for Urban Education, 1969. 60 pp.

A description and evaluation of a cooperative school-work project conducted in New York City (1968-69) under the Manpower Development Training Program.

Folk, Hugh. *The Transition from School to Work.* Princeton, Woodrow Wilson School of Political and International Affairs, 1968.
An analysis of the economics of youth unemployment.

Frank, Louis. *l'Education Domestique des Jeunes Filles; ou, La Formation des Mères.* Paris, Larousse, [1904]. xxiv, 547 pp. illus.
Deals with domestic education in all countries; types of schools, etc. An elaborate presentation of the subject.

Fuller, Alice M. Housekeeping and Household Arts . . . Manila, Bureau of Printing, 1911. 178 pp. illus.
A manual intended for girls in the elementary schools of the Philippine islands.

Functional Education for Disadvantaged Youth. Edited by Sterling M. Mc-Murrin. New York, Committee for Economic Development, 1971. 120 pp. (Supplementary paper no. 32)
Contains four papers by Ralph W. Tyler, Garth L. Mangum, Seymour L. Wolfbein and Howard A. Matthews. These papers were commissioned by the Committee for Economic Development as a part of the general study in urban education which resulted in the policy statement called Education for the Urban Disadvantaged: from Preschool to Employment (See entry under title)

Garbin, Albeno P. and others. *Problems in the Transition from High School to Work as Perceived by Vocational Educators.* Columbus, Ohio, Ohio State University, Center for Vocational and Technical Education, 1967. 82 pp.
Opinions of outstanding vocational educators from various geographical regions of the U. S., in regard to the social and psychological problems faced by youth adjusting to the world of work. Of the 49 specific problems identified, 40% of the educators cited these: 1) Unrealistic aspirations and expectations; 2) poor attitudes toward work and working; 3) lack of responsibility, maturity and self discipline; 4) lack of knowledge of the real demands of work.

Gardner, John W. "From High School to Job." In *Annual Report, Carnegie Corporation of New York, 1959-60.* (New York, 1960.) pp. 11-20.
What should be done, and what could be done, for that segment of American youth whose formal schooling ends with high school. The discussion includes suggestions for effective "transitional experiences" from high school to job. The work-study program is included among the examples.

Gerner, B. *Die Fortbildungs, und fachschulen in den gröszeren Örten Deutchlands* . . . Leipzig, A. Hahn, 1904. 458 pp.

Gillette, John Morris. *Vocational Education.* New York, Cincinnati [etc.], American Book Company, [c1910]. vii, 303 pp.

Author sets out in summary form the development of vocational training and its many manifestations in modern and contemporary life and thought.

Ginzberg, Eli and others. *Occupational Choice; an Approach to a General Theory.* New York, Columbia University Press, 1951. 271 pp.

The data reported in this book is based on 91 interviews with students from the sixth grade to graduate school. It has value for those determining vocational subjects to be taught and provides information on the process involved by the student in making the choice for his life's work.

Goldmark, Josephine. *Fatigue and Efficiency.* Introduction by Frederic S. Lee . . . New York, Charities Publication Committee, 1912. xvii, 591 pp. (Russell Sage foundation)

An epoch-making book. Analyzes fatigue, its nature and effects. Seeks to explain the phenomena of overwork in working people. Of value to educators, especially those engaged in preparing young people for industrial pursuits.

Gordon, Margaret S., ed. *Higher Education and the Labor Market.* New York, McGraw-Hill, 1974.

Graney, Maurice R. *The Technical Institute.* New York, The Center for Applied Research in Education, Inc., 1964. 111 pp.

A study of the technical institute in American higher education and its role in providing trained manpower. Divided into five chapters, this book presents an historical background of the technical institute, its relationship to present day technology, and its organization, administration, curricula, and faculty. The last chapter is devoted to the technical institute student's place in industry and society.

Great Britain. Board of Education. *Manual Instruction in Public Elementary Schools.* London, Printed for H. M. Stationery Off., by Eyre & Spottiswoode, 1910. iv, 34 pp.

Great Britain. Board of Education. *Manual Instruction in Secondary Schools.* London, Printed for H. M. Stationery Off., by Wyman and Sons, Limited, 1908. 2 pp. (Its Circular 547)

Originally issued as Circular 603 in July, 1905, and revised in June, 1908. Signed: W. N. Bruce.

Great Britain. Board of Education. *Special Reports on Educational Subjects.* v. 15 [16,19] School Training for the Home Duties of Women . . . London, Printed for H. M. Stationery Office, by Wyman & Sons, Limited, 1905-7. 3 v. illus., plans, tables, diagrs. ([Parliament. Papers by command] Cd. 2498,2963,3860)

Contains bibliographies.

Part I discusses the scheme of public education in the United States, with history and development of domestic science teaching. Takes up in detail the methods of teaching, equipment, curricula, etc., in state school, elementary and secondary; and in private institutions. Describes social agencies for the promotion of domestic science instruction. PartII is an elaborate presentation of house-wifery instruction in state-supported schools in Belgium. Part III treats of the domestic training of girls in Germany and Austria.

Great Britain. Board of Education. Consultative Committee. *Report . . . on Attendance, Compulsory or Otherwise, at Continuation Schools.* Presented to Parliament by Command of His Majesty. London, Printed for H. M. Stationery Office, by Eyre and Spottiswoode, Ltd., 1909. 2 v. ([Parliament. Papers by command] Cd. 4757-4758)

Contents — 1. Report and appendices.(Adopted by the committee, May 7th,1909) — 2. Summaries of evidence.

See also Great Britain. Board of Education. Compulsory Continuation Schools in Germany. London, 1910. 75 pp. (Educational Pamphets, no. pp 18)

Great Britain. Education Department. *Education and Industry in the United States,* by H. T. Mark. Special Reports on Educational Subjects, v. 2, part 2. London, Eyre and Spottiswoode, 1902. pp. 101-228.

Treats of manual and industrial training in the public elementary schools; industrial training in ordinary high schools, manual-training high schools, and commercial schools; industrial and commercial instruction in colleges and universities; trade schools; truant and reform schools.

Gives the testimony of Dr. W. T. Harris before the Industrial commission, January 1899, regarding education from the viewpoint of industry.

Great Britain. Foreign Office Germany. *Report on Commercial Instruction in Germany* . . . London, Printed for H. M. Stationery Office, by Harrison and Sons, 1904. 109 pp. ([Parliament. Papers by command] Cd. 2237. No. 619 miscellaneous ser. Diplomatic and consular reports)

Great Britain. Foreign Office. Germany. *Report on Technical Instruction in Germany: Supplementary and Miscellaneous.* Presented to both Houses of Parliament by Command of His Majesty, March, 1905. London, Printed for H. M. Stationery Office, by Harrison & Sons, 1905. 78 pp. (Parliament. Papers by command. Cd. 2237-11)

Report by Frederick Rose.

Great Britain. National Conference on Industrial Training of Women and Girls, London, October 6, 1908. *Report.*

Greenleigh, Arthur. *Opening the Doors; Job Training Programs. A Report to the Committee on Administration of Training Programs.* New York, Greenleigh Associates, Inc. 1968. Part I: 163 pp.; Part II: 292 pp.

A study of the administration of training programs financed by federal funds. Its purpose was to determine if there was any waste, duplication and inefficiency in the administration of these programs, and, if so, to supply recommendations for administrative change. Part Two of this research is a complete documentation of what was found, accompanied by a series of statistical data.

Gregory, Benjamin C. *Better Schools* . . . New York, The Macmillan Company, 1912. xi, 238 pp.
    Chapter V deals with manual training; chapter VI with industrial education. Author makes the following "broad and simple classification of the ends of education: (1) Those which relate to making the child self-supporting, and (2) those which look to his culture, happiness, power, and character." Advocates vocational education. Quotes from a number of prominent writers to show the value of industrial training.

Griessman, B. Eugene and Kenneth G. Densley. *Review and Synthesis of Research on Vocational Education in Rural Areas.* Columbus, Ohio, Ohio State University, Center for Vocational and Technical Education, 1969. 84 pp.
    This work is divided into two parts. The first is entitled "A Sociologist's Perspective of Vocational Education" and the second part is called "Vocational Education in Rural America: An Educator's Perspective." A comprehensive bibliography of all research reviewed is to be found on pages 70-84.

Gysbers, Norman C., et al. *Career Guidance.* Worthington, Ohio, Charles A. Jones Publishing Co., 1973.

Hailmann, William N. *German Views of American Education, with Particular Reference to Industrial Development. Collated from the Reports of the Royal Prussian Industrial Commission of 1904.* 2nd ed. Washington, Government Printing Office, 1907. 55 pp. (U. S. Bureau of Education. Bulletin no. 2, 1906)
    Synopsis of the report made by German specialists who visited the United States in 1904. Comparisons with German schools given.
    See Reiseberichte über Nord-Amerika erstattet von Kommissaren des königlichen preussischen ministers für handel und gewerbe. Berlin, 1906.

Hall, Clyde W. *Black Vocational, Technical and Industrial Arts Education: Development and History.* Chicago, American Technical Society, 1973.

(Halliday, Samuel Dumont.) *History of the Agricultural College Land Grant, Act of July 2, 1862* . . . Ithaca, N. Y. Ithaca Democrat Press, 1905. 63 pp.

Hamermesh, Daniel S. *Economic Aspects of Manpower Training Programs: Theory and Policy.* Lexington, Mass., D. C. Heath and Co., 1971. 145 pp.
    A study meant for the social scientist and economist, but of value to the educators involved in federal manpower training programs. An economic analysis is used to "discuss the possible roles and effects of government intervention in the area of manpower training."

Hamlin, Herbert M. "Adult Occupational Education." In *Handbook of Adult Education in the United States,* edited by Malcolm S. Knowles. (Chicago, Adult Education Association of the U. S. A., 1960) pp. 542-550.

Brief summary and bibliography on adult vocational education now in the United States and the public policy for its training, prospects, and current needs.

Haney, James P. *A Symposium on Industrial Education.* (Asbury Park, N. J., Kinmonth Press), 1907. 58 pp. (National society for the promotion of industrial education. Bulletin no. 3)

Presents in concise and personal form the opinions of employers and employees in regard to industrial education.

Haney, James Parton. *Vocational Training and Trade Teaching in the Public Schools.* Philadelphia, American Academy of Political and Social Science, (1909). 23-32 pp. (Publications of the American academy of political and social science, no. 570)

Reprinted from the Annals of the American academy of political and social science for January, 1909.

"While trade . . . teaching as such can not be advocated for the immature pupils of the elementary schools, preparatory vocational training must come to be seen as a necessary preliminary to the development of what may be termed the clientele of the trade school."

Hanus, Paul H. *Public Trade Schools.* A stenographic report of a Commencement Address delivered May 1909. (Winona Technical Institute. Bulletin, August 1910)

Hanus, Paul Henry. *Beginnings in Industrial Education, and Other Educational Discussions.* Boston and New York, Houghton Mifflin Company, 1908. ix, 199 pp.

Partly reprinted from various periodicals.

Contents. — Industrial education. — Industrial education, under state auspices, in Massachusetts. — What kind of industrial school is needed? — Industrial education and social progress. — The industrial continuation schools of Munich. — Professional preparation of high school teachers. — School instruction in religion. — The country schoolmaster in Bavaria.

"The author's presentation is strong and deserves a wide reading." — *Manual Training Magazine.* December 1908, pp. 188.

Hanus, Paul Henry. *The Technical Continuation Schools of Munich.* Boston, School of Printing, North-end Union, 1906. 14 pp.

Harby, Samuel Farkas. *A Study of Education in the Civilian Conservation Corps Camps of the Second Corps Area, April 1933-March 1937.* Ann Arbor, Mich., Edwards Brothers, Inc., 1938. 264 pp.

Originally written as a doctoral dissertation at Columbia University. This study seeks to find out what educational opportunities were offered to the enrollees, the extent and nature of the enrollees' response to his form of vocational education, and how well the programs fulfilled their aims in training unemployed youth.

Harris, Norman C. "Skilled Manpower and the Community College." In *Higher Education in an Age of Revolution,* Edited by G. Kerry Smith. (Washington, Association for Higher Education, 1962.) pp. 110-113.

One of the papers presented at the 17th annual National Conference on Higher Education. It briefly and concisely states the reasons why the junior college is able to "provide education for the world of work."

Harvey, Lorenzo Dow. *Report of the Commissioner Appointed by the Legislature in 1901 . . . to Investigate . . . Courses of Instruction in Manual Training and Domestic Economy, Adapted to Graded Schools; and to Recommend a Plan for the Organization of a Training School for the Preparation of Teachers of These Subjects . . .* Madison, Democrat Printing Co., 1902. 45 pp.

Commissioner, L. D. Harvey. Courses for girls: pp. 60-66.

Hawkins, Layton S. and others. *Development of Federal Legislation for Vocational Education.* Compiled from "Development of Vocational Education," U. S. Department of Health, Education, and Welfare. Chicago, American Technical Society, 1962. 110 pp.

Selection of material from the 1951 work "Development of Vocational Education" by L. S. Hawkins, C. A. Prosser, and J. C. Wright. Brought up to date with additional material covering legislation from 1947 to the passage of the Manpower Development and Training Act of 1962.

Hawkins, Layton S., Charles Prosser and John C. Wright. *Development of Vocational Education.* Chicago, American Technical Society, 1951.

A massive resource on historical backgrounds, programs, federal legislation, and trends.

Hays, Willet Martin. *Country Life Education.* (Washington, Government Printing Office), 1907. 13 pp. (U.S. Department of Agriculture. Office of experiment stations. Circular 73)

Address before the Pennsylvania state board of agriculture, 1907.

Healy, C. *Career Counseling in the Community College.* Springfield, Mo., Charles C. Thomas, 1974. 140 pp.

Counseling in the occupationally and vocationally oriented community college.

Henniger, G. Ross *The Technical Institute in America.* New York, McGraw-Hill, 1959. 276 pp.

Findings of the 1957-58 National Survey of Technical Institute Education conducted under the auspices of the American Society for Engineering Education. This study bridges the 30 years from the original 1928-29 study made by ASEE, known then as the Society for the Promotion of Engineering Education.

Henry, Nelson B., ed. *Vocational Education.* (National Society for the Study of Education, 42nd. Yearbook, Part I). Chicago, University of Chicago Press, 1943.

A comprehensive review of legislation, programs, and problems affecting vocational education. The Yearbooks for 1905, 1912, 1916, and 1924 also were addressed to vocational education.

Herr, Edwin L., ed. *Vocational Guidance and Human Development.* Boston, Houghton Mifflin, 1974.

Herrick, Cheesman A. *Meaning and Practice of Commercial Education.* New York & London, The Macmillan Company, 1904. xv, 378 pp.

Select bibliography: pp. 350-70.

"The kind of education urged in this book, it is believed, will teach men the meaning of business and raise commerce above narrow commercialism. Commerce we must have. Two main sources of the book are the announcements and reports of schools and expressions from business men and students of education."

Curricula set forth in appendix.

Herrick, Cheesman Abiah. *Aims of the William Penn High School for Girls; Address at the Dedication of the William Penn Building, December 10, 1909.* (Philadelphia? 1909.) 11 pp.

Hesburgh, Theodore M., et al. *Patterns for Lifelong Learning.* San Francisco, Jossey-Bass, 1973.

Hiatt, James S. *The Child, the School, and the Job.* Philadelphia, (1912). 12 pp. (Public education association. Study no. 39) Cover title.

Reprinted from the *City Club Bulletin,* December 27, 1912.

A study of child wage earners between 14 and 16 years of age, as they apply to the city of Philadelphia. Study based on the school census of June, 1912. Presents a number of interesting statistical charts and tables.

The following conclusions are drawn: "1. That the problem of the working child is not an immigrant problem, since over 50 per cent of those reported as at work are of the second generation of American birth. 2. That this is not the problem of the boy alone, since over 49 per cent of the workers are girls. 3. That the vast majority of children who leave school at fourteen to enter industry go into those kinds of employment which offer a large initial wage for simple mechanical processes, but which hold out little or no opportunity for improvement and no competence at maturity. 4. That wages received are so low as to force a parasitic life. 5. That but slight advancement is offered the fifteen-year-old over the fourteen-year-old child worker."

High School Teachers' Association of New York City. *Choosing a Career; a Circular of Information for Boys.* New York, Students' Aid Committee, [1909]. 22 pp.

High School Teachers' Association of New York City. *Choosing a Career; a Circular of Information for Girls.* New York, Students' Aid Committee, [1909]. 26 pp.

High School Teachers' Association of New York City. *Students' Aid Committee. Directing Young People in the Choice of a Vocation.* (Brooklyn, N. Y.), Printed for the Students' Aid Committee, (1910), 16 pp.

High School Teachers' Association of New York City. *Year-book, v. 5, 1910-1911.* 142 pp.
Contains papers on vocational guidance in the high schools of New York, pp. 17-25; final report of the subcommittee on a preparatory course for boys entering commercial life, pp. 85-105.

Hill, David S. *Introduction to Vocational Education; a Statement of Facts and Principles Related to the Vocational Aspects of Education below College Grade.* New York, Macmillan, 1932. 483 pp.
Useful as an historic study on vocational education in the public high school in the post-World War I period. Contains courses of study for various branches of vocational training then in existence.

Hill, Frank Ernest. *The School in the Camps; the Educational Program of the Civilian Conservation Corps.* New York, American Association for Adult Education, 1935. 84 pp.
A valuable reference written while the camps were in existence and full operation.

Hodge, George B. *Association Educational Work for Men and Boys . . .* New York & London, Association Press, [1912]. 256 pp.
Describes work of the Y. M. C. A. in the field of vocational education. Illustrated with 50 charts or graphs; also half-tones showing the various kinds of work in operation. Educational statistics compiled from Government and state reports: books and periodicals, etc.

Holland, John L. *Making Vocational Choices: A Theory of Careers.* Englewood Cliffs, N. J., Prentice Hall, 1973.

Holland, Kenneth and Frank E. Hill. *Youth in the CCC Camp.* Washington, American Council on Education, 1942. 263 pp.
This book was the result of a 5-year study sponsored by the American Youth Commission. It includes a survey and evaluation of the social and educational work of the CCC and a report on an experimental program in 10 selected camps.

Holmes, William H. *School Organization and the Individual Child . . .* Worcester, Mass., The Davis Press, 1912. 205 pp.
Discusses the value of manu-mental work in developing the exceptional child, Chapter 14. Chapter 12 contains useful information on wage earning and after-care of mentally defective children.

Hooper, Frederick and James Graham. *Commercial Education at Home and Abroad . . .* London & New York, Macmillan and Co., Ltd., 1901. xv, 267 pp. illus.
Discusses materials for a scheme of commercial education for Great Britain, also suggested curricula for all grades of educational institutions.

Contains chapter on commercial education on the Continent, and the position in the United States in 1901.

Householder, Daniel L. and Alan R. Suess. *Review and Synthesis of Research in Industrial Arts Education.* 2nd ed. Columbus, Ohio, Ohio State University, Center for Vocational and Technical Education, 1969. 63 pp.

The research reviewed concentrates mainly on periodical articles and unpublished doctoral dissertations, published for the 1966-1968 period. A comprehensive bibliography on all research reviewed is to be found on pages 46-63.

Howard, Earl D. *The Cause and Extent of the Recent Industrial Progress of Germany.* Boston and New York, Houghton Mifflin Co., (1907). xiii, 147 pp. [Hart, Schaffner & Marx prize essays.I]

Bibliography: pp. [xi]-xiii.

In a chapter on industrial education stress is laid upon the intimate relation of school training to vocation. The character and extent of the general and industrial continuation schools are described.

Contains a resume of industrial conditions in Germany before 1871; shows the remarkable progress made subsequent to that date. The relation of school training to the intended vocation is treated.

Hoyt, Kenneth B. and Jean R. Hebeler. *Career Education for Gifted and Talented Students.* Salt Lake City, Olympus Publishing Co., 1974.

Hoyt, Kenneth B., et al. *Career Education: What It Is and How to Do It.* Salt Lake City, Olympus Publishing Co., 1974.

Hughes, Everett C., et al. *Education for the Professions of Medicine, Law, Theology, and Social Welfare.* New York, McGraw-Hill, 1973.

Hunter, William L. and Everett G. Livingston. *A Guide to Magazine Articles on Industrial Arts Education and Vocational Industrial Education.* Ames, Iowa, Iowa State College, Industrial Arts Dept., 1934. 75 pp.

A list of the major articles on industrial education appearing between January 1, 1920, and January 1, 1934. Has author and subject index.

Illinois University, College of Education. *Curricula Content for Technical Education.* William John Schill. Principal Investigator. Urbana, 1964. 139 pp. (Cooperative research report No. 2048)

A sample survey interviewing technicians in 500 manufacturing establishments "to find out what a technician does and what knowledges are related to his job." The resulting data should prove useful to those determining the curriculum content of technical vocational courses.

Indiana. Commission on Industrial and Agricultural Education. *Report . . . December, 1912.* Indianapolis, Wm. B. Burford, Contractor for State Printing and Binding, 1912. 133 pp.

Will A. Yarling, chairman.

Recommendations include 17 items concerning "the establishment of vocational schools, the machinery of administration, compulsory attendance,

teacher training and related points." **Reviewed in** *Vocational Education,* 2:
251-55, January 1913.

Appendices contain a digest of laws relating to industrial education, also
drafts of bills proposed — vocational education in industries, agriculture and
domestic science; apprenticeship; and certification of the compulsory attendance laws. Views of organized labor and manufactures given.

Indiana Town and City Superintendents' Association. Committee on Manual,
Domestic and Vocational Training. *Report. November Meeting, 1908.* [n. p.,
1908.] 18 pp. table.

Chairman, W. A. Jessup.
Bibliographies: p. 12, 17.

"Industrial Education in the United States." In *History of Manual and Industrial School Education* by Lewis Flint Anderson. (New York, Appleton,
1926). pp. 135-251.

This history of industrial education in the Untied States is part II of this
work. It covers developments from the period preceding the Civil War to
1925. Useful as a history of industrial education institutions for Negroes.

*Industrial Education: Studies by F. H. Sykes . . . F. G. Bonser . . . H. C.
Brandon . . .* New York City, Teachers College, Columbia University, 1911.
61 pp.

Contents. — Industrial arts education and industrial training [by] F. H.
Sykes. — Modifications within public or general school programs to meet in-
dustrial needs [by] F. G. Bonser. — The cost of industrial education in the
United States; a study of 50 typical schools [by] H. C. Brandon.

International Labour Office. *Automation and Other Technological Developments.* Report of the Director General. Geneva, Switzerland, The Office,
1957. 105 pp. (Report I — part I)

A review of technological changes in modern society, the impact of these
changes upon the education and training of youth and adults. Information
applicable to and typical of what is found in the United States.

International Labour Office. *Vocational Training of Adults in the United
States.* Geneva, Switzerland, the Author, 1948. 223 pp. (Its Vocational
Training Monograph, No. 3)

Contents: General introduction; the Federal-State vocational education
program; apprentice training (including Federal financial aid); in-plant
training conducted by private undertaking; training within industry for
supervisors; training conducted by trade unions; and provision for special
training needs.

Itasca Conference on the Continuing Education of Women. Itasca State
Park, Minnesota, 1962. *Education and a Woman's Life. Proceedings.* Edited
by Lawrence E. Dennis, Washington, American Council on Education, 1963.
153 pp.

Sponsored by the American Council on Education, with assistance from
the Carnegie Corporation of New York and the University of Minnesota this
conference discussed the theory and practice of continuing education for
women and describes the pilot projects in vocational training in the area.

Johnson, Palmer O. and O. L. Harvey. *The National Youth Administration.* Washington, U. S. Government Printing Office, 1938. 121 pp.

This report is useful in its discussion of the means used to train unemployed youth and the types of work-study programs used as a relief measure.

Johnston, Charles H., ed. *High School Education* . . . New York, Scribner's Sons, 1912. xxii, 555 pp.

Bibliography: pp. 471-531.

Discusses commercial education, vocational training, practical arts for girls, etc., etc.

Johnstone, John W. *Volunteers for Learning: a Study of the Educational Pursuits of American Adults.* Chicago, National Opinion Research Center, 1963. 148 1, 12 pp. (NORC report No. 89)

The first of a series of studies about the nature of adult education in America. Points out governmental activity in two phases: vocations and home family life.

Johnstone, John W. and Ramon J. Rivera. *Volunteers for Learning; a Study of the Educational Pursuits of American Adults.* Chicago, Aldine Publishing Co., 1965. 624 pp.

Research conducted by the National Opinion Research Center on the nature of adult education in America. Information on vocational training of adults is mainly found in the chapter: "Why People Take Courses and What They Get From Them." (pp. 142-162)

Jones, Arthur J. *The Continuation School in the United States.* Washington Government Printing Office, 1907. 157 pp. (U. S. Bureau of Education. Bulletin no. 1, 1907)

Bibliography: pp. 145-49.

Advocates the need of such schools by statistics showing the rapid decline of school attendance after the age of industrial worth is reached. It indicates briefly how much more extensive and efficient German and English schools of this type are than our own. The work of many typical American schools is described, and finally the place and purpose of the continuation school in our system of education are defined.

Kahler, Alfred and Ernest Hamburger. *Education for an Industrial Age* Ithaca, N. Y., Cornell University Press, 1948. 334 pp.

This book was published for the Institute of World Affairs and is an evaluation of vocational education and training in the United States as they relate to the mobility of the labor force and employment stability. As a comparison, investigations into apprenticeship and other types of in-service training were made for selected foreign countries. Germany, Great Britain, Switzerland, and the Soviet Union were chosen, each country representing a special kind of training.

Kandel, Isaac Leon. *Federal Aid for Vocational Education; a Report to the Carnegie Foundation for the Advancement of Teaching.* New York, 1917.

127 pp. (The Carnegie Foundation for the Advancement of Teaching. Bulletin No. 10)

Contents: The legislative history of Federal aid for vocational education; constitutional and educational precedents, and subsequent developments of the Morrill Act.

Kansas City, Mo. Board of Education. *Committee on Vocation Schools Report . . .* (Kansas City, Mo. 1911.) 48 pp.

Kaufman, Jacob J. and Morgan V. Lewis. *The Potential of Vocational Education: Observations and Conclusions Based on a Study of Three Selected Cities in Pennsylvania.* University Park, Pa., The Pennsylvania State University, The Institute for Research on Human Resources, 1968. 160 pp.

Vocational education and occupational training in three city public secondary schools were studied. The cities remain unidentified and are designated simply as small, medium-sized and large. Partial contents of chapters: Vocational Education and Educational Opportunities, Evaluation Education Programs, Employment Experiences of Graduates.

Kaufman, Jacob J. (Project director) and others. *A Cost-effectiveness Study of Vocational Education; a Comparison of Vocational and Nonvocational Education in Secondary Schools.* University Park, Pa., Pennsylvania State University. Institute for Research on Human Resources, 1969. 302 pp.

This study provides a framework and related data in an attempt to answer the question: "Should the U. S. invest more money in vocational education, given alternative investment opportunities in other educational curricula?"

Kaufman, Jacob' J. and others. *The Role of the Secondary Schools in the Preparation of Youth for Employment.* University Park, Pa., Institute for Research on Human Resources, Pennsylvania State University, 1967. 339 pp.

A study focused on 25 schools in nine communities located in the northeastern section of the U. S. Made two years after the Vocational-Education Act of 1963 had been implemented, the survey attempts to give concrete evidence of what has been accomplished by the schools in training youth for jobs.

Kazanas, H. C., et al. *The Philosophy and Foundations of Vocational Education.* New York, MSS Information Corp., 1973.

Keeling, Frederic. *The Labor Exchange in Relation to Boy and Girl Labour.* London, P. S. King & Son, 1910. 76 pp.

Bibliography: pp. 73-76.

Keller, Franklin J. *The Double-purpose High School: Closing the Gap between Vocational and Academic Preparation.* New York, Harper, 1953. 207 pp.

A book primarily for those responsible for providing courses in occupational training along with preparation for college entrance.

Keller, Franklin, J. *Principles of Vocational Education; the Primacy of the Person.* Boston, D. C. Heath, 1948. 402 pp.

Philosophical principles underlying vocational education and a discussion of the aims and objectives of the ideal program.

Kerschensteiner, Georg. *Three Lectures on Vocational Training . . .* Delivered in America under the Auspices of the National Society for the Promotion of Industrial Education. Chicago, Published by the Commercial Club of Chicago, 1911. 52 pp.

The fundamental principles of continuation schools, pp. 1-16.

The organization of the continuation school in Munich, pp. 17-29.

The technical day trade schools in Germany, pp. 30-52.

Kinne, Helen. *Equipment for Teaching Domestic Science.* Boston, Whitcomb & Barrows, 1911. v, 96 pp. illus.

Estimates, descriptions, and suggestive lists given for complete equipment for instruction in domestic science.

Kliever, Douglas E. *The Vocational Education Act of 1963: A Case Study in Legislation.* Washington, Brookings Institution, 1965.

A review of federal legislation for vocational education, with exhaustive examination of 1963 Act.

Krug, Edward A. *The Shaping of the American High School, 1880-1920.* New York, Harper, 1964; and *The Shaping of the American High School, 1920-1941.* Madison, University of Wisconsin Press, 1972.

Invaluable historical contexts for the study of vocational, industrial arts, and practical arts education.

Land, Samuel L. *Trade Associations: Their Services to Education; a Study of the Function of the National Trade Association in the Promotion of Training in Industry.* New York, Heating and Piping COntractors National Association, 1931. 141 pp.

Useful as a historical source of information concerning the efforts of trade associations to establish and maintain educational training programs for workers. Describes also the relationships of these organizations to Federal, State, and local boards for vocational education.

Larson, Milton E. *Review and Synthesis of Research: Analysis for Curriculum Development in Vocational Education.* Columbus, Ohio, Ohio State University, Center for Vocational and Technical Education, 1969. 75 pp.

A "state of the art" paper reviewing research findings and other contributions as reported in books, periodicals, manuals and guides and published for the period 1963-1969.

Larsson, Gustav. *American Sloyd, 1888-1900.* Boston, Sloyd Training School, 1900. 39 pp.

Describes work in the free normal classes in the Sloyd training school.

Laselle, Mary A. and Katherine E. Wiley. *Vocations for Girls,* with an Introduction by Meyer Bloomfield. Boston, New York (etc.), Houghton Mifflin Company, (1913). x, 139 pp.

"The object of this book is to give to young girls, and those responsible for the guidance of girls, some definite information as to conditions of work in the more common vocations."

Lathrop, F. W. "The Organization of Vocational Education for Youth and Adults." In *The National Society for the Study of Education, 44th Yearbook: American Education in the Postwar Period, part II: Structural reorganization.* (Chicago, University of Chicago Press, 1945.) pp. 84-96.

Contents: Vocational education prior to the war; wartime expansion of vocational education; liberal and cultural content in vocational curriculums; and some recent changes in vocational or related fields.

Lavergne, F. *Les Ecoles et les Oeuvres Municipales d'Enseignement.* Paris, France, P. Mouillot, 1900.

Evening schools, France.

Laws Relating to Vocational Education and Agricultural Extension Work Compiled by Gilman G. Udell. Washington, U. S. Govt. Print Off., 1971. 1000 pp.

Contains a chronological listing of the laws since 1917, and each entry is accompanied by brief references to a legislative history of it.

Lazerson, Marvin. *Origins of the Urban School: Public Education in Massachusetts, 1870-1915.* Cambridge, Harvard University Press, 1971.

Includes chapters on "Manual Training: The Search for Ideology"; "Manual Training and the Restoration of Social Values"; "From the Principles of Work to the Teaching of Trades"; "The Politics of Vocationalism"; and "Vocationalism and the Equality of Educational Opportunity."

Lazerson, Marvin and W. Norton Grubb, eds. *American Education and Vocationalism: A Documentary History, 1870-1970.* New York, Teachers College Press, Columbia University, 1974.

Representative documents, with essay introduction and valuable bibliographical essay.

Leake, Albert H. *The Vocational Education of Girls and Women.* New York, Macmillan, 1918. 430 pp.

A study done at the time when vocational training for women was in its initial stages. Part I is devoted to home economics training, and Part II discusses "women in industry outside the home," the problems of the unskilled woman who must work to support herself and family and the types of vocational schools then in existence for women.

Leavitt, Frank M. *Examples of Industrial Education.* Boston, Ginn. 1912.

Summarizes the ideology of the industrial education movement, with examples. See also, Arthur D. Dean, *The Worker and the State* (New York, Century Company, 1910).

Leavitt, Frank M. and Edith Brown. *Prevocational Education in the Public Schools.* Boston, Houghton Mifflin, 1915.
   The only substantial historical source on prevocational training.

Leavitt, Frank Mitchell. *Some Examples of Industrial Education.* Boston, New York (etc.), Ginn and Company, (1912). 330 pp.
   Contents. 1. Significance of the movement for industrial education. 2. Manual training and industrial education. 3. The demand — an analysis. 4. The demand of organized labor. 5. The demand of educators. 6. The demand of social workers. 7. The revision of educational ideals involved in the movement for industrial training. 8. A plan for immediate reorganization. 9. Examples of more fundamental reorganization. 10. Prevocational work in grades 6-8. 11. The intermediate or separate industrial school. 12. Vocational high schools. 13. The trade school. 14. Part-time cooperative schools. 15. The continuation school. 16. Vocational guidance. 17. State legislation. 18. Concerning agricultural education.
   Chapter 8 presents a plan for meeting "the immediate needs of the present generation of school children without modifying, in any radical way, the prevailing systems of school organization."

Le Blanc, René. *L'Enseignement Professional en France au Début du xx Siecle.* Paris, E. Cornely et Cie., 1905. 338 pp.

Le Blanc, René. *La Réforme des Écoles Primaires Supérieures.* Paris, Librairie Larousse, (1907). 216 pp. illus.
   "Enseignement technique primaire, agricole, industriel, commercial, maritime, ménager."

Lecht, Leonard A. *Manpower Needs for National Goals in the 1970's.* New York, Praeger, 1969. 183 pp.
   A study undertaken by the Center for Priority Analysis of the National Planning Association. In Chapter seven "The implications for education and job training" (pp. 100-119) a discussion is given of the present role of vocational education, and its adequacy in providing job training.

Lederer, Muriel. *The Guide to Career Education.* New York, Quadrangle/New York Times, 1974.

Lee, Edwin A. *Objectives and Problems of Vocational Education.* New York, McGraw, 1928. 451 pp.
   An evaluation of the Smith-Hughes Act, 10 years after its passage and enactment by leading educators written in individual essays.

Leighbody, Gerald B. *Vocational Education in America's Schools: Major Issues of the 1970's.* Chicago, American Technical Society, 1972.
   Evaluation of programs, and recommendations, with notices of 1968 Amendments of Vocational Education Act.

Lembke, Fr. Der ländliche Fortbildungs-schulunterricht, Praparationen and Aufgaben. Im Anschluss an den "Lehrplan für ländliche Fortbildungsschulen in Preussen" . . . Leipzig, Quelle & Meyer, 1909. 105 pp.

Levitan, Sar A. *Antipoverty Work and Training Efforts: Goals and Reality.* - Ann Arbor, Michigan, University of Michigan, Institue of Labor and Industrial Relations, No. 3)
   This study of federal antipoverty programs was done in cooperation with the National Manpower Policy Task Force. It reviews the operation of federally-supported manpower programs as the Job Corps, the Neighborhood Youth Corps and the Work Experience and Training programs, and represents only the views of the author. The last chapter is entitled "Goals and Their Implementation."

Levitan, Sar A. *Vocational Education and Federal Policy.* Kalamazoo, Michigan, W. E. Upjohn Institute for Employment Research, 1963. 29 pp.
   Partial contents: Development of Federal aid for vocational education; scope of federally supported vocational education; and the role of the Federal Government in improving vocational education.

Levitan, Sar A. and G. L. Mangum. *Federal Training and Work Programs in the Sixties.* Ann Arbor, Michigan, The University of Michigan and Wayne State University, Institute of Labor and Industrial Relations, 1969. 465 pp.
   A compilation of a series of policy papers by the authors, tracing the development of manpower programs for the disadvantaged and a description of the federally funded manpower programs now in existence. Part three is devoted to the Vocational Education Act of 1963.

Lexis, W. H. R. ,A. *Das technische Unterrichtswesen.* Berlin, A. Asher & Co., 1904 3 parts. (Das Unterrichtswesen im deutschen Reich. Band 4)
   Contents. — 1. Teil. Die technischen Hochschulen. 2. Teil. Die Hochschulen fur besondere Fachgebiete. 3. Teil. Der mittlere und niedere Fauchunterricht.

Liles, Parker. "Retraining for New Jobs." In *Recent and Projected Developments Affecting Business Education. National Business Education Yearbook, v. 2, 1964.* (Washington, National Business Education Association (NEA), 1964.) pp. 51-71.
   A discussion of the problem and cause of unemployment and a comprehensive review of the Area Redevelopment Act of 1961 and the Manpower Development Training Act, 1962, with emphasis on the latter. The responsibilities on the State and local levels in implementing the training program under this law are also included.

Lindman, Erick L. *Financing Vocational Education in the Public Schools.* Los Angeles, University of California, Graduate School of Education, 1970. 234 pp. (National Educational Finance Project. Special Study No. 4)
   This study is one of eleven satellite studies which comprise the National Education Finance Project, described as "the most comprehensive study of school finance on all levels of education since the 1930's." Topics treated here

include the federal contributions to vocational education, projections of vocational educational enrollments and costs for 1980, the allocation of federal vocational education funds within states.

Little, J. Kenneth. *Review and Synthesis on the Placement and Follow-up of Vocational Education Students.* Columbus, Ohio State University, 1970.
    Critical review of literature and reports.

Lockette, Rutherford E., ed. *Industrial Arts in Senior High Schools.* 22nd. Yearbook. American Council on Industrial Arts. Bloomington, McKnight Publishing Co., 1973.

London. County Council. Education Committee. *The Apprenticeship Question.* Report of the Section of the Education Committee . . . London, Printed for the London County Council, by Jas. Truscott and Son, Ltd., (1906). 45 pp.
    R. A. Bray, chairman.
    Discusses situation in England, Germany, France, and the United States. Advocates the part time system and evening continuation schools as a substitute for apprenticeships.

London. County Council. Education Committee. *Report on Eight Years of Technical Education and Continuation Schools (Mostly Evening Work) in Two Parts.* Presented to the Education Committee on the 11th December, 1912 . . . London, James Truscott and Son, Ltd., (1912). 120 pp.
    Two-thirds of the children of London who leave the elementary schools enter unskilled occupations. Report says that the great weakness of the evening schools is the instability of attendance. Mr. Bray, in his memorandum on the subject, declares that nothing but compulsion will successfully cope with the 40,000 ineffectives.

London. School Board. *Report [Prepared under the Direction of the Late School Board for London) with Regard to Industrial Schools, 1870 to 1904.* (London). Alexander & Shepheard (1904). 56 pp. plates.
    London. County Council.

London. Technical Education Board. *Report of the Special Sub-committee on Technical Instruction for Women.* (Presented to the Technical Education Board, 7th December, 1903.) (London), J. Truscott and Son, 1903. 23 pp.
    Chairman, J. R. Macdonald.

Long, Cloyd Darl. *School-leaving Youth and Employment; Some Factors Associated with the Duration of Early Employment of Youth Whose Formal Education Ended at High School Graduation or Earlier.* New York, Teachers College, Columbia University, 1941. 84 pp.
    An earlier study of a new common problem — the "school dropout." This research centered around six schools located in Connecticut and New Jersey. It contains the findings of what the schools and communities did to help out of school youth from a period of 1934-38, and what became of the young people who had dropped out of school.

Lyon, Otto. *Die Fortbildungsschule für Mädchenl; Vortrag auf dem 8. deutschen Fortbildungsschultage in Stettin am 1 Oktober 1905* . . . Leipzig. B. G. Teubner, 1906. 24 pp.

McCarthy, John A. *Vocational Education: America's Greatest Resource.* Chicago, American Technical Society, 1951. 397 pp.
  At the time of the publication of this book, the author was assistant commissioner of education, Department of Education in New Jersey. In addition to an historical account of Federal vocational education legislation, material on the philosophy and organization of vocational programs is given.

McCollum, Sylvia G. "Needed Directions in Vocational Resources Development for the Noncollege Bound." In *Human Resources Development,* edited by Edward B. Jakubauskas and C. Phillip Baumel. (Ames, Iowa, Iowa State University Press, 1967) pp. 126-133.
  This and other chapters in the book "Human Resources Development" was developed from a conference held at Iowa State University, Oct. 13-14, 1966 on the subject of developing human resources for manpower. The "needed directions" discussed are those in the fields of research for curriculum development for job-related education.

Macdonald, James W. *Report upon Business and Industrial Education in the High Schools of Massachusetts.* 37 pp. Cover-title.
  Reprinted from the 69 Report of the State board of education, January 1906. Largely statistical.

McKeever, William A. *Assisting the Boy in the Choice of a Vocation.* Manhattan, Kans., 1909. 15 pp.
  Reprinted from the *Industrialist,* v. 35, no. 41, June 16, 1909.

McLeod, T. H., ed. *Post-Education in a Technological Society.* Montreal, McGill-Queen's University Press, 1973.

Maennel, Bruno. *The Auxiliary Schools of Germany. Six Lectures* . . . Trans. by Feltcher B. Dresslar. Washington, Government Printing Office, 1907. 137 pp. (U. S. Bureau of Education. Bulletin no. 3, 1907)
  Bibliography: pp. 125-31.
  The original work is entitled "Vom hilfsschulwesen: Sechs vortrage von Dr. B. Maennel, Rektor. Druck und Verlag von B. G. Teubner in Leipzig, 1905." 140 pp. It forms the 73rd volume of the series, "Aus Natur und Geisteswelt; Sammlung wissenschaftlich-gemein verständlicher darstellungen." The work is dedicated to W. Rein, Ph. D., Litt. D., professor of pedagogy in the University of Jena.

Maine. Committee on Industrial Education. *Report of the Committee on Industrial Education, 1910.* Augusta, Kennebec Journal Print, 1910. 72 pp. fold. diagr.
  Contains report and recommendations of special committee created by the legislature of 1909. To be found also as Chapter I in annual report of the state superintendent for 1910.

Mangum, Garth L. *MDTA, Foundation of Federal Manpower Policy.* Baltimore, Johns Hopkins Press, 1968. 184 pp.

An evaluation of the Manpower Development and Training Act of 1962, and all of the amendments of this Act through 1966. Information is given on how the law was implemented to "deliver service", and the contributions and costs of the programs that were eventually established.

Mangum, Garth L. *Reorienting Vocational Education.* Ann Arbor, Michigan, Institute of Labor and Industrial Relations, 1968. 56 pp. (Policy Papers in Human Resources and Industrial Relations No. 7)

"This evaluation of the results of the Vocational Education Act of 1963 is part of a larger project to evaluate federal manpower policies and programs directed by the author under a grant from the Ford Foundation". Contents: "Origin and Achievements of the 1963 Act"; "The Status of Vocational Education"; "Innovations in Vocational Education"; "Reorienting Vocational Education."

Mangum, Garth L. and Otto Progan. *Education for Employment.* Ann Arbor, University of Michigan, Institute of Labor and Industrial Relations, 1969. 120 pp.

The historical trends leading to formal training for employment and the current status of this type of training. Included also are the Report of the Advisory Council on Vocational Education, 1968 and the potential of the Vocational Education Amendments of 1968.

Manitoba. Royal Commission on Technical Education and Industrial Training. *Report . . . August 26, 1910.* Winnipeg, Manitoba, 1912. 78 pp. illus.

Many manufacturers, contractors, and skilled mechanics representing the various trades appeared before the Commission. "From whatever point of view the witnesses spoke, they were one in saying that the conditions to be met required the establishment of some well-considered scheme of vocational training based upon and accompanied by the essentials of a good general education."

Contains a resume of the aims and methods of industrial education in educational centers in the United States and Eastern Canada.

Manpower Information for Vocational Education Planning. *Report of a Conference Held at the Ohio State University's Center for Vocational and Technical Education, June 12 and 13, 1969.* Edited by Robert C. Young. Columbus, Ohio, Ohio State University, Center for Vocational and Technical Education, 1969. 170 pp.

Papers prepared for the conference, followed by comments from those in attendance. Sessions were held on such topics as forecasting occupational employment for state vocational education planning and occupational education and training requirements.

Mapp, Edward C., comp. *Books for Occupational Education Programs.* Ann Arbor, Michigan, R. R. Bowker, 1971. 250 pp.

A guide to 9,000 books covering subjects in 131 technical and vocational fields.

Marland, Sidney P., Jr. "Career Education. In *U. S. Congress. Senate. Committee on Appropriations. Hearings on HR. 15417, 92d Cong. 2d sess, Fiscal Year 1973. Pt. I.* (Washington, U. S. Govt. Print. Off. 1972) pp. 147-163. (Committee Print)

Testimony of the U. S. Commissioner of Education given at the Senate hearings on the FY 1973 HEW Budget.

Marshall, F. Ray and Vernon M. Briggs, Jr. *The Negro and Apprenticeship.* Baltimore, Johns Hopkins Press, 1967. 283 pp.

This book is based on a 1965 study of Negro participation in apprenticeship programs in ten large cities, having large Negro populations. Included is a discussion on the causes for the small numbers of Negro apprentices and recommendations on how to bridge this gap.

Marshall, Florence M. *Industrial Training for Women . . .* (Asbury Park, N. J., Kinmonth Press), 1907. 59 pp. (National society for the promotion of industrial education. Bulletin no. 4)

Martin, George Henry. *Industrial Education and the Public Schools; an Address before the Massachusetts Teachers' Association,* Boston, November 27. 1908. Boston, Wright & Potter Printing Co., State Printers, 1908. 20 pp.

An excellent presentation of the elementary school problem of industrial education.

Maryland. Commission on Industrial Education. *Report of the Commission to Make Inquiry and Report to the Legislature of Maryland Respecting the Subject of Industrial Education, 1908-1910.* Baltimore, G. W. King Printing Co. State Printers, (1910), 121 pp. illus.

Discusses among other things the practicability of introducing industrial instruction, or extending it, in the schools of Maryland, city and rural, with forms of industrial education for colored children. Gives replies to circular letter addressed to citizens of Maryland and others.

Mason, William P., comp. *Report of a National Seminar on the Scope of the Responsibilities of Vocational Education in Large Cities. Final Report.* Cleveland, Ohio, Cleveland Public Schools, 1969. 98pp.

Compilation of the major speeches delivered at the July 1968 Seminar, attended by directors of state departments of vocational education, city vocational education directors, city school superintendents and U. S. Office of Education personnel.

Massachusetts. Board of Education. *Information Relating to the Establishment and Administration of State-aided Vocational Schools.* Issued . . . December 1, 1911. Boston, Wright & Potter Printing Co., State Printers, 1911. 57 pp. (Board of Education. Bulletin no. 3)

Massachusetts. Bureau of Labor Statistics. *Industrial Education for Working Girls.* Boston, 1905. 38 pp. (pt. 1 of Annual Report)

Massachusetts. Bureau of Statistics of Labor. *The Apprenticeship System.*

Part I, Annual Report for 1906. Boston, 1906. 86 pp.

Replies to a questionnaire sent to employers and officers of trade unions in Massachusetts regarding status of apprenticeship, its regulation, condition, restriction of numbers, and value for training workmen.

Massachusetts. Commission on Industrial Education. *Industrial Continuation Schools for Gardeners' Apprentices, Munich.* Boston, Wright & Potter Printing Co., State Printers, 1907. 6 pp. (Its Bulletin no. 6)

Gives history of the origin of the school, plan of organization, statistics, etc. The instruction covers the whole business of the gardener, including industrial arithmetic and bookkeeping, civics, botany, reading, and drawing.

Massachusetts. Commission on Industrial Education. *Industrial Continuation Schools for Jewelers' and Gold and Silver Workers' Apprentices, Munich.* Boston Wright & Potter, 1907. 12 pp. (Bulletin no. 1)

Industrial Continuation Schools for Jewelers' and Gold and Silver Workers' Apprentices, Munich. Boston, Wright & Potter, 1907. 12 pp. (Bulletin no. 1)

Massachusetts. Commission on Industrial Education. *Industrial Continuation Schools for Machinists' Apprentices, Munich.* Boston, Wright & Potter Printing Co., State Printers, 1907. 12 pp. (Its Bulletin no. 3)

The instruction in physics and machinery, as well as in materials and shop work, is given by a skilled machinist, the remaining instruction is undertaken by teachers of the common and continuation schools.

Massachusetts. Commission on Industrial Education. *Industrial Continuation Schools for Machinists' Apprentices, Munich.* Boston, Wright, & Potter, 1907. 11 pp. (Bulletin no. 5)

Massachusetts. Commission on Industrial Education. *Industrial Continuation Schools for Male Commerical Employees, Munich.* Boston, Wright & Potter Printing Co., State Printers, 1907. 12 pp (Its Bulletin no. 2)

The subjects of instruction include arithmetic, exchange, bookkeeping and accounts current, **commercial** correspondence and reading, commercial geography and the study of goods, life and citizenship, stenography, and penmanship. Under the head of goods, "the individual raw products and the manufactured articles are considered as regards their source, manufacture and qualities."

Massachusetts Commission on Industrial Education. *Industrial Continuation Schools for Mechanicians' Apprentices, Munich.* Boston, Wright & Potter Printing Co., State Printers, 1907. 15 pp. (Its Bulletin no. 4)

Apprentices, who during their four years of required attendance on the school have not done well, may be required, upon the solicitation of their master or of the school, to attend all or part of the instruction in any one class.

Massachusetts, Commission on Industrial Education. *Industrial Education, under State Auspices, in Massachusetts.* Boston, Wright & Potter Printing Co., 1908. 13 pp. (Its Bulletin no. 8)

Massachusetts. Commission on Industrial and Technical Education. *The Agricultural School.* Boston, Wright & Potter, 1907. 11 pp. (Bulletin no. 7)

Massachusetts. Commission on Industrial and Technical Education. (*First annual*) *Report . . . March 1907.* Boston, Wright & Potter Printing Co., State Printers, 1907. 71 pp. (Public document no. 76)
   Paul H. Hanus, chairman.
   Advocates co-operation with local authorities in the founding of schools for technical and industrial education. Shows that considerable progress had been accomplished in the matter of establishing in several cities of the state of the industrial schools contemplated by the law.

Massachusetts. Commission on Industrial and Technical Education. *Report . . . 1906.* Boston, Wright & Potter Printing Co., State Printers, 1906. 196 pp. [General Court] Senate no. 349
   Carroll D. Wright, chairman.
   Reprinted by Columbia University, Teachers College. Educational reprints, no. 1.
   Outlines system of education. Gives the status of vocational education in Massachusetts. Presents report of the sub-committee on the Relation of children to the industries. Statistics gathered during the investigation. In-dustrial education in Europe. Submits for consideration of the legislature the draft of a bill providing for industrial and technical schools, with the recom-mendation that a second commission be appointed to extend the investigation of methods of industrial training and of local requirements, and advising and assisting in the introduction of industrial instruction by means of a system of independent schools. With some modifications the recommended legislation was adopted by the State. The new commission was appointed August 31, 1906.

Massachusetts. Commission on Industrial and Technical Education. *Report on the Advisability of Establishing One or More Technical Schools or Indus-trial Colleges . . .* Boston, Wright & Potter, 1908. 38 pp. (Bulletin no. 11)

Massachusetts. Commission on Industrial and Technical Education. *Report on the Relations of European Industrial Schools to Labor.* By Charles H. Winslow. Boston, Wright & Potter, 1908. 22 pp. (Bulletin no. 10)

Massachusetts. Commission on Industrial and Technical Education. *Second Annual Report . . . January 1908.* Boston, Wright & Potter Printing Co., State Printers, 1908. 682 pp. (Public document no. 76)
   Paul H. Hanus, chairman.
   A notable report. Evening industrial schools established by the commis-sion in five cities. Requests for others under advisement. Nearly 1,000 pupils

in attendance upon these schools. In reviewing the work accomplished during the year, the Commission says that "during the past year the interest in industrial education steadily increased among all classes and in all directions. Both employers and employed are meeting on the common ground of mutual interest." The report gives voluminous data on industrial education in foreign countries; the relations of European industrial schools to labor, etc. Describes special schools in the United States; and the attitude of the manufacturing interest in 2 Massachusetts cities toward industrial education. Fully illustrated.

Massachusetts. Commission on Industrial and Technical Education. *Some Representative American Industrial and Manual Training Schools.* Boston, Wright & Potter, 1908. 87 pp. illus. (Bulletin no. 9)

Massachusetts. Commission on Industrial and Technical Education. *Third Annual Report . . . January 1909.* Boston, Wright & Potter Printing Co., State Printers, 1909. 186. pp.
    Day industrial schools established in 2 cities and evening industrial in 11 cities of the state.
    By an act of the legislature, approved May 28, 1909, the commission on industrial education was abolished, likewise the existing state board of education. The powers and duties of each body were given to a new board of education, created in conformity with the provisions of the act.

Mays, Arthur B. *The Concept of Vocational Education in the Thinking of the General Educator, 1845 to 1945.* Urbana, Illinois, University of Illinois Press, 1946.
    A theoretical and critical assessment with detailed historical backgrounds. See also the author's *Principles and Practices of Vocational Education* (New York: McGraw-Hill, 1948).

Mays, Arthur B. *Principles and Practices of Vocational Education.* New York, McGraw-Hill, 1948. 303 pp.
    A college text useful for its coverage of the history of vocational training in the United States and for the bibliographies on the various types of vocational programs. It is also the revised edition of the author's earlier work "An Introduction to Vocational Education" published in 1930. (New York, Century Co., 1930. 323 pp.)

Medsker, Leland L. *The Junior Colleges: Progress and Prospect.* New York, McGraw-Hill, 1960. 367 pp.
    A study of 76 public 2-year colleges in 15 States, including treatment of the terminal and vocational training offered by these institutions.

Meyer, Ernest C. *Industrial Education and Industrial Conditions in Germany.* Washington, Government Printing Office, 1905. 323 pp. (U. S. Department of Commerce and Labor. Bureau of Statistics. Special consular reports. v. 33)
    Bibliography: pp. 145-47.
    An elaborate and exhaustive study of the subject. The appendices con-

tain descriptions of schools in France; Zittau, Germany; Japan and London.

Michigan Political Science Association. *Convention of Educators and Business Men, Ann Arbor, Mich., February 5-7, 1903.* Ann Arbor, 1903. vii, 229 pp. (Publications of the Michigan Political Science Association. v. 5, no. 2, June 1903)
    Discusses every phase of the subject. Among other things the character of instruction in history, economics, mathematics, statistics, accounting and law needed by students in commerce.

Michigan. State Commission on Industrial and Agricultural Education. *Report.* Lansing, Published by the Commission, 1910. 95 pp. tables.
    Chairman, Walter H. French.
    Appendix C — Authorities: pp. 92-95.

Michigan State University. College of Education. *Vocational Education in a Robot Revolution,* edited by George L. Brandon. East Lansing, the College, 1957. 37 pp.
    The socioeconomic changes and the growth of automation, and the effect of these factors on vocational education. This report also presents the challenges of automation to the leaders in the field of vocational training.

Michigan State University. College of Education. Educational Research Series. *Vocational Curricula in Michigan by Sigmund Nosow.* East Lansing, 1963. 50 pp. (Its ER series No. 17)
    A study of the work force and unemployment in Michigan and how the factors of each relate to vocational training offered in the schools.

Michigan State University. College of Education. Educational Research Series. *Vocational Education: Its Effects on Career Patterns of High School Graduates.* East Lansing, 1963. 182 pp. (Its ER series No. 18)
    "A career pattern study of 116 metropolitan Lansing public and parochial high school graduates who have been on the labor market from June 1956 to December 1962 — a 78-month work period."

Michigan State University. College of Education. Educational Research Series. *Vocational Education: Philosophy and Objectives.* East Lansing, 1962. 32 pp. (Its ER series No. 6)
    Report of Task Force No. 1 in the overall Michigan Vocational Education Evaluation Project. It defines the objectives desirable in teaching vocational education in Michigan secondary schools.

Miller, Leslie W. *The Claims of Industrial Art, Considered with Reference to Certain Prevalent Tendencies in Education . . .* Boston, School of Printing, North-end Union. 1908. 15 pp.
    Address before the Philobiblon club of Philadelphia, February 27, 1908.

Miller, Rex, and Lee H. Smalley, eds. *Selected Readings for Industrial Arts.* Bloomington, McKnight and McKnight Publishing Co., 1963. 360 pp.

A selection of 34 articles representing essential readings for members of the industrial arts teaching profession. Contents are arranged under these headings: "History," "Content and Organization," "Teaching Techniques," "The Future."

Minneapolis Commercial Club. Educational Committee. *A Plea for the Rearrangement of the Public School System of the City of Minneapolis* [1910] *folder.*
    A. E. Zoñne, chairman.

Minnesota. University. College of Education. *Education 1967; a Statewide Study of Elementary, Secondary and Area Vocational-technical Education in Minnesota.* By the Bureau of Field Statistics and Services, Otto E. Domian, Director. Minneapolis, 1967. 440 pp.
    A useful study for those planning a similar survey on a statewide basis, including area vocational schools. Data gathered on vocational, technical and adult education is to be found in Chapter IV, pp. 130-154)

Mittenzweh, L. *Die Berufswahl.* Leipzig, Dürr, 1910. xv, 217 pp.

Moll-Weiss, Augusta. *Les Ecoles Ménagères à l'Étranger et en France . . .* Paris, A. Rousseau, 1908. xxvi, 344 pp. illus.

Moore, Bernice Milburn. "The Case for Education for Home and Family Living." In *Education for a Changing World of Work. Report of the Panel of Consultants on Vocational Education. Appendix III.* (Washington, U. S. Government Printing Office, 1963) pp. 53-71.
    A report of the Texas Cooperative Youth Study in which 13,000 high school youths from 185 Texas high schools expressed their feelings and attitudes of personal worth, social competence, and other factors of their family life. One salient point brought out: ". . . youth from culturally handicapped parents do have a more difficult time remaining in school." Since the youths of this generation will be parents of the next, it is necessary to provide them with sufficient education in home and family living to insure a greater measure of success in their role as parents.

Moore, Harris W. *Manual Training Toys for the Boy's Workshop.* Peoria, Ill., The Manual Arts Press, (1912). 111 pp. illus.
    "Dedicated to the boy who likes to tinker 'round."

Mosely Educational Commission. *Report.* London, Co-operative Printing Society, 1904. 400 pp.
    Contains reports of 26 English educators who were brought to the United States in 1903 by Sir Alfred Mosely to investigate American methods of education. A number of papers treat directly of technical and industrial education; the attitude of the employer of labor and trade-unions. Comparisons drawn between conditions in England and this country.

Mumm, Elizabeth von. *Die Pflichtfortbildungsschule des weiblichen Geschlechts in hygienischer Beziehung* . . . Bonn, M. Hager, 1906. 14 pp.

Munroe, James P. *New Demands in Education.* New York, Doubleday, Page and Co., 1912. 312 pp.

Contains chapters on industrial education, vocational training, and manual training. Author does not consider it the function of the public school to impart strictly trade processes, but to develop good morals, good health, power of concentration, manual power, and command of the tools of communication. He advocates trade schools.

Münsterberg, Hugo. *Psychology and Industrial Efficiency.* Boston and New York, Houghton Mifflin Company, 1913. 321 pp.

Shows the value of psychological tests. But notwithstanding the value of laboratory methods for determining industrial efficiency, the writer thinks that vocational guidance, if it shall ever be a closed and perfected system, will yet demand the supplementary services of the labor investigator, the sanitary expert, etc. This book is well reviewed in the *Survey,* 30: 95-96, April 19, 1913.

Münsterberg, Hugo. *Vocation and Learning.* University City, St. Louis, Mo., The Peoples University (1912). 289 pp.

An analysis of the demands made by the various vocations, considering not merely the technical requirements, but especially the deeper inner demands of our occupations and professions. In addition to a presentation of general principles, the following vocations are individually analyzed: Engineer, farmer, business man, teacher, domestic worker, secretary, librarian, journalist, physician, lawyer and politician, architect.

(National Academy of Engineering). Advisory Committee on Issues in Educational Technology. *Issues and Public Policies in Educational Technology.* Boston, Lexington Books, 1974.

National Advisory Committee on the Junior College. *A National Resource for Occupational Education.* Washington, American Association of Junior Colleges, 1965. 9 pp.

A policy statement on the role of the junior college and its possible responsibilities in providing occupational education to meet America's manpower needs.

National Association of Manufacturers of the United States of America. Committee on Industrial Education. *Industrial Education, Continuation and Trade Schools, Apprenticeship, State and Local Control, Pre-vocational Courses in Elementary Schools. Report . . . Seventeenth Annual Convention, New York City, May 21, 1912.* (n. p., 1912) 39 pp. (No. 28) Cover title.

H. E. Miles, chairman.

Reiterates demand for continuation schools. Day classes for those in employment, and no loss of wages, these to be for children between 14 and 16 years of age. For those from 16 up, night work is permissible. "It is advisable that, as in Wisconsin, the development of industrial education be put into the hands of a special state board of industrial education."

National Association of Manufacturers of the United States of America. Committee on Industrial Education. *Report . . . Fourteenth Annual Meeting, New York, May 17-19, 1909.* (n. p., 1909) 19 pp. Caption title.
    Anthony Ittner, chairman.
    States the attitude of the manufacturers toward the trade-unions. Quotes largely from other reports.
    "Your committee has had correspondence with all the officers and managers of the principal industrial and trade schools throughout the country and they all agree with us that a much higher grade mechanic can be graduated from a trade school than can be produced through the apprenticeship system in the old way."

National Association of Manufacturers of the United States of America. Committee on Industrial Education. *Report . . . Sixteenth Annual Meeting, New York City, May 15-17, 1911.* [n. p., 1911] 11 pp. Caption title.
    H. E. Miles, chairman.
    The Association at this meeting passed a resolution favoring the establishment in every community of continuation schools for the benefit of children (14 to 18 years of age) engaged in the industries.
    Attention was called by the committee to the fact that—"Almost all of the children who enter the industries enter at the age of 14. The working people of the country who wish their children to enter the industries take them out of school, knowing from experience that if they stay in school until 16 they will have passed the psychological time when industry beckons—will have acquired other tastes, and will never enter the industries. The American-born mechanic, then, is the boy who entered the shop at 14, grown up. Therefore, as good citizens and as employers, it is for us to give especial consideration to the educational problem as it concerns children of 14 to 16"

National Child Labor Committee. *(Proceedings of the Eighth Annual Conference Held at Louisville, Ky., January 25-28, 1912)* New York, National Child Labor Committee, 1912. 223 pp.(*Child Labor Bulletin*, vol. 1, no. 1)
    Contains: 1. E. O. Holland: Child labor and vocational work in the public schools, pp. 16-23. 2. Helen T. Woolley: Child labor and vocational guidance, pp. 24-37. 3. Alice P. Barrows: The dangers and possibilities of vocational guidance, pp. 46-54. 4. W. H. Elson: Relation of industrial training to child labor, pp. 55-65. 5. M. Edith Campbell: Economic value of education, pp. 66-72. 6. R. K. Conant: The educational test for working children, pp. 145-48.

National Conference on Research. Oklahoma State University, Stillwater, Oklahoma. 1968. *The 1968 Vocational Education Amendments. Proceedings [of a conference].* Stillwater, Oklahoma, Oklahoma State University, Coordinating Unit for Research in Vocational Education, 1969. 152 pp.

One of nine national conferences held on various phases of the 1968 Vocational Education Amendments. Brief summaries of these papers may be found in the *American Vocational Journal*, v. 45, March 1970: 39-46.

National Conference on Vocational Guidance. *First.* Boston, November 15-16, 1910.

Under auspices of the Boston chamber of commerce and the Vocation bureau of Boston. Forty-five cities sent delegates. Manufacturers, workmen, business men, social workers, and educators participated in the discussions.

The activities of vocational guidance, as outlined at this conference, are as follows: First, giving information about vocations in general and about opportunities for work in the immediate vicinity, and also concerning opportunities for receiving vocational instruction. The second group relates to children, when it is necessary to make the transition from school to work, and advising as to the importance of wise choice between temporary employment, however remunerative, and positions which offer opportunity for advancement. The third group relates to the guidance and sympathetic counseling of the young worker subsequent to his entry into his new duties. A fourth group looks to the establishment of vocation bureaus for the collection of information about opportunities for boys and girls in the trades and stores, as well as the provision for vocational training, and the classification of this information in forms available for ready reference.

The opinion was expressed that ultimately this function should be taken over by the public schools.

See *Survey*, 25: 319-20, November 26, 1910 (Bloomfield, Meyer) also *School Review*, 19: 57-62, January 1911 (Leavitt, F. M.)

National Conference on Vocational Guidance. *Second.* New York, October 23-26, 1912.

Topics discussed: Placement; Follow-up; Study of occupations; Scholarships; Vocational analysis; Opportunities for vocational training; Methods of vocational direction; and Relation of vocational guidance to the employer.

Reviewed at length by W. T. Bawden, in Vocational education, 2: 209-17, January 1913. On the subject of "finding jobs for boys and girls," the sentiment of the majority of those participating in the discussion was "in favor of making every effort to retain children under 16 in school, in order to train them for more skilled occupations."

The following definite questions regarding vocational training in the schools were raised by the conference:

"Shall industrial training aim to fit children for particular trades, or shall it educate them in elementary processes and underlying principles?

"Shall it begin early in the child's school life, or at the age of fourteen when so many now break away from the prescribed curriculum?

"Shall it be grafted on the present elementary courses, or be taught in separate institutions?

"Can industry be prevented from compelling the schools to give just enough training to meet industry's immediate needs, and no more?

"Is it advisable to raise the compulsory school age two years, or with the curriculum in its present state is this simply prescribing a larger dose of something already seen to be inadequate and unsuitable?

"On the other hand, will raising the age limit, by throwing back upon the schools thousands of boys and girls who now go to work as soon as they can, force the schools to a quicker adjustment of education to needs?"

It was declared to be fundamentally wrong "that any untrained child, without knowledge of industrial processes or skill in the use of tools, whose aims are vague and aptitudes unknown, should be allowed to work. It is an aggravation of this wrong to allow such a child to take a job which will not supplement previous education, or open the way to skill and independence. Yet children are going into just such work to-day. Therefore, we are but tolerating an intolerable situation when we accept school and industry on this basis and try to put each individual into the best job available for him. Our task is twofold. We must reconstruct our system of education so that it will fit youth for the work which it will have to do; we must also study the processes and needs of industry so thoroughly that every child shall have the maximum of information on which to base his choice of work. Then, perhaps, we must go· even farther and reorganize industry in such a way that it will hold positive cultural values for those who devote to it their full energies of mind and body."

An excellent resume of the conference is contained in Survey, 29: 225-28, November 23, 1912. One of the subjects under discussion was "Why children leave school." Attempts have been made to ascertain why so many children leave school as soon as the law permits. The Survey commenting upon this says:

"A recent inquiry of the Federal Government conducted in six cities proceeded upon the basis that any family which had a per capita income of less than $1.50 a week would need outside assistance to keep its children in school. It was found that in 25 per cent of the 524 families studied the income was below this amount, and it was therefore concluded that 25 per cent of the children in this group left school because of 'economic pressure' within the home. Findings of the Vocational guidance survey of New York (now called the Vocational education survey and a part of the Public education association) which corroborated this study were made public for the first time at the conference."

(National Education Association). *Report of the Committee on the Place of Industries in Public Education.* Washington, The Association, 1910.

Professional educators' expressions of approval of certain aspects of vocationalism.

National Education Association. U. S. Department of Rural Education. *Vocational Education for Rural America.* Edited by Gordon I. Swanson. Washington, 1959. 354 pp. (Its Yearbook 1958-59)

A discussion of the social and economic forces influencing vocational education for youth in rural and small urban areas, and of what should be done to change the contents of their educational programs in the field of vocational training.

National Education Association of the United States. National Council of Education. Committee on Industrial Education in Schools for Rural Communities. *Preliminary Report . . . to be discussed Monday Morning, June 29,*

1908. (Chicago, Printed by the University of Chicago Press, 1908.) 64 pp.
Advance print from volume of Proceedings, Cleveland meeting.
Contents. —Historical statement. —Waterford high school, Waterford, Pennsylvania (by) D. J. Crosby. —Cecil County agricultural school, Calvert, Maryland (by) D. J. Crosby. —The John Swaney consolidated country school in Magnolia township, Putnam County, Illinois (by) O. J. Kern. —The congressional district agricultural schools of Georgia (by) O. J. Kern.

National Education Association of the United States. National Council of Education. Committee on Industrial Education in Schools for Rural Communities. *Report . . . July 1905.* Published by the Association, 1905. 97 pp.
L. D. Harvey, chairman.
An argument for the establishment of industrial education as a distinct feature of work in schools adapted to the requirements of rural communities. Discusses two types of elementary schools, the one-teacher district school, and the consolidated district school having no high school work. Four types of secondary schools adapted to rural communities considered: the consolidated school presenting one or more years of high school work; the rural high school of the county, township, etc., character; the village high school with a large percentage of pupils from the country; the agricultural high school, industrial and academic. Courses of study outlined.
Appendices contain studies of particular schools in Wisconsin and Minnesota. W. M. Hays contributes a paper, prepared by request of the committee, on "Industrial course in the consolidated rural school, the agricultural high school, and the agricultural college articulated into a unified scheme."

National Manpower Council. *Education and Manpower.* Edited by Henry David. New York, Columbia University Press, 1960. 326 pp.
A selection of chapters and articles from the publications of the National Manpower Council. Those chapters dealing directly with the relationship of manpower and vocational training are "Issues in vocational education" (pp. 127-147) and "Types of vocational schooling" (pp. 148-177)

National Manpower Council. *Improving the Work Skills of the Nation; Proceedings of a Conference on Skilled Manpower, Held April 27-May 1, 1955 at Arden House, Harrimon Campus of Columbia University.* New York, Columbia University Press, 1956. 203 pp.
Ten papers by various educators, businessmen, and others discussing policy objectives and other subjects to improving the Nation's supply of skilled workers mainly through the cooperation of the school, the community, and industry.

National Manpower Council. *A Policy for Skilled Manpower; a Statement by the Council with Facts and Figures Prepared by the Research Staff.* New York, Columbia University Press, 1954. 299 pp.
See part II (pp. 37-299) on "Facts and Issues about Skilled Manpower," including types of vocational training offered in industry, educational institutions, and the Armed Forces.

National Metal Trades Association. *Synopsis of Proceedings of the Twelfth Annual Convention, April 13-14, 1910, New York City.* (n. p. 1910.) 168 pp.
Contains: 1. W. B. Hunter: The Fitchburg plan of industrial education, pp. 25-31. 2. Herman Schneider: Growth of co-operative system, pp. 32-35. 3. F. B. Dyer: A plea for continuation schools, pp. 36-41. 4. Report of Committee on industrial education, pp. 42-45. 5. C. A. Bookwalter: Winona technical institute, pp. 58-61. 6. J. H. Renshaw: Cincinnati's continuation school, pp. 91-93. 7. D. S. Kimball: Industrial education. pp. 161-64.

National Society for the Promotion of Industrial Education. *Circular of Information; Constitution, State Branches, Officers and Members.* New York City, National Society for the Promotion of Industrial Education, 1908. 44 pp. (Its Bulletin no. 7)

National Society for the Promotion of Industrial Education. *A Descriptive List of Trade and Industrial Schools in the United States.* Prepared by Edward H. Reisner. New York City, National Society for the Promotion of Industrial Education, August 1910. 128 pp. (Its Bulletin, no. 11)
An effort "to bring together in brief form the main facts relating to the organization, administration, methods of instruction and courses of study of trade and industrial schools in the United States."

National Society for the Promotion of. Industrial Education. *Education of Workers in the Shoe Industry.* Prepared by Arthur D. Dean. New York City, National Society for the Promotion of Industrial Education, 1908. (Its Bulletin no. 8)

National Society for the Promotion of Industrial Education. *Industrial Education* . . . Communication from C. R. Richards, President of the National Society for the Promotion of Industrial Education, Transmitting Reports by a Committee of the Society on the Subject, together with Resolutions Urging upon Congress an Appropriation to Enable the Department of Education to Develop Schools for Industrial Training . . .(Washington, Government Printing Office, 1910) 8 pp. (United States) 61st Cong., 2d sess. Senate. Doc. 516.

National Society for the Promotion of Industrial Education. *Industrial Training for Women.* Prepared by Florence M. Marshall. New York City, National Society for the Promotion of Industrial Education, 1907. (Its Bulletin no. 4)
Contents. — A study of the changed position of women in industry; Opportunities of women in industry; What trade training is accomplishing; Suggested schemes for industrial training.

National Society for the Promotion of Industrial Education. *Legislation upon Industrial Education in the United States, Prepared by Edward C. Elliot and C. A. Prosser.* New York, National Society for the Promotion of Industrial Education, 1910. 76 pp. (Its Bulletin, no. 12)
Part 1 gives the general legislation regarding industrial education in

public elementary and secondary schools. Part 2 the terminology in legislation, trend of legislation, state commissions, etc. Part 3 is an analysis of the legislation for state industrial and trade educational systems. Part 4 an analysis of the legislation providing for manual training.

National Society for the Promotion of Industrial Education. *Principles and Policies That Should Underlie State Legislation for a State System of Vocational Education. A Tentative Statement of Principles and Policies Formulated at a Meeting of a Committee . . . in Annual Convention, at Philadelphia, December 1912 . . .* Philadelphia (?), the Author, 1913. 6 pp.

A list of 31 guidelines for the establishment of State departments of vocational education.

National Society for the Promotion of Industrial Education. *Proceedings of First Annual Meeting, Chicago, January 23-25, 1908. Part I.* New York City, National Society for the Promotion of Industrial Education, 1908. 68 pp. (Bulletin no. 5)

Contains: 1. C. W. Eliot — Industrial education as an essential factor in our national prosperity, pp. 9-14. 2. J. W. Van Cleave — Industrial Education from the standpoint of the manufacturer, pp. 15-21, 3. H. S. Pritchett — The aims of the national society for the promotion of industrial education, pp. 22-29. 4. C. D. Wright — The apprenticeship system as a means of promoting industrial efficiency, pp. 30-33. 5. W. R. Warner — The apprenticeship system of to-day, p. 34-39. 6. W. B. Prescott — The value of a thorough apprenticeship to the wage earner, pp. 40-50. 7. J. F. Deems — Trade instruction in large establishments, pp. 51-55. 8. L. W. Miller — The necessity for apprenticeship, pp. 56-60.

National Society for the Promotion of Industrial Education. *Proceedings . . . Part 2,* New York City, National Society for the Promotion of Industrial Education, 1908. 104 pp. (Bulletin no. 6)

Contains: 1. C. F. Perry — The trade school as a part of the public-school system, p. 6-19. 2. M. P. Higgins — The type of the trade school to meet American needs, pp. 20-25. 3. Graham Taylor — The effect of trade schools on the social interests of the people, p. 26-30. 4. Anna G. Spencer — The social value of industrial education for girls, pp. 39 — 45. 5. C. W. Ames — Necessity for many kinds of trade schools, pp. 46-48. 6. Luke Grant — The wage earner's attitude toward industrial education, pp. 49-55. 7. E. G. Hirsch — The moral aspect of industrial education, pp. 56-60. 8. L. D. Harvey and others — The true ideal of a public-school system that aims to benefit all, pp. 61-75.

National Society for the Promotion of Industrial Education. *Proceedings of Second Annual Meeting, Atlanta, Ga., Nov. 19-21, 1908.* New York, National Society for the Promotion of Industrial Education, 1909. 151 pp. (Bulletin no. 9)

Contains: 1. T. C. Search — The founding of the school of industrial art in Philadelphia, pp. 18-36. . E. E. Brown — Unifying influence of industrial art, pp. 36-41. 3. C. D. Wright — Industrial education as an essential factor in our national prosperity, pp. 42-49. 4. E. P. Bullard, Jr. — Industrial training through the apprenticeship system, pp. 51-63. 5. M. W. Alexander — An effective apprenticeship program, pp. 63-70. 6. J. M. Shrigley — Organization and management of trade schools, pp. 78-90. 7. Florence M. Marshall — How to conduct a trade school for girls, pp. 90-100. 8. C. R. Davis — The Federal government and industrial education, pp. 101-112. 9. Press Huddleston — The wage earner's benefit from an effective system of industrial education, pp. 112-115. 10. Anna C. Hedges — Women's work in industrial education, pp. 116-122. 11. T. M. Balliet — The importance of industrial education in the public schools, pp. 135-142.

National Society for the Promotion of Industrial Education. *Proceedings of the Third Annual Meeting, Milwaukee, Wis., December, 1909.* New York, National Society for the Promotion of Industrial Education, 1910. 204 pp. (Its Bulletin no. 10)

National Society for the Promotion of Industrial Education. *Proceedings of the Fourth Annual Convention, Boston, Massachusetts.* Part I. Trade Education for Girls. Part II. Apprenticeship and Corporation Schools. Part III. Part Time and Evening Schools. Part IV. The Social Significance of Industrial Education. New York, National Society for the Promotion of Industrial Education, 1911. 91 pp. (Its Bulletin no. 13, pt. 1-4)

Contains: (Part 1) 1. Susan M. Kingsbury: The needle trades, pp-1-6. 2. D. F. Edwards: The department stores, pp. 6-12. 3. L. W. Prince: What the schools can do to train girls for work in department stores, pp. 12-16. 4. E. M. Howes: What schools can do to train for needle work, pp. 17-20. 5. H. R. Hildreth: How the Manhattan trade school for girls meets trade demands, pp. 20-26. 6. W. A. Hawkins: What more should the schools do to meet the demands pp. 26-28. 7. F. M. Marshall and C. A. Prosser: What more can schools do to meet the new requirements. pp. 40-45, 47-51.

(Part 2) 1. M. W. Alexander: Apprenticeship and corporation schools, pp. 53-56. 2. Tracy Lyon: How the Westinghouse company trains its apprentices, pp. 57-61. 3. F. W. Thomas: Educating apprentices on the Santa Fe, pp. 61-69. 4. S. F. Hubbard: A co-operative apprenticeship school, pp. 70-76. 5. G. C. Cotton: A half-time system of apprentice instruction, pp. 76-81.

(Part 3) 1. W. B. Hunter: The Fitchburg plan, pp. 93-108. 2. A. L. Safford: The Beverly industrial school, pp. 108-22. 3. F. B. Dyer: Industrial education in Cincinnati, pp. 123-28. 4. C. A. Prosser: Massachusetts independent evening industrial schools, pp. 129-42.

(Part 4) 1. J. P. Munroe: The social meaning of industrial education, pp. 181-83. 2. T. N. Carver: The economic significance of industrial education, pp. 183-87. 3. E. B. Butler: Industrial education and the community, pp. 188-96. 4. Howell Cheney: The school and the shop from an employer's point of view, pp. 196-208. 5. C. H. Winslow: Labor's demands on industrial education, pp. 208-13.

A notable address of this session was that of Howell Cheney, who discussed the cause of the lack of progress in children when first entering industrial life, which he attributed to the unrelated nature of the school work which has gone before. He desired to know whether low-grade industrial work might not be made educational. He called attention to the fact that every machine process is the development of a hand process. He remarked that if children possessed some knowledge of these processes and some appreciation of the possibilities of high-grade machine work, even toil in the factory might be made relatively desirable.

National Society for the Promotion of Industrial Education. *Proceedings of the Fifth Annual Meeting, Cincinnati, Ohio, November 2-4, 1911.* New York, National Society for the Promotion of Industrial Education, 1912. 239 pp. (Its Bulletin no. 15)

Contains: 1. How shall the obligation to provide industrial education be met. The obligation of the employer (by) H. E. Miles, pp. 29-37; The obligation of the employee (by) Frank Duffy, pp. 38-48. 2. J. P. Munroe: President's address, pp. 49-56. 3. Herman Schneider: Co-operative plan of the University of Cincinnati, pp. 59-67. 4. P. A. Johnston: Vocational plans in the high school, pp. 68-79. 5. J. H. Renshaw: The Cincinnati continuation school for apprentices, pp. 80-95. 6. J. L. Shearer: The Ohio mechanics' institute, pp. 96-103. 7. A. L. Williston: Evening trade and industrial schools, pp. 105-8. 8. C. P. Cary: Part-time schools, pp. 119-22. Discussion, pp. 122-25. 9. David Sneddin: Report of Committee on national legislation, pp. 126-34. 10. C. A. Prosser: The training of the factory worker through industrial education, pp. 137-55. 11. E. G. Cooley. The argument for industrial education from the success of Germany, pp. 178-92. 12. J. P. Frey: A trade union view of industrial education, pp. 193-97. Discussion, pp. 197-200. 13. Should trade schools for youth above 16 years of age be provided at public expense (by) J. P. Munroe; (by) C. G. Pearse, pp. 204-18; (by) G. M. Forbes, 219-26..

The article on The Cincinnati continuation school for apprentices, by J. H. Renshaw, is illustrated with half-tone cuts, showing pupils at work. He says: "The continuation school is distinctively a creation of Cincinnati and is a copy of no other school in the world. . . . It differs from the German plan in that it uses no machine equipment. The school is based upon the principle that the productive power of a youth in a shop does not depend solely upon the hours he works, but that his attitude toward his work and his intelligence in his work are the determining features. To this end the manufacturers' organizations, the labor organizations, and the school authorities decided two and a half years ago to shorten the hours of labor without decreasing the pay. The working week of the boys was shortened one-half day and their weekly pay was maintained. The half day of rest from work was to be spent in a schoolroom under educational and cultural influences."

National Society for the Promotion of Industrial Education. *Proceedings of the Organization Meetings.* (New York, C. S. Nathan, 1907.) 44 pp. (Its Bulletin no. 1)

Contains addresses by N. M. Butler, A. Mosely, Jane Addams, F. A. Vanderlip, etc.

National Society for the Promotion of Industrial Education. *Report of the Committee of Ten on the Relation of Industrial Training to the General*

System of Education in the United States. New York City, National Society for the Promotion of Industrial Education, (1910). 16 pp.

Includes Preliminary report of the Committee of ten, H. S. Pritchett, chairman, submitted at the second annual meeting of the Society, Nov. 19-21, 1908, and Final report, submitted at the third annual meeting, Dec. 2-4, 1909.

National Society for the Promotion of Industrial Education. *A Symposium on Industrial Education.* Prepared by James P. Haney. New York City, National Society for the Promotion of Industrial Education, 1907. (Its Bulletin no. 3)

Opinions of employers and employees regarding industrial education. A questionnaire was sent to 300 manufacturers and representatives of organized labor. The replies received are highly interesting.

National Society for the Promotion of Industrial Education. New York State Branch. *Proceedings of the Second Annual Convention, Held at Rochester, N. Y., November 19, 1909.* Brooklyn, N. Y., Guide Printing and Publishing Company, 1910. 98 pp.

Contains: 1. J. F. McElroy: President's address, pp. 7-8. 2. B. R. Rhees: The national importance of industrial education, pp. 9-17. 3. Mary S. Woolman: Industrial education for girls, pp. 18-23. 4. E. G. Miner: Industrial education from the point of view of the manufacturer, pp. 24-33. 5. P. M. Strayer: Industrial education from the point of view of the workman, pp. 34-47. 6. Charles De Garmo: Industrial education in relation to race development, pp. 48-57. 7. G. M. Forbes: The factory school of Rochester, pp. 58-67. 8. A. D. Dean: Preparatory trade schools in other parts of New York State, pp. 68-71. 9. C. W. Cross: The apprenticeship system of the New York Central lines, pp. 78-86. 10. G. H. Vose: Industrial schools in Beverly, Mass., pp. 91-98.

National Society for the Promotion of Industrial Education. New York State Branch. *The Trade Continuation Schools of Munich.* A Lecture by Dr. Georg Kerschensteiner, Director of Education, Munich, Bavaria, and the Translation of the Curricula of Selected Schools as Given in the Official Report for 1910. New York City, National Society for the Promotion of Industrial Education, 1911. (Its Bulletin, no. 14)

The author says: "The essential features of the compulsory trade continuation schools of Munich are thus summed up in these four points: (a) practical work is made the center of interest; (b) the active sympathy and cooperation of employers on the one hand, and of trade societies and guilds on the other, is enlisted on behalf of the schools; (c) the time of instruction is sufficient in amount and excellent in quality; (d) every opportunity that presents itself for training the citizen is utilized."

In addition to the above class of schools, there are in Munich 12 local continuation schools in which boys are enrolled "who are not yet apprentices, but who are engaged in casual and unskilled labor, or who can not be provided with a special continuation school because these numbers are too few."

National Society for the Study of Education. *Sixth Year-book.* Part I. Vocational Studies for College Entrance. Chicago, University of Chicago Press, 1907. 79 pp.

Discusses the purport of vocational studies; the educational values and relationship of the value developed in vocational studies to the standards appropriate for college admission.

Originally the Herbart Society; name changed to the National Society for the Scientific Study of Education, and finally to the present title.

National Society for the Study of Education. *Eleventh Year-book.* Part I. Industrial Education: Typical Experiments Described and Interpreted. Part II. Agricultural Education in Secondary Schools. Chicago, University of Chicago Press (1912). 2 v. 124, 113 pp.

Contains interesting papers on the vocational high school; the part-time co-operative plan of industrial education; vocational guidance: classification of plans for industrial training, etc.

Part 1 gives various types of vocational schools. Chapter 1 presents a classification of plans for industrial training, by Frank M. Leavitt. Each chapter of the year-book is by a different author and describes for the most part the given type of school with which the author is connected. Comparison is made with other institutions of similar character, and conclusions drawn "as to the relation of the particular type of school to the solution of the industrial education problem."

National Society for the Study of Education. *Twenty-third Yearbook.* Part II: Vocational Guidance and Vocational Education for the Industries, prepared by A. H. Edgerton . . . Edited by Guy M. Whipple. Bloomington, Ill., Public School Publishing Co., 1924. 435 pp.

Partial contents: Guidance problems in large cities; guidance activities in small city systems; day and evening industrial courses in smaller cities; and training foremen and other leaders in industry.

National Society for the Study of Education. *Forty-second Yearbook, 1943.* Part I: Vocational Education. Chicago, University of Chicago Press, 1943. 494 pp.

Partial contents: Legislative commitments affecting vocational education; vocational education through nonschool governmental agencies; and vocational programs in different educational institutions.

National Society for the Study of Education. *Sixty-fourth Yearbook, 1965.* Part I: Vocational Education, edited by Melvin Barlow, Chicago, University of Chicago Press, 1965. 301. pp.

Developed during the period of vocational education changes, the yearbook's production was interrupted by the passage of the Vocational Education Act of 1963. Each of the 13 chapters are devoted to different phases of vocational education in the United States. In chapter 8, for example, the impact of Federal legislation and policies is discussed by Major Mobley and Melvin Barlow, and much information is given about the period between the passage of the Smith-Hughes law to the enactment of the Vocational Education Act of 1963.

National Society for Vocational Education. *Bulletin No. 1-36.* New York, 1907-23.

Valuable source material for tracing the development of vocational education in America. These bulletins also contain the proceedings of the annual meetings held by this organization. First organized at Cooper Union,' New York, November 16, 1906, by prominent businessmen and educators, the organization was first known as the Society for the Promotion of Industrial Education. In 1917, with the passage of the Smith-Hughes Act, it became known as the National Society for Vocational Education. Merging with other groups, this organization became a part of the American Vocational Association in 1925.

Nearing, Scott. *Social Adjustment.* New York, The Macmillan Company, 1911. xvi, 377 pp.

Discusses, among other social questions, the educational remedies for maladjustment.

The Negro Problem. A Series of Articles by Representative American Negroes of To-day. New York, James Pott & Co., 1903. 234 pp.

Contains a valuable paper on industrial education, by Booker T. Washington.

New England High School Commercial Teachers' Association. *Report of the Ninth Annual Convention . . . Held at Simmons College, Boston, Mass., October 21, 1911.* 34 pp.

Contains: 1. A. J. Meredith: The professional and technical training of commercial teachers, pp. 5-9. 2. W. A. Hawkins: Bread and butter education, pp. 10-12. 3. A. E. Holmes: What a business man expects of his stenographer and bookkeeper, pp. 13-19. 4. W. M. Cole: Some connotations of teaching for business, pp. 20-24.

New Jersey. Commission on Industrial Education. *Report . . . 1908.* Trenton, N. J., MacCrellish & Quigley, State Printers, 1909. 177 pp.

Data obtained through correspondence and personal interviews with employers and workers everywhere in the state. Results of investigations show that the apprenticeship system has been virtually abandoned as a means of instructing the young in various trades. There is "a lack of skilled and efficient workmen, and this will be largely increased unless a better means of vocational training is found." Schools have not been able to offer vocational instruction. Fully 95 per cent of the pupils leave school between the ages of 14 and 17, and without any idea as to what trade or vocation they should pursue. They drift into occupations, rather than choose those most suited to their abilities, the result being an arrested progress. The trades have become so specialized that there is but little opportunity for a novice to go beyond the narrow limits of the work to which he is assigned, unless he has supplementary training. Commission reported that trade schools are undesirable at present, being too expensive a form of education. "The average person leaves school early in life to go to work, and the necessity of earning his daily bread prevents him from attending a day trade school." Only a small percentage of the manufacturers of New Jersey favor partial-time day industrial schools. Recommends the passage of an act creating a commission on industrial education, to consist of five citizens, at least three of whom shall be engaged in industrial occupations. Commission to make and enforce rules and regulations for employment of teachers in the industrial schools which may be established. Recommends establishing industrial schools in communities by boards of education, school committees, or like bodies.

Appendix contains an excellent resume of industrial education and manual training in America; and a paper on the money value of industrial education, giving among other data graphic statistics showing the average weekly earnings of graduates of the Newark technical school, a state institution of secondary grade.

New Jersey. Commission on Industrial Education. *Report . . . 1910.* Trenton, N. J., MacCrellish & Quigley, State Printers, 1910. 7 pp.

New South Wales. Commission on Primary, Secondary, Technical, and Other Branches of Education. *Report of the Commissioners on Agricultural, Commercial, Industrial, and Other Forms of Technical Education . . .* Sydney, William A. Gullick, Government Printer, 1905. 853 pp. illus.

A voluminous report, describing conditions in New South Wales, Europe and America.

"The aim of this report is to disclose the state of trade, commercial, agricultural, technical and industrial education generally, both in its lower and higher forms, and the state of the relation of these to the development of a state university . . . Throughout, the commissioners have attacked their task from what may be called the comparative standpoint."

New York City. Committee on Vocational Schools and Industrial Training. *Report.*
      Chairman, Frederick R. Coudert.

New York (State) Education Department. *Course of Study and Syllabus for Elementary Schools; Drawing and Manual Training . . .* Albany, New York (State) Education Department, 1908. 107-143 pp. illus., plates, diagrs.
      "Books of reference for preacademic grades:" pp. 142-43.

New York (State) Education Department. Division of Trade Schools. *Albany Vocational School.* (Albany, N. Y., 1909.) 15 pp.

New York (State) Education Department. Division of Trades Schools. *(Circular of definitions.)* Albany, 1908. 3 pp.
      Arthur D. Dean, chief, Division of Trades Schools.

New York (State) Education Department. Division of Trades Schools. *Evening Industrial Improvement Schools . . .* (Albany, N. Y.,1909) 11 pp.
      Bibliography: pp. 9. List of schools: pp. 10-11.

New York (State) Education Department. Division of Trades Schools
Evening Industrial Improvement Schools . . .(Albany, N. Y., 1909) 11 pp.
    Bibliography: pp. 10-21.
    Text of law providing for the establishment and maintenance of in-
dustrial and trade schools, with notes on the law.

New York (State) Education Department. Division of Trades Schools. *Schools
of Agriculture, Mechanic Arts and Home Making*. Albany, N. Y., November
1, 1910. 23 pp.
    A selected list of books on agricultural and related subjects: pp. 13-23.

Norton, Thomas Lowell. *Public Education and Economic Trends*.
Cambridge, Mass., Harvard University, Graduate School of Education, 1939.
196 pp.
    A group of seven lectures delivered at the Harvard Graduate School of
Education in April and May of 1939 on the relationship of education to the
changing character of the American economy and the demands of the labor
market.

Noyes, William. *Handwork in Wood*. Peoria, Ill., Manual Arts Press, 1910.
231 pp. illus.
    "General bibliography": pp. 4-6.

Oberman, Carl E. *A History of Vocational Rehabilitation in America*.
Minneapolis, University of Minnesota Press, 1965.
    Comprehensive history with valuable information on vocational
education movement.

Occupational Education: Planning and Programming. Edited by Arnold
Katz. Menlo Park, California, Stanford Research Institute, 1967. 2 vols. At
head of title: "A Research Study Prepared for the U. S. Office of Education."
    These two volumes contain the results of surveys made in six states and
eleven communities, plus proceedings of a conference. The identification of
objectives and goals of vocational education are presented in volume I.
Statements on program structure, benefit and cost analysis, evaluation and
organization appear in the second volume.

(Office of Science and Technology: Executive Office of the President). *Youth
Transition to Adulthood: Report of the Panel on Youth of the President's
Science Advisory Committee*. Washington, U. S. Government Printing Office, 1973.
    Chaired by James Coleman, "the Panel has identified issues and
proposed recommendations." Includes materials on the demography of
youth, economic problems of youth, the scope of formal schooling, etc.

Ontario. Education Department. *Education for Industrial Purposes*. A
Report by John Seath, Superintendent of Education for Ontario. Printed by
Order of the Legislative Assembly of Ontario. Toronto, L. K. Cameron,
1911. 390 pp. illus.

Writer, in introduction, says that the present importance of the problem of industrial education is the result of three main causes: 1. The rivalry amongst the nations for commerical supremacy. 2. The imperfect provision for training skilled workmen. 3. The modern extension of the scope of education to include vocational as well as cultural training, administered and maintained wholly or largely at the public expense."

Describes conditions in Ontario, England, Scotland, France, Switzerland, Germany and United States.

See also National Association of Education Officers. *Education in Relation to Industry.* A report on technical, trade, applied art, manual training, domestic, commercial, and public schools in Canada and the United States. By the following commission on behalf of the National Association of Education Officers: W. P. Donald, J. B. Johnson, J. E. Pickles, Percival Sharp. Leeds, Glasglow and Belfast, E. J. Arnold & Son (1912) ix, 187 pp.

This representative commission of English chief education officers visited Canada and the United States in the summer of 1911, to investigate the relationship existing between the educational institutions and the industrial and commercial occupations of the people. A stay of several days was made in turn in Quebec, Montreal, Ottawa, Toronto, Detroit, Buffalo, Philadelphia, New York, and Boston, and a short visit was paid by one of the members to Chicago and St. Louis.

Orth, Samuel Peter. *Industrial Education . . .* Cleveland, Printed at the Technical High School Printshop, (1909). 6 pp.

Address, dedication of the Cleveland technical high school.

Paddelford, Fred L. *Short Addresses on Industrial Training, The American Boy [Handle with Care]; Thanksgiving; Industry the Golden Pass Key.* Golden, Colorado, (The Industrial School Press, 1909). (72) pp.

Page, Carroll S. *Vocational Education. Speech . . . Delivered in the Senate of the United States, June 5, 1912, on Senate Bill 3, to Co-operate with the States in Encouraging Instruction in Agriculture, the Trades and Industries, and Home Economics in Secondary Schools. etc.* Washington, Government Printing Office, 1912. 134 pp. (U. S.) 62d Cong., 2d sess. Senate. Doc. 845)

Discusses provisions of the bill. Emphasizes the importance of vocational education. Says: "It is a question which will, in my judgment, settle in great measure the quality of our citizenship in the generation upon which we are now entering. It is a question which will profoundly affect the cost of our food supply as well as the amount which our workers may earn with which to meet that higher cost of living which is upon us. It is a question which involves appropriations from the National treasury aggregating nearly $15,000,000 annually." . . . . "I believe I voice the sentiment of hundreds upon hundreds of the more thoughtful educators and publicists of our land to-day, who give it as their opinion that the curriculum of the elementary or graded school is largely impracticable and does not fit for the great struggles of life that are before them the 92 per cent of our boys and girls who never pass beyond the eight grades."

The appendix contains indorsements of the Page bill from prominent educators, editors, and public men.

Pallone, Nathaniel J. *No Longer Superfluous; the Educational Rehabilitation of the Hard-core Unemployed.* South Bend, Ind., South Bend Community School Corporation, 1965. 60 pp.

This report was prepared through the research program of the U. S. Office of Manpower, Automation, and Training and describes a project sponsored by MDTA funds. The information here is centered on the learning outcomes of the trainees, their experiences with the curriculum offered, and the reorientation of their attitudes.

Paquier, J. B. *L'Enseignement Professionel en France; Son Histoire.-Ses différentes Formes, Ses Resultats.* Paris, A. Colin, 1909. 342 pp.

Parkyn, George W. *Towards a Conceptual Model of Lifelong Education.* Paris, UNESCO, 1973.

Parsons, Frank. *Choosing a Vocation.* Boston, Houghton, Mifflin Co., 1909. 165 pp.

Contains valuable suggestions for the teacher in upper grades and high schools.

Patten, Thomas H., Jr. *Manpower Planning and the Development of Human Resources.* New York, John Wiley and Sons, 1971. 737 pp.

This work attempts to provide "a framework for placing developments in industrial education and training in perspective." In doing this, the author brings together the important literature in these fields published during the 1960's. Of special note are the chapters entitled: "Apprentice and Technical Training" and "Public Policy on Manpower, Training and Vocational Education."

Patterson, William F. *Educating for Industry; Policies and Procedures of a National Apprenticeship System.* New York, Prentice-Hall, 1946. 229 pp.

A survey of the apprenticeship system in the United States, including the role played by the Federal Government in introducing the national apprenticeship system. An extensive bibliography on the subject is to be found on pp. 155-184.

Pellison, Maurice. *Les Oeuvres Auxiliaires et Complémentaires de l'École en France.* Paris, Imprimerie Nationale, 1903. 161 pp.

Schools in France.

Pearlman, Richard. *On-the-job Training in Milwaukee-Nature, Extent and Relationship to Vocational Education.* Milwaukee, University of Wisconsin, Industrial Relations Research Institute, 1969. 37 pp. (Center for Studies in Vocational and Technical Education Research Report)

A study of the training provided by 245 Milwaukee companies for their employees to determine to what degree this on-the-job training complemented, duplicated, or substituted for the general vocational training provided by the Milwaukee schools.

Phoenixville, these case studies furnish information on the programs used, the development of the curriculum, the teachers employed, and the types of trainees attending. The final chapter is titled: "Employment and Societal Effects of Retraining Programs."

Perkins, Agnes F., ed. *Vocations for the Trained Woman.* Boston, Woman's Educational and Industrial Union, 1910. 28 pp.
    Opportunities other than teaching available for women.

Pennsylvania State University. Department of Vocational Education. *Pennsylvania Meets the Challenge of Retraining; Case Studies of a Three Pronged Attack.* By Carl J. Schaefer and John M. Shemick. University Park, Pennsylvania, the Author, 1964. 85 pp.
    The final report of a research project sponsored in part by the Ford Foundation. Centered upon three areas of Wilkes-Barre, Pottsville, and

Person, Harlow Stafford. *Industrial Education; a System of Training for Men Entering upon Trade and Commerce.* Boston & New York, Houghton, Mifflin and Company, 1907. 86 pp. (Hart, Schaffner & Marx Prize essays)
    Deals with the training required by young men who would fit themselves for the higher positions in industry or commerce, and the need of providing such training in the United States. The need is now generally admitted. The author's opinion clearly is that while commercial training should be offered in high schools, collegiate courses, and professional departments, the ideal conditions can be found only in distinctly professional instruction, open solely to those who have already completed a liberal education. The question here raised is a large one, about which, as is well known, there is serious difference of opinion.
    "It sets forth briefly the economic conditions which hold in the kingdom of Wurttemberg, the natural resources of the country, and the system of transportation. It then traces the development in this environment of the system of industrial schools and the service which they render in the upbuilding and maintenance of the State."
    It also includes a brief description of other industrial and commercial schools of the kingdom, and an outline of the activities of the Wurttemberg central bureau for industry and commerce.

Pressland, Arthur John. *The Continuation Schools of Switzerland.* London (etc.), Sherratt & Hughes, 1908. pp. 547-75.
    Reprinted from Continuation schools in England and elsewhere. Ed. by M. E. Sadler. Chapter XX.

Proceedings of the National Society for the Promotion of Industrial Education. *Bulletins* (New York: 1907-)
    Founded in Boston in 1907, the NSPIE was the lobby and chief organ of the alliance between educators and industrialists. At the federal level, the NSPIE influentially promoted national aid to vocational education. Renamed the National Society for Vocational Education in 1920.

Prosser, Charles A. and Charles R. Allen. *Vocational Education in a Democracy.* New York, Century Co., 1925. 580 pp.

A discussion of the principles underlying vocational education of secondary grade, the policies which should be adopted to make this form of training successful, and suggestions for methods in carrying out these policies.

Prosser, Charles Allen. *Evening Industrial Schools, by Charles A. Prosser, with the Collaboration of M. R. Bass.* Rev. ed. Chicago, American Technical Society, 1951. 372 pp.

Although designed as a textbook for students of vocational education, this work provides a history of the forms of vocational training given to workers in the past, how demands of technological change have brought about changes also in the structure, and purpose of additional training for workers already employed.

Prosser, Charles Allen and Thomas H. Guigley. *Vocational Education in a Democracy.* Chicago, American Technical Society, 1949. 575 pp.

A revision of a work first published in 1925 by C. A. Prosser and C. R. Allen. It updates this earlier work, describing the development of vocational education and subsequent Federal legislation in this field since 1925.

Public Sociological Library, New York City. *On Vocational Guidance . . . .* - New York City, Charity Organization Society of the City of New York, 1911. (4) pp. (Library bulletin no. 2)

Purdue University. Division of Education. Studies in Education. *Vocational Education in Public Schools as Related to Social, Economic, and Technical Trends. Part I:* The Analysis of Trends and Concepts. By F. J. Woerdehoff and others. Lafayette, Ind., 1960. 116 pp.

The initial phase of this study. It is concerned with "the identification of social, economic, and technical trends related to vocational education and the ranking of trends in terms of . . . in planning programs of vocational education."

Purdue University. Division of Education. Studies in Education. *Vocational Education in Public Schools as Related to Social, Economic and Technical Trends. Part II:* The Appraisal of Programs of Vocational Agriculture and Industrial Education. Frank J. Woerdehoff, Norbert J. Nelson, and John K. Coster, Project Directors. Lafayette, Ind. 1960. 489 pp., 91 (Cooperative research project No. 385)

Results of a study of a sample of Indiana high schools "to identify factors related to the desirable characteristics" of agricultural and industrial vocational education.

Rakestraw, Clarence Edward. *Training High School Youth for Employment.* Chicago, American Technical Society, 1947. 217 pp.

Although somewhat dated, this work is still of value. The author, a staff member of the U. S. Office of Education at the time this was written, describes the book as "a plan under which vocational training on a cooperative part-time basis can be offered in high schools."

Rathmann, Carl Gustav. *The Mission of Manual Training; an Address . . . before the Graduating Class of the Manual Training School of Washington University, June 23, 1909. With an Appendix Containing the Opinions of Educators in England, Germany, Austria and Australia.* (St. Louis), The Managing Board of the School, (1909). 23 pp.

Ravenhill, Alice, ed. *Household Administration, Its Place in the Higher Education of Women . . .* New York, H. Holt and Company, 1911. x, 324 pp. illus.
    Contains papers by noted writers on the subject of domestic science. Introduction by Catherine Schiff, is a brief historical sketch of woman's position in the family.

Ravner, Pearl (Cooper). *Training Mature Women for Employment, the Story of 23 Local Programs.* Prepared in the Division of Research of the Women's Bureau by Pearl C. Ravner with the assistance of Jean A. Wells and Annie Lefkowitz. Washington, U. S. Department of Labor, Women's Bureau, 1955. 46 pp. (U. S. Women's Bureau. Bulletin No. 256.)
    "This report provides examples of projects established by community organizations to meet the training needs of women ranging in economic standing from those receiving public assistance to those able to pay tuition fees at private schools."

Reber, Louis E. *Industrial and Continuation Schools, Their Foundation, Organization, and Adjustment to the Life of the Community.* Madison, Published by the Board, 1912. 18 pp. (Wisconsin. State Board of Education. Bulletin no. 5)
    Reviews work accomplished in other cities — Chicago, Cincinnati, and Cleveland, etc. — and emphasizes the need of industrial education.
    The writer says: "In Wisconsin, as elsewhere in this country, the greatest present need is for the continuation school. . . . Wisely vocationalized public schools and well-organized continuation schools will do much toward dignifying all occupations, and thus will create contented and happy classes where discontent now frequently exists."

Research Council of the Great Cities Program for School Improvement. *New Programs in Vocational Education.* Chicago, The Author, 1964. 45 pp.
    Statement describing vocational education programs developed by the member Great Cities since 1962. These cities are: Baltimore, Boston, Chicago, Cleveland, Detroit, Houston, Los Angeles, Milwaukee, New York City, Philadelphia, Pittsburgh, St. Louis, and Washington, D. C.

Research Council of the Great Cities Program for School Improvement. *Report Submitted to the Panel of Consultants on Vocational Education in the Large Cities of America.* Chicago, The Author, 1962. 102 pp.
    "This document . . . is a status study of vocational education in the member cities. It includes a statement of policy with regard to vocational education, a summary of current practices, and information relating to enrollment and review of basic problems."

Reuther, Walter P. "Education and Poverty." In *The Unfinished Journey; Issues in American Education.* (New York, John Day, 1968) pp. 53-68.

The late American labor leader states in this chapter that "no avenue should be left unexplored in seeking a more relevant education for poor children. . . . One of the major implications of such a stand is a thoroughgoing overhaul of vocational education." Reasons for this opinion are given as well as practical suggestions.

Rever, Philip R. *Scientific and Technical Careers: Factors Influencing Development during the Educational Years.* Iowa City, The American College Testing Program, 1973.

Rhees, Benjamin Rush. *The National Importance of Industrial Education* (New York?, 1909.) 11 pp.

Address, second annual convention, New York State branch National Society for the Promotion of Industrial Education.

Rhode Island. Commissioner of Public Schools. *Special Report, Relating to Industrial Education . . .* March 28, 1911. Providence, E. L. Freeman Co., 1911. 102 pp.

Commissioner, Walter E. Ranger.

Bibliography: pp. 97-102 (Supplement II)

Richards, Charles R. *Industrial Training; a Report on Conditions in New York State.* Albany, State Department of Labor, 1909. 394 pp. (New York. Bureau of Labor Statistics. 26th annual report for 1908, Part I)

Bibliography: pp. 357-94.

Contents. — General summary. — Conditions of entrance and advancement in individual industries. — Attitude of labor unions toward industrial and trade schools. — Comments by employers on industrial training. — Rules and agreements of labor unions in regard to apprentices and helpers. — Laws of New York State relating to child labor, compulsory education, apprenticeship, and industrial education. — Institutions offering courses in industrial training in New York State.

Richards, Charles R. *Selected Bibliography on Industrial Education.* Asbury Park, N. J. Kinnmonth Press, 1907. 32 pp. (National Society for the Promotion of Industrial Education. Bulletin no. 2)

Contains 107 well-annotated titles on the various phases of industrial education.

Righter, Leonard and others. *Educational Survey Preparatory to Organization of Vocational Education,* by Leonard Righter . . . *Social Phases of Industrial Life and Vocational Guidance,* by Robert J. Leonard. With an Introduction by Frederick G. Bonser. New York City, Teachers' College, Columbia University, 1913. 64 pp. diagrs. (Teachers College Record. vol. XIV, no. 1)

Bibliography: p. 43.

The author of the first paper describes the manner in which the survey, used for many purposes at the present time, may be adapted to educational purposes, especially to the adjustment of the school curriculum to meet the needs of the community. The second paper emphasizes the need for the development in the schools of a knowledge of industrial conditions and the importance of industries in the national life.

Roberts, Roy W. *Vocational and Practical Arts Education.* New York, Harper, 1957. 637 pp.
   A study of vocational and practical arts education in the public secondary schools and their relationship to other areas of the curriculum. Includes accounts of the development of federally aided programs.

Roberts, Roy W. *Vocational and Practical Arts Education; Historical Development and Principles.* 2d ed. New York, Harper, 1965. 569 pp.
   An updated edition of the 1957 work.

Roberts, Roy W. *Vocational and Practical Arts Education: History, Development and Principles.* 3rd. ed. New York, Harper and Row, 1971. 500 pp.
   Valuable mostly as a college textbook. The third revised edition has appendixes of statistical tables on enrollments in vocational education 1918-1967, expenditures for various types of vocational education, 1918-1967 and a section giving the Vocational Education Amendments of 1968.

Robison, Emily, comp. *Vocational Education.* Second and revised edition by Julia E. Johnson. New York, H. W. Wilson Co., 1920. 359 pp.
   First published in 1917, this book offers a valuable compilation of early source material on vocational education in the United States. In this revised edition, a bibliography of some 300 references has been added.

Roman, Frederick W. *Die deutschen gewerblichen und kaufmännischenFortbildungs-und Fachschulen und die industriellen, kommerziellen Schulen in den Vereingten-Staaten von Nord-Amerika. Ein Vergleich.* Leipzig, Duncker & Humbolt, 1910. x, 214 pp.
   A comparison between German continuation schools and industrial schools in the United States.

Rosenberg, Jerry M. ed. *New Conceptions of Vocational and Technical Education.* New York, Teachers College Press, 1967. 86 pp.
   Papers from the National Conference on the Need for a Renewed Conception of Vocational and Technical Education, held in May 1965, under the sponsorship of Teachers College, Columbia University. Emphasis of the conference was seen in the discussion of work-study programs and vocational education of the unskilled.

Rouillon, Louis. *Economics of Manual Training, a Study of the Cost of Equipping and Maintaining Handwork in the Elementary and Secondary Schools.* New York, Derry-Collard, 1905. 174 pp.
   Tables of the average cost are given. Gives plans of training school buildings at Kansas City, Mo.; Boston, Mass.; Chicago, Ill., and others.

Row, Robert Keable. *The Educational Meaning of Manual Arts and Industries.* Chicago, Row, Peterson and Company, (1909). 248 pp. illus. diagrs.

Russell, John Dale and associates. *Vocational Education. Staff Study Number 8.* Prepared for the Advisory Committee on Education. Washington, U. S. Government Printing Office, 1938. 325 pp.
    This monograph was originally prepared as a staff study for the Advisory Committee on Education appointed by President Franklin Delano Roosevelt on September 19, 1936. Under its original assignment, the Committee was known as the President's Committee on Vocational Education. In the introduction the authors state the scope and purpose of this work: "This study undertakes to survey in a fairly broad way the whole plan of organization for the federally reimbursed program of vocational education, the outcomes of this service, the needs of the country for occupational preparation, and the manner in which these needs may best be met."

Sadler, Michael Ernest, ed. *Continuation Schools in England and Elsewhere; Their Place in the Educational System of an Industrial and Commercial State.* Manchester, University Press, 1907. xxvi, 779 pp. tab. (fold.) (Publications of the University of Manchester. Educational series, no. 1)
    An important volume, in which are collected careful and competent accounts of the history and present status in Great Britain, of the various agencies for "further education," with 8 brief chapters on such schools in the chief European countries and the United States. The contributions of 18 different authors have been carefully edited by Professor Sadler (himself a considerable contributor), and the result is a veritable cyclopedia of information hitherto widely scattered or quite inexistent.

Saint, Avice. *Learning at Work: Human Resources and Organizational Development.* Chicago, Nelson-Hall, 1974. 332 pp.
    A discussion of on-the-job training, with illustrations drawn from a variety of studies of training in corporate and government settings.

Sargent, Walter. *Fine and Industrial Arts in Elementary Schools.* Boston, New York (etc.), Ginn and Company, (1912). 132 pp. illus.
    Contents. — 1. Educational and practical values of the fine and industrial arts. 2. A survey of the progression of work through the grades. 3 — 7. Grades I to VIII.

Sayward, William Henry. *The Relation of the Trade School to the Trade; an Address . . . Delivered at the Graduation Exercises of the North-end Union Plumbing School, Boston, May 15, 1908.* Boston, Printed at the School of Printing, North-end Union, 1908. 14 pp.

Schaefer, Carl J. and Jacob J. Kaufman. *New Directions for Vocational Education.* Lexington, Mass., D. C. Heath, 1971.
    Valuable review of programs, trends, and needs, with critical assessments of reports and literature. Originated as a report prepared for the Massachusetts Advisory Council on Education.

Schaefer, Carl J. *and* Jacob J. Kaufman. *New Directions for Vocational Education: A State Model. A Report Prepared for the Massachusetts Advisory Council on Education.* Lexington, Mass., Health Lexington Books, 1971. 295 pp.

This research was initiated with a two-fold purpose: 1) to evaluate the present system of vocational and technical education in the State; 2) to recommend a master plan for the coordination and expansion of this type of training. Recommendations for teacher preparation are included.

Schneider, Herman. *Fundamental Principles of Industrial Education.* (New York, 1909.) 307-16 pp.

A paper presented at a special meeting of the American Institute of Electrical Engineers, New York, April 16, 1909.

Subject to final revision for the *Transaction.*

Sears, William P., Jr. *The Roots of Vocational Education; a Survey of the Origins of Trade and Industrial Education Found in Industry, Education, Legislation, and Social Progress.* New York, John Wiley & Sons, 1931. 310 pp.

This comprehensive study is divided into three parts. Part I is a summary of the social forces that created the needs for vocational education, beginning with a social history of England and the founding of the American Colonies extending to the late 1920's. In Part II titled "The Educational Evolution," the author traces the growth of industrial vocational education in industry and educational institutions. Part III is devoted to the contributions of social agencies and educators to vocational education in the United States.

Sewell, D. O. *Training the Poor: a Benefit-cost Analysis of Manpower Programs in the U. S. Antipoverty Program.* Kingston, Ontario, Queen's University, Industrial Relations Centre, 1971. 153 pp. (Research ser. no. 12)

An evaluation of the North Carolina program Manpower Improvement through Community Effort. (MITCE)

Shadwell, Arthur. *Industrial Efficiency. A Comparative Study of Industrial Life in England, Germany and America.* New ed. London, New York (etc.), Longmans, Green, and Co., 1909. xx, 720 pp.

Contains a critical analysis and comparison of the organization, ideals and methods of public elementary education in England, Germany, and the United States. Chapter xvii treats directly of technical education, describes schools for industrial and technical instruction, emphasis being laid especially on the schools of Germany and England, and the effect of these schools on the industrial problem. An illuminating book on many points. Gives a searching study of social conditions in the three countries.

Shaffer, Helen B. *Jobs for Young People.* Washington, Editorial Research Reports, 1961. pp. 501-517. (Editorial research reports, 1961, v. 2, No. 2, July 12, 1961)

Contents: Changed outlook for young job-hunters; job handicaps of undereducated youths; and programs to prepare youths for work.

Siercks, H. *Das deutsche Fortbildungsschulwesen, nach seiner geschichtlichen Entwicklung und in seiner gegenwartigen Gestalt.* Leipzig, G. J. Goschen, 1908. 176 pp. [Sammlung Goschen (392)]
    Literatur: pp. 5-6.

Smith, Harold T. *Education and Training for the World of Work; a Vocational Education Program for the State of Michigan.* Kalamazoo, W. E. Upjohn Institute for Employment Research, 1963. 165 pp.
    A study of "what should be expected of vocational and technical education in our present-day society, . . . what institutions, what administrative organization and what financial structure are needed in Michigan before these expectations can be fulfilled."

Smith, Leo F. and Lawrence Lypsett. *The Technical Institute.* New York, McGraw-Hill, 1956.
    Review of various types of institutes and their programs.

Smith, Ross H. *Development of Manual Training in the United States.* Lancaster, Pa., Intelligencer Printing Co., 1914.
    An early history with considerable detail on programs.

Smoker, David S. *Vocational Education: Innovations Revolutionize Career Training.* Washington, D. C·, National School Public Relations Association, 1971. 64 pp. (At head of title: Education U. S. A. Special Report).
    Brief but concise assessment of vocational education in the U. S., the inadequacies of the system, what should be done for greater efficiency. Includes information on what particular states are doing to change the structure of their vocational training programs.

Snedden, David S. *American High Schools and Vocational Schools in 1960.* New York Teachers College, Columbia University, 1931. 122 pp.
    An essay written from a Utopian point of view as to what could be expected of American secondary school organization and vocational training in a 30-year period. The author uses a mythical "Chinese National Board of Education" report for his forecasts. Useful as a "Brave New World" study in the field of education. Title on cover: "Secondary Schools, 1960."

Snedden, David S. *The Problem of Vocational Education.* Boston, New York (etc.), Houghton Mifflin Company, (1910). vi, 86 pp. (Riverside educational monographs, ed. by H. Suzzallo)
    A concise but comprehensive survey of present conditions and prospects. Discusses definitions of a liberal education; the need of vocational education; state support, types, and pedagogical divisions of vocational education. Treats of the relation of vocational education to manual training, problem of women in industry, and a variety of related topics. Dr. Snedden is a recognized authority in this important educational field.

Snedden, David S. *Vocational Education.* New York, Macmillan, 1920. 587 pp.

A discussion of what was considered "current problems in vocational education" when that type of training was just beginning. It includes all forms of vocational educational programs with chapters also on the administration of vocational education and the training of teachers for vocational schools. Appendix A (pp. 515-533) has statistics taken from the 1910 census on the number of workers engaged in specified gainful occupations, occupations that have long since been displaced by automation.

Snedden, David, S. and others. *Vocational Education; Its Theory, Administration and Practice.* Boston, Houghton Mifflin, 1912. pp. 85, 207, 75.
     A collection of three monographs on the status of vocational education in the early part of the 20th century. Contents: "The problem of vocational education" by David Snedden; "The people's schools: a study in vocational training" by Ruth Mary Weeks; and "The improvement of rural schools" by Ellwood P. Cubberly.

Social Educational Research and Development, Inc. *Vocational Education: A Feasibility Study for the Suburbs of Tomorrow.* Vol. I. Conducted for the Educational Development Cooperative. Silver Spring, Md., the author, 1968.
     The Educational Development Cooperative (EDC) is comprised of 14 high school districts and 50 elementary schools districts in Cook County, Illinois, The purpose of the study conducted for this Cooperative was to ascertain the possibilities and problems involved in locating a broadly based vocational program among the 14 high school districts.

Society for the Promotion of Engineering Education. *American Industrial Education; What Shall It Be? Preliminary Report of a Committee of the Society.* In Proceedings of the New York Meeting, July 2-3, 1900. pp. 1-71.

Society for the Promotion of Engineering Education. *A Study of Technical Institutes; a Collateral Project to the Investigation of Engineering Education.* Lancaster, Pa., Lancaster Press, Inc., 1931. 281 pp.
     A 1928—1929 national survey made of postsecondary technical training schools in the United States, their historical development and status for that period of time. This study also includes information on technical schools in France, Great Britain and Germany.

Society for the Promotion of Engineering Education. Committee on Industrial Education. *Report* . . . (n. p., 1908.) pp. 363-405.
     Reprinted from its Proceedings, 16.
     Prepared by Arthur L. Williston, chairman.

Some Industrial Arts Books. A. L. A. Publishing Board, 1909. 16 pp.
     "These books have been of popular use in the St. Joseph (Mo.) public library and will be of value to other libraries." *Library Journal,* March 1908, p. 119.

Somers, Gerald G. and others. *The Effectiveness of Vocational and Technical Programs; a National Follow-up Survey.* Madison, University of Wisconsin,

Center for Studies in Vocational and Technical Education, 1971. 263 pp.

"A national sample of vocational students who graduated from high school, post-secondary school and junior college vocational programs in 1966 were surveyed three years later to determine the effectiveness of their vocational education."

Somers, Gerald G. and J. Kenneth Little, eds. *Vocational Education: Today and Tomorrow*. Madison, University of Wisconsin Press, 1971.

Critical essays on aspects of vocational education with some program assessment.

Somers, Gerald G. and Ernst W. Stromsdorfer. *A Cost-effectiveness Study of the In-school and Summer Neighborhood Youth Corps*. Madison, University of Wisconsin, Industrial Relations Research Institute, Center for Studies in Vocational and Technical Education, 1970.

A report prepared for the Manpower Administration of the U. S. Dept. of Labor. The study is a nation-wide šample of NYC participants from projects in operation during fiscal years 1965/66 and 1966/67.

Spring, Joel. *Education and the Rise of the Corporate State*. Boston, Beacon Press, 1972.

Develops the thesis that the basic faiUling of the schools resulted from their uncompromising adaptation to the structure and needs of modern, industrial society. Includes a foreword by Ivan Illich.

Stadt, Ronald W., et. al. *Managing Career Education Programs*. Englewood Cliffs, N. J., Prentice Hall, 1973.

Starr, Harold and others. A *System for State Evaluation of Vocational Education*. Columbus, Ohio, The Center for Vocational and Technical Education, Ohio State University, 1970. 181 pp. Appendix.

The final report of a project designed to furnish a model for state divisions to use in evaluating programs which satisfy state and federal accountability requirements. A six page bibliography on state directed evaluation systems is to be found on pages 53-58.

Stephens, W. Richard. *Social Reforms and the Origins of Vocational Guidance*. Washington, Brookings Institution, 1970.

Vocational education and its relationships to social reform, educational change, and the guidahce of youth.

Stevenson, John B. *An Introduction to Career Education*. Worthington, Ohio, Charles A. Jones Publishing Co., 1973.

Stombaugh, Ray. *A Survey of the Movements Culminating in Industrial Arts Education in Secondary Schools*. New York, Teachers College, Columbia University, 1936. 192 pp.

This study covers the period from 1871, with the establishment of the Boston Whittling School, up to 1936. Eight "trends" or movements are discussed.

Struck, F. Theodore. *Foundations of Industrial Education.* New York, John Wiley, 1930.
   Includes materials on historical backgrounds. Influential statement by leader in field.

Struck, F. Theodore. *Vocational Education for a Changing World.* New York, John Wiley & Sons, 1945. 550 pp.
   Although a textbook, this work, prepared by a former head of the Department of Industrial Education at Pennsylvania State College, covers the history and development of vocational education of less than college, covers the history and development of vocational education of less than college grades. It also includes the policies of labor and management as they relate to vocational education and the attitude of many trade and educational associations toward education for work. Each chapter contains excellent bibliographies related to topics discussed.

Swanson, J. Chester, ed. *Development of Federal Legislation for Vocational Education.* 2nd. ed. Chicago, American Technical Society, 1966.
   Historical overview with extensive information on the Vocational Education Act of 1963.

Swanson, John C., project director. *A Nationwide Study of the Administration of Vocational-technical Education at the State Level.* Berkeley, University of California, School of Education, 1967.
   Research performed under contract with the U. S. Office of Education, appearing in seven volumes, each with a distinctive author. Partial contents: Program evaluation and review technique by Sara Pierce; The current status of state-level organization by J. C. Swanson; Analysis of expenditures for vocational-technical education programs by John Ross. (All parts of this study available also in microfiche form through the ERIC system)

(Symposium) *Social Education Quarterly,* June 1907. 97 pp.
   Contains: 1. The place of industrial education in the common school system, by F. P. Fish. 2. Industrial education in a prairie state, by E. B. Andrews. 3. American industrial training as compared with European, by f. A. Vanderlip. 4. The problem of industrial education, by C. R. Richards. 5. The needs from the manufacturers' standpoint, by M. W. Alexander. 6. The importance of industrial education to the workingman, by John Golden. 7. Bearings of industrial education upon social conditions, by R. A. Woods.

Technician Education Yearbook, 1973-1974. Ann Arbor, Prakken Publications, 1973.

Tennyson, W. Wesley, et. al. *Vocational Development and Guidance.* New York, MSS Information Corp., 1974.

Terminal Education in Higher Institutions with Special Reference to the Readjustment of Higher Education to Meet Current National Needs. Proceedings of the Institute for Administrative Officers of Higher Institutions, 1942. Vol. 14. Edited by John Dale Russell. Chicago, University of Chicago Press, 1942. 198 pp.

A collection of 18 papers presented at the 19th session of the Institute for Administrative Officers of Higher Institutions. Contributions consist of an overall view of terminal education in various vocational fields, particularly at the junior college level and the readjustments of higher education to meet national manpower needs, with emphasis on the country's war effort.

Tesconi, Charles A. and Van Cleve Morris. *The Anti-Man Culture: Bureautechnocracy and the Schools*. Urbana, University of Illinois Press, 1972.

Asserts that the schools are the "perpetuator" of bureautechnocracy even as they are its creature. Bureautechnocracy advocates assimilation; the adjustment of individuals to modern, industrial society; and the adoption of scientific methodologies.

Texas. Governor's Conference on Technical-Vocational Education. *A Concerned Texas. A Report of the Governor's Conference on Technical-Vocational Education*. By the Advisory Council for Technical-Vocational Education in Texas. March 23-24, 1970. Austin, 1970. 115 pp.

Proceedings of a Conference sponsored by state and federal agencies, business firms, associations and educational institutions, providing "a forum for exchange of ideas". Main topics were centered on the "Concers" for the further expansion of technical-vocational education, and for the continuing need for updating and improving present programs.

Thomas, Lawrence G. *The Occupational Structure and Education*. Englewood Cliffs, Prentice Hall, 1956. 502 pp.

A study of the relationship of American vocational training and the occupational structure in our economy. This "occupational structure" is discussed in regard to income, prestige, and job satisfaction, qualifications demanded by employers, and the contribution of vocational schools to it.

Thrasher, Max Bennett. *Tuskegee, Its Story and Its Work. With an Introduction by Booker T. Washington*. Boston, Small, Maynard & Co., 1901. xvi, 215 pp. illus.

Tolman, William H. *Social Engineering; a Record of Things Done by American Industrialists Employing upwards of One and One-half Million of People. With an Introduction by Andrew Carnegie*. New York & London, McGraw-Hill Book Company, 1909. viii, 384 pp.

Discusses among other topics vocational education, pp. 257-97. Shows what the various manufacturing companies have done to further the education of employees.

The Transition from School to Work; a Report Based on the Princeton Manpower Symposium, May 9-10, 1968. Princeton, N. J. Princeton University, Industrial Relations Section, 1968. 282 pp.

The objective of the symposium was to summarize "the dimensions of the youth unemployment problem and to discuss the roles and responsibilities of schools, private enterprise, trade unions, voluntary agencies and various levels of government in development of better bridges between school and work for non-college bound youth."

Triche, Andrew. *A Comparative Study of Vocational Education in the 48 States.* State College, Pennsylvania, School of Education, Pennsylvania State College, 1935. 47 pp. (Penn State studies in education. No. 15)
     Originally written as a doctoral dissertation. Contains 1930 statistics pertinent to vocational education, arranged by State. Includes enrollment figures, expenditures, etc.

True, Alfred C. *A History of Agricultural Education in the United States, 1785-1925.* Washington, Government Printing Office, 1929.
     Comprehensive history of vocational agriculture in the public schools.

Truman, Max. *l'Éducation Populaire; les Oeuvres Complémentaires de l'École* . . . 3d rev et augm . . . Paris, V. Lecoffre, J. Gabalda & Cie, 1907. 426 pp.
     Bibliographie: pp. 407-12.

(UNESCO). *Technical and Vocational Teacher Education and Training.* Paris, UNESCO, 1973. 240 pp.
     Directed primarily toward the needs of developing countries. Provides information, analysis, and guidelines in the education and training of teachers.

(UNESCO). *Television for Higher Technical Education of Workers: Final Report on a Pilot Project in Poland.* Paris, UNESCO, 1973.

U. S. Advisory Committee On Education. *Report of the Advisory Committee on Education. Message from the President of the United States, Transmitting the Report of the Advisory Committee on Education Appointed in September 1936 to Study the Experience Under the Existing Program of Federal Aid and Vocational Education.* Washington, U. S. Government Printing Office, 1938. 148 pp. (85th Cong. 3d sess. House. Doc. No. 529) Issued also without document note under title: "Report of the Committee."
     Message from President F. D. Roosevelt on the relation of vocational education to existing economic and social conditions and the need to expand the program.

U. S. Advisory Committee on Education. *Report of the Committee, February 1938.* Washington, U. S. Government Printing Office, 1938. 243 pp.
     Official report of the Committee to President F. D. Roosevelt. Contains a general summary of education in our national life and a recommended program, mainly in vocational training.

U. S. Bureau of Adult, Vocational and Technical Education. *Prevocational Exploratory Programs in Manpower Development and Training.* Washington, U. S. Govt. Print. Off., 1970. 60 pp.
     The "prevocational exploratory program" is designed to help the trainee

"whose education and experience is inadequate to prepare him either to make a vocational choice or to profit from job training." Included in this study are chapters on launching prevocational programs and implementation of the initial moves.

(United States Bureau of Education). *The Apprenticeship System in Its Relation to Industrial Education.* Washington, Government Printing Office, 1908. (Bulletin, 1908, No. 6. Carroll D. Wright.)
  Historical backgrounds of the apprentice system and critical appraisal by the Commissioner of Labor.

United States. Bureau of Education. *Bibliography of Education in Agriculture and Home Economics.* Washington, Government Printing Office, 1912. 62 pp. (Its Bulletin no. 10, 1912).
  The bibliography of home economics (pp. 41-56) is divided into nine parts as follows: General; elementary schools; rural schools; secondary schools; club study; colleges and ‘universities; foreign countries; bibliography; periodicals. It is well-annotated and indexed. The School of Household Arts of Columbia University, Teachers College, published in 1910 an annotated list of books relating to domestic science.

United States. Bureau of Education. ·*Consular Reports on Continuation Schools, in Prussia.* Washington, Government Printing Office, 1913. 30 pp. (Its Bulletin no. 9, 1913)
  Contains interesting data on vocational training in Magdeburg; part-time for industrial workers in Prussia; the city continuation and trade school of Brunswick; continuation schools of Barmen; and part-time shoe schools in Breslau. Reports made by United States consuls.

United States. Bureau of Education. *Synopses of Courses of Study in Eighteen Manual Training High Schools.* Washington, Government Printing Office, 1902. 20 pp.

United States. Bureau of Labor. "Conditions under Which Children Leave School to Go to Work." In its *Report on Condition of Women and Child Wage-earners in the United States.* Washington, Government Printing Office, 1910. v. 7. 309 pp. (61st Cong., 2 sess. Senate. Document no. 645)
  Contents. — 1. Reason for leaving school and going to work. 2. Circumstances possibly influential in causing children to leave school. 3. Industrial experience of children. 4. Legal conditions affecting the employment and school attendance of children. 5. Retardation, repeating, and elimination.
  An intensive study of 622 children in seven different localities, taken from two northern and two southern states. Domestic, educational, industrial, legal, social and hygienic conditions discussed. Throws light on the difficulty experienced by boys in-securing chances to learn trades.

United States. Bureau of Labor. "Industrial Education." In its *Annual Report of the Commissioner of Labor, 1910.* Washington, Government Printing Office, 1911, 822 pp.

Bibliography: pp. 519-39.

Comprehensive study of industrial education in all its phases. Discusses at length apprenticeship schools; vocational guidance; legislation regarding industrial education, etc. "The data for this report were gathered mainly by special agents of the Bureau of Labor on a schedule of inquiries. The information was collected during the latter half of the year 1910 and relates to conditions at that time. . . . A very few schedules were secured by correspondence."

Chapter xvii contains voluminous statistics of Trades and subjects taught and time devoted to schoolroom work and to practice.

United States. Bureau of Labor. *17th Annual Report of the United States Commissioner of Labor, 1902.* Washington, Government Printing Office, 1902. 1333 pp.

An exhaustive compilation of material regarding trade and technical education in the United States. Describes institutions for industrial education in the United States. Chapter 2 deals with the attitude of employers, graduates and labor unions toward such institutions. A study is made of industrial education in Austria, Belgium, Canada, France, Germany, Great Britain, Hungary, Italy and Switzerland.

A synopsis of the report, prepared for the exhibit of the bureau at the Louisiana purchase exposition, is contained in Bulletin no. 54, of the U. S. Bureau of Labor. Washington, September, 1904. pp. 1369-1417. The text is copiously illustrated.

U.S. Bureau of Labor Statistics. *Occupational Manpower and Training Needs: Information for Planning Training Programs for the 1970's.* Washington, U. S. Government Print. Off., 1971. 81 pp. (Its Bulletin 1701)

This study contains information on how to use projections of occupational requirements and supply, and training in planning education and training programs. It includes data and statistics on the types of vocational schools in existence and the federal manpower programs in this field. The last chapter "Relating Training to Occupational Needs" gives information on all professional and related occupations, and the training requirements of these positions.

U. S. Commission on National Aid to Vocational Education. *Vocational Education. Report . . . Together with the Hearings Held on the Subject Made Pursuant to the Provisions of Public Resolution No. 16, 63rd Congress.* (S. J. Res. 5). In two volumes. Washington, U. S. Government Printing Office, 1914. 292 pp. (63d Cong., 2d sess. House Doc. No. 1004)

A report of the status of vocational education in the United States in 1914, and the reasons for Federal participation in this kind of training. Volume II gives the testimony of prominent educators, industrialists, and members of the Armed Forces on vocational programs in existence at the time and the demand for expansion.

United States. Congress. House. Committee on Agriculture. *Vocational Education. Hearing before the Committee on Agriculture . . . on H. R. 23581, April 23-26, 1912.* Washington, Government Printing Office, 1912. 152 pp.

John Lamb, Chairman.
Treats of technical education, domestic economy, and agricultural education.

U.S. Congress. House. Committee on Education. *Development of Vocational Education in the Several States. Hearing . . . before the Committee on Education on H. F. 9201 [H. R. 12241], a Bill to Provide for Further Development of Vocational Education in the Several States.* February 7 March 20 and 21, 1928. Washington, U. S. Government Printing Office, 1928. 87 pp. (70th Cong., 1st sess.)
Contains testimony and statements by leading educators and others on the needs of vocational education at the time and reasons for expanding it.

U. S. Congress. House. Committee on Education and Labor. *Occupational Education Act of 1971. Hearing before the General Subcommittee on Education, 92d Cong., 1st sess. on H.R. 7429 and sections of S. 659, Sept. 20, 1971.* Washington, U. S. Govt. Print. Off., 1971. 109 pp.

U. S. Congress. House. Committee on Education and Labor. *Partnership of Learning and Earning Act of 1968. Hearings before the General Subcommittee on Education 90th Cong., 2d sess. on H. R. 15066, Feb. 20-Mar. 21, 1968.* Washington, U. S. Govt. Print. Off., 1968. 830 pp.

U. S. Congress. House. Committee on Education and Labor. *Reports on the Implementation of the Vocational Education Amendments of 1968 [by the] General Subcommittee on Education.* Washington, U. S. Government Printing Off., 1971. 868 pp. (At head of title: Committee Print).

U. S. Congress. House. Committee on Education and Labor. *Vocational Education Amendments of 1966. Hearings before the General Subcommittee on Education, 89th Cong., on H. R. 15444 and H. R. 15445, June 9-August 18, 1966.* 2 pts. Washington, U. S. Govt. Print. Off., 1967. 912 pp.

U. S. Congress. House. Committee on Education and Labor. *Vocational Education Amendments of 1968. Hearings before the General Subcommittee on Education, 90th Cong., 2d sess. on H. R. 16460, Pts. I and II, May 1-16, 1968.* Washington, U. S. Govt. Print. Off., 1968. 1078 pp.

U. S. Congress. House. Committee on Education and Labor. *Vocational Education Amendments of 1969. Hearing before the General Subcommittee on Education, 91st Cong., 1st sess. on H. R. 13630, Sept. 25, 1969.* Washington, U. S. Govt. Print. Off., 1969. 380 pp.

U. S. Congress. House. Committee on Education and Labor. *Vocational Education Improvement Act Amendments of 1967. Hearings before the General Subcommittee on Education, 90th Cong., 1st and 2d sess., on H. R. 8525 and Related Bills. Pts. I-III, Apr. 12, 1967-Feb. 1, 1968.* Washington, U. S. Govt. Print. Off., 1968. 926 pp.

(U. S. Congress, House of Representatives, 63rd Congress, 3rd Session, 1914, House Document 1004): *Report of the Commission on National Aid to Vocational Education.*

The Commission's recommendations were written into law with the passage of the Smith-Hughes Act of 1917.

United States. Congress Senate. *A Bill to Provide for Co-operation with the States in Promoting Instruction in Agriculture, the Trades and Industries, and Home Economics in Secondary Schools; in Preparing Teachers for These Vocational Subjects in State Colleges of Agriculture and the Mechanic Arts, in State Normal Schools, and in Other Training Schools for Teachers Supported and Controlled by the Public; in Maintaining Extension Departments of State Colleges of Agriculture and the Mechanic Arts; in Maintaining Branches of State Experiment Stations; and to Appropriate Money and Regulate its Expenditure.* [Washington, Government Printing Office, 1912] 28 pp. (62 Congress, 2d session. Senate 3. Calendar no. 348 [Report no. 405])

Introduced by Senator Page April 6, 1911; reported with amendments Feb. 26, 1912; text of original bill and reported amendments withdrawn, and substitute reported placed on calendar, June 14, 1912; ordered reprinted July 24, 1912.

A special committee of the National Society for the Promotion of Industrial Education, David Snedden, chairman, appointed to consider the above bill, made an interesting report to the executive committee of the society. Discussing the uncertainty which prevails as to what constitutes vocational education, the committee came to the conclusion that the Page bill should contain "a series of definitions indicating the types of education contemplated and the standards applicable to its administration," etc. They accordingly drafted, by way of suggestion, a measure which incorporated the principles suggested by them.

The Page bill would appropriate $3,000,000 annually to extension work; $3,000,000 a year to aid district agricultural schools; $3,000,000 to introduce the teaching of agriculture, trades and domestic science in the rural schools; and $3,000,000 to teaching trades and domestic science in the city schools. The money given from the Federal treasury for these purposes must be supplemented by an equal sum from the state. The state must evince its sincere purpose to co-operate in the work by giving its half.

United States. Congress. Senate. Committee on Agriculture and Forestry. *Vocational Education. Hearings before the Committee on Agriculture and Forestry . . . April 12 and 13, 1910, on the Bill (S. 4675) to Co-operate with the States in Encouraging Instruction in Agriculture, the Trades, and Industries . . .* Washington, Government Printing Office, 1910. 82 pp.

United States, Congress. Senate. Committee on Agriculture and Forestry. *Vocational Education. Report of the Committee . . . United States Senate . . . on Senate Bill 3 . . .* Washington, Government Printing Office, 1912. 75 pp. (62d Cong., 2d sess. Senate. Dept. 405)

Calendar no. 348.

United States, Congress. Senate. Committee on Agriculture and Forestry.-
*Vocational Education. Report of the Subcommittee . . . United States
Senate, Sixty-second Congress, on Senate Bill 3 . . .* Washington, Govern-
ment Printing Office, 1912. 71 pp.

U.S. Congress. Senate. Committee on Labor and Public Welfare. *Education
Amendments of 1971: Report, August 3, 1971, on S.659 to Amend the
Higher Education Act of 1965, the Vocational Education Act of 1963 and
Related Acts, and for Other Purposes, Together with Supplemental and In-
dividual Views.* Washington, U. S. Government Printing Off., 1971. 584 pp.
(92d Cong., 1st sess., S. rept. no. 92-346)

U. S. Congress. Senate. Committee on Labor and Public Welfare. *Education
Legislation 1968. Hearings before the Subcommittee on Education, 90th
Cong., 2d sess. on S. 3098 and S 3099, in eight parts.* Pt. I Mar. 12, 1968; Pt.
II Mar. 13, 25-26, 1968; Pt. III Mar. 27, 1968; Pt. IV Mar. 28-29, 1968; Pt.
V Apr. 2, 1968; Pt. VI Apr. 3-5, 1968. Pts. VII and VIII Appendixes 1-4.
Washington, U. S. Govt. Print. Off., 1968. 6,584 pp. (S. 3098 included the
National Vocational Student Loan Act of 1965 and and S. 3099 contained the
amendments to the Vocational Act of 1963)

U. S. Congress. Senate. Committee on Labor and Public Welfare. *Manpower
Development and Training Legislation, 1970. Hearings before the Subcommittee on Employment, Manpower and Poverty, 91st Cong., 1st and 2d
sess. on S. 2838. Pt. I. Nov. 4, 1969-Feb. 9, 1970.* Washington, U. S. Govt.
Print. Off., 1970. 741 pp.

U. S. Congress. Senate. Republican Policy Committee. *The Forgotten Youth.*
Remarks in the Senate. Congressional Record (daily ed.), v. 109, March
1963: 3965 — 3967 (Part I included in Senate hearings on Youth Employment
Act [S.1])
    A study of vocational education in the United States, what it has con-
tributed, and the problems involved.

United States. Department of Commerce and Labor. Bureau of Labor.
Conditions of Entrance to the Principal Trades. Washington, Government
Printing Office, 1906. 100 pp. (Bulletin no. 67, November 1906)
    A study of the changes in organization and processes of modern indus-
try. Position of the helper system in highly specialized machine industries.
Treats of the decadence of the apprenticeship system.

United States. Department of Commerce and Labor. Bureau of Statistics.
Industrial Education and Industrial Conditions in Germany. Washington,
Government Printing Office, 1905. 323 pp. illus. (Special consular reports. v.
33)
    Industrial education: pp. 5-147.
    A comprehensive survey of the subject. Contains a study of the ad-
ministration of industrial education. Describes the various schools, methods
of instruction, curricula, and the attitude of the people and government

toward industrial education in general. For discussion of continuation schools, see pp. 145-47.

(U. S. Department of Health, Education, and Welfare). *Education for a Changing World of Work*. Washington, Government Printing Office, 1964.
    The historical development of vocational education and a review of existing programs. Report of John F. Kennedy's Panel of Consultants on Vocational Education.

(U. S. Dept. of Health, Education and Welfare). *Research in Industrial Education: Summaries of Studies, 1930-1955*. Vocational Division Bulletin No. 264. Trade and Industrial Series No. 65. Washington, U. S. Government Printing Office, 1957.

(U. S. Dept. of Health, Education and Welfare). *Research in Industrial Education: Summaries of Studies, 1956-1959*. Vocational Division Bulletin No. 293. Trade and Industrial Education Series No. 72. Washington, U. S. Government Printing Office, 1961.

(U. S. Dept. of Health, Education and Welfare). *Research in Industrial Education: Summaries of Studies, 1960-1961*. Vocational Division Bulletin No. 299. Trade and Industrial Education Series No. 75. Washington, U. S. Government Printing Office, 1962.

(U. S. Department of Health, Education, and Welfare). *Vocational Education: The Bridge between Man and His Work*. Prepared by the Advisory Council on Vocational Education. Washington, Government Printing Office, 1968.
    Influential report and the basis for the Vocational Education Amendments of 1968. See also, Garth Mangum, *Reorienting Vocational Education* (1968).

U. S. Department of Health, Education and Welfare. Office of the Secretary. *Education and Training; Report of the Secretary of Health, Education and Welfare to the Congress on the Manpower Development and Training Act*. Washington, U. S. Govt. Print. Off., 1962-. "Prepared in the Office of Education for the Secretary of Health, Education and Welfare." Subtitle for each year varies. See entries under "Education and Training."
    Reviews all programs under the Manpower Development and Training Act, with particular emphasis on certain aspects accomplished for that year.

U. S. Department of Labor. Manpower Administration. *Breakthrough for Disadvantaged Youth*. Washington, U. S. Govt. Print. Off., 1969. 256 pp.
    Analytical reports of 55 early projects (1963-1966) developed under MDTA. These projects are discussed here in regard to their successes as well as their shortcomings.

U. S. Department of Labor. Manpower Administration. *The Neighborhood Youth Corps; a Review of Research by Marjorie Egloff*. Washington, U. S. Govt. Print. Off., 1970. 56 pp.

Divided into two parts, this review consists of: a) a summary and analysis of the studies and b) a brief comment on the individual titles.

U. S. Department of Labor. Office of the Secretary. *Report of the Secretary of Labor to the Congress on Research and Training Activities in Accordance with Section 309 of the Manpower Development and Training Act. A Report and Evaluation of Research, Trainees, Training Programs, and Training Activities.* Washington, U. S. Government Printing Office, 1963.

Issued annually. Title varies. Reports for 1964 and 1965 entitled "Manpower Research and Training under the Manpower Development and Training Act of 1962."

U. S. Federal Board for Vocational Education. *Annual Report, 1917/18-1932/33.* Washington, U. S. Government Printing Office, 1917-33.

First report contains initial development of Smith-Hughes Act and its implementation in the various States. Continuing reports are on the progress made in the States in the development of vocational education under this legislation and its amendments.

U. S. Federal Board for Vocational Education. *Bulletin No. 1-171.* Washington, U. S. Government Printing Office, 1917-33.

Statement of Policies issued as Bulletin No. 1, 1917, May 1922 (rev. ed.) and December 1926.

United States Industrial Commission. *Relations and Conditions of Capital and Labor Employed in the Manufactories and General Business. Report. v. 7.* Washington, Government Printing Office, 1901.

Contains considerable data regarding apprenticeship.

U. S. National Advisory Council on Vocational Education. *Notes and Working Papers Concerning the Administration of Programs Authorized under the Vocational Education Act of 1963, PL 88-210, as Amended.* Washington, U. S. Govt. Print. Off., 1968. 430 pp. (At head of title: 90th Cong., 2d sess. Committee print)

A report prepared for the Subcommittee on Education of the Committee on Labor and Public Welfare, U. S. Senate.

U. S. National Advisory Council on Vocational Education. *Vocational Education Amendments of 1968, Public Law 90-576.* Washington, 1969-.

Each of the three reports issued (July 15, 1969, November 15, 1969, July 10, 1970) contains criticism and recommendations on the 1968 Amendments. These reports are submitted to the Secretary of the Department of Health, Education and Welfare for transmittal to the Congress.

U. S. National Advisory Council on Vocational Education. *Vocational Education: the Bridge between Man and His Work. General Report of the Advisory Council on Vocational Education, 1968.* Washington, U. S. Govt. Print. Off., 1968. 220 pp.

A thorough assessment of vocational education in U. S. and the gains made through the implementation of the Vocational Education Act of 1963. Five recommendations are made to chart the course for future planning.

U. S. Office of Education. *Art and Industry. Education in the Industrial and Fine Arts in the United States.* By Isaac Edwards Clarke. Washington, U. S. Government Printing Office, 1885-98. 4 vols. in 5. (Printed also as 46th Cong. 2d sess. Senate. Ex. Doc. No. 209, pt. 1-4).

Contents: Part I—Drawing in public schools; Part II—Industrial and manual training in public schools; Part III—Industrial and technical training in voluntary associations and endowed institutions; Part IV—Industrial and technical training in schools of technology and in U. S. land-grant colleges.

U. S. Office of Education. *Career Education.* Washington, U. S. Govt. Print. Off., 1971. 10 pp.

A brochure containing brief facts and statistics on the present state of career education in the U. S., including an example of a "Career Education Model."

U. S. Office of Education. *Digest of Annual Reports of State Boards for Vocational Education to the Office of Education, Division of Vocational Education.* Washington, U. S. Government Printing Office, 1933.

Supersedes the annual reports of the U. S. Federal Board for Vocational Education published from 1917 to 1932. Contains condensed versions of the annual reports which the States are required to make on the past year's accomplishments, receipts, and expenditures.

U. S. Office of Education. *Educationally Deficient Adults; Their Education and Training Needs.* Washington, U. S. Government Printing Office, 1965. 60 pp.

The reprint of a survey conducted by the Information and Training Services, a Division of McGraw-Hill, Inc., New York, and authorized by the Division of Vocational and Technical Education, U. S. Office of Education. Dealing mainly with the educational and training needs of educationally deficient adults, this report also furnishes guidelines for a plan to meet these needs and the materials that might be used in providing vocational training for jobs.

(United States Office of Education). *Federal Cooperation in Agricultural Extension Work, Vocational Education, and Vocational Rehabilitation.* Washington Government Printing Office, 1933. Bulletin, n. 15, Lloyd E. Blauch.

The movement to secure federal aid for vocational education between 1910 and 1920.

U. S. Office of Education. *Industrial Education in the United States. A Special Report Prepared by the U. S. Bureau of Education.* Washington, U. S. Government Printing Office, 1883. 319 pp. (Printed also as 47th Cong., 2d sess., Senate. Ex. Doc. No. 25)

The first part of this detailed report, prepared in response to a Senate

resolution of December 15, 1882, gives an overall summary of the status of industrial education in the land-grant colleges, private institutions, and in
elementary and secondary schools. Part II (appendixes) is devoted to the individual land-grant colleges, giving a brief history of each, courses of study,
and statistics on enrollments and expenditures. Includes illustrations also of
the schools and the floor plans of the main buildings.

U. S. Office of Education. *Technological Advances and Skilled Manpower;
Implications for Trade and Industrial Education. An Annotated Selected
Bibliography.* Washington, U. S. Government Printing Office, 1956. 67 pp.
(Its Misc. 3509 Rev. Nov. 1, 1956)

Compiled by Mr. Howard K. Hogan, Consultant in the Division of
Vocational Education, this bibliography lists items representing the views,
primarily, of management, labor, and education on the subject of vocational
education as it relates to the production of skilled manpower.

U. S. Office of Education. *Training the Hard-core Unemployed: a Demonstration-research Project at Virginia State College, Norfolk Division. (An in-
terim Report.)* Washington, U. S. Government Printing Office, 1964. 101 pp.
(Its Cooperative Research Monograph No. 13).

A report on the demonstration-research project conducted at the Norfolk Division of Virginia State College to find methods of training both the
semiliterate and the literate unskilled worker.

U.S. Office of Education. *Vocational Division Bulletin, No.* — Washington
U. S. Government Printing Office, 1934 —

Continues the numbering of the bulletin formerly issued by the U. S.
Federal Board for Vocational Education.

U. S. Office of Education. *The Vocational Education Amendments of 1968.*
Washington, U. S. Govt. Print. Off., 1969. 12 pp.

A brief informative booklet on the 1968 amendments of the Vocational
Education Act, and a description of the programs authorized by this
legislation.

U. S. Office of Education. *Vocational Education and Changing Conditions;
Changing Economic and Social Conditions and Their Effect upon Vocational
Education.* By Charles Allen Prosser. Washington, U. S. Government
Printing Office, 1934. (Its Vocational Education Bulletin No. 174. Gen-
eral Series No. 5)

A survey made by the Federal Board for Vocational Education in the U. S.
Office of Education and its outcome is described thus: "The economic and social trends which appear to be of significance for vocational education have
been identified, listed, and classified . . . as they bear on different types of
vocational training . . . ."

U. S. Office of Education. *Vocational Education and Occupations.*
Washington, U. S. Govt. Print. Off., 1969. 292 pp.

This publication is a dictionary, defining nearly 22,000 occupations, arranged by group jobs in nine broad categories. The information given describes job market information in terms of vocational educational programs.

U. S. Office of Education. *Vocational Education in the Next Decade.* Washington, U. S. Government Printing Office, 1961. 197 pp.

National needs and objectives in vocational education are defined in this report and from these definitions guidelines may be obtained in evaluating State or local programs of vocational education.

U. S. Office of Education. *Vocational Education in the Years Ahead; a Report of a Committee to Study Postwar Problems in Vocational Education.* Washington, U. S. Government Printing Office, 1945. 329 pp. (Its Vocational Bulletin No. 234).

Report of a committee appointed by U. S. Commissioner of Education, John W. Studebaker. Divided into nine chapters and an appendix, the report covers all phases of vocational training up to 1945.

U. S. Office of Education. *Vocational-technical Education for American Industry.* By Lynn A. Emerson. Washington, U. S. Government Printing Office, 1958. 25 pp. (Its circular No. 530, 1958)

Contents: Vocational-technical occupations (definition and classification); education for vocational-technical occupations (growth of, institutions providing training); bibliography (selected references, annotated references;) organizations interested in technical education (list of 19 organizations with brief description of each).

U. S. Office of Education. *Work Experience Education Programs in American Secondary Schools,* By DeWitt Hunt. WAshington, U. S. Government Printing Office, 1957. 94 pp. (Its Bulletin 1957, No. 5).

Partial contents: Significant publications on work experience education; the development of work experience as a part of secondary education in American schools; types of work experience programs.

U. S. Office of Manpower, Automation and Training. *Developing Human Resources through Occupational Training. A Report of Occupational Training under the Area Redevelopment Act for the Fiscal Year Ending June 30, 1964.* (Washington, U. S. Government Printing Office, 1964) 35 pp.

Contents: Putting the program in perspective; the training program in operation; investing in human resources; training in action; program appraisal, emphasis, and direction; statistical appendix.

U. S. Office of Manpower, Automation and Training. *Manpower and Automation Research Sponsored by the Office of Manpower, Automation and Training through June 30, 1965.* Washington, U. S. Government Printing Office, 1965. 133 pp.

Research projects listed include those on vocational education, vocational school graduates, the impact of technological change on vocational training, and the problems encountered in training unemployed youth.

U. S. Office of Manpower, Automation and Training. *Training Disadvantaged Groups under the Manpower Development and Training Act.* By Chester W. Hepler and others. Washington, U. S. Department of Labor, 1963. 24 pp. (Its Manpower Evaluation Report No. 1)

"This report evaluates the extent to which training programs established under the act are meeting the need for marketable skills among disadvantaged groups — persons who, because of certain personal characteristics or lack of suitable work skills, are markedly disadvantaged in the competition for available jobs."

U. S. Office of Manpower, Automation and Training. *Unemployment and Retraining; an Annotated Bibliography of Research.* Washington, U. S. Government Printing Office, 1965. 31 pp.

A brief but well-annotated bibliography relating to "social psychological factors in job training and hard-core unemployment."

U. S. President. *Manpower Report of the President and a Report on Manpower Requirements, Resources, Utilization and Training.* Prepared by the U. S. Department of Labor. Transmitted to the Congress . . . Washington, U. S. Govt. Print. Off., 1963.

This report is published annually since 1963. It contains a supplement entitled "Statistics on Manpower".

U. S. Task Force on Occupational Training in Industry. *A Government Commitment to Occupational Training in Industry; Report.* Washington, U. S. Govt. Print. Off., 1968. 114 pp.

A survey of training needs and programs operated by private industry. Recommendations are made as to how the federal government could assist in promoting such programs.

University of the State of New York. *Commercial Education in High Schools .* . . Albany, University of the State of New York, 1903. 127 pp. (College department . . . Bulletin 23)

86142⁰ — 13 — 5

[Van Cleave, James Wallace] *Industrial Education as an Essential Factor in Our National Prosperity.* Washington, Printed for Private Distribution by Mrs. A. M. Wilcox, [1908]. 8 pp.

Speech delivered at the annual banquet of the National Society for the the Promotion of Industrial Education, Chicago, January 23, 1908.

Advocates free industrial high schools, fully equipped, to be open night as well as day to the boys who have taken the manual training course in the primary schools. "Manifestly no apprenticeship system in the United States ever had or which it ever could invent would enable us to rise to the demands of the present and the approaching situation."

Vanderlip, Frank Arthur. *The Urgent Need of Trade Schools . . .* [Indianapolis, Printed at Winona Technical Institute, 1906.] 15pp.

Venn, Grant. *Education and Work: Post Secondary Vocational and Technical Education.* Washington, American Council on Education, 1964.

Derives from a conference called by the American Vocational Association (Washington, September, 1962) whose consensus was that "some assessment of the place of occupational education within education as a whole and within a new technological economy would have to be made." Excellent review of federal role in vocational education.

Venn, Grant. *Man, Education and Manpower,* Washington, D. C., American Association of School Administrators, 1970. 281 pp.

During the 1960's, the federal support given to develop educational manpower "tended to bypass the schools and postsecondary institutions, institutions best able to develop new skilled and technical manpower." According to the author this book is an attempt to define the action that should be taken to support education in its task of developing our human resources and preventing human failure where job training is concerned.

Vocation Office for Girls, Boston. *Vocations for Boston Girls...*Boston, The Girls Trade Educational League, [1912], (Bulletin no. 4).

Contains references.

Vocational Education and Training under a Comprehensive Manpower Policy. Proceedings of a conference May 13 and 14, 1970. Prepared by the Center for Studies in Vocational and Technical Education. Madison, University of Wisconsin, 1971. 101 pp.

This conference was held in August 1970 and is one of a series established under a grant from the Ford Foundation. Main topics discussed were "Problems of Decentralization and Block Grants", "An Evaluation of the New Manpower Legislation", "Problems and Prospects of a Coordinated Working Relationship", "Absolute Poverty, Relative Poverty and the Task of Manpower Training Programs," "Implications for Political Responsibility and Public Policy".

Vocational Education. Report of a Conference Sponsored by the Brookings Institution. Published as a Supplement to the *Journal of Human Resources.* v. 3, 1968. 140 pp.

Includes five papers presented at the Conference held on April 17-18, 1967. (For reviews of individual papers of pertinent interest see entries under G. G. Somers, M. K. Taussig, A. J. Corazzini and J. K. Kaufman in Pt. II.)

Vocational Education: Social and Behavorial Perspectives; a Report Prepared for the Massachusetts Advisory Council on Education. Edited by Carl J. Schaefer and Jacob J. Kaufman. Lexington, Mass., Heath Lexington Books, 1971. 208 pp.

"Major papers and the responses to these papers, which were presented at a symposium conducted in Boston, Mass., on November 28 and 29, 1967".

Vocational Education; Today and Tomorrow. Edited by Gerald G. Somers and J. Kenneth Little. Madison, University of Wisconsin, Center for Studies in Vocational and Technical Education. 1971 358 pp.

A group of twelve papers by acknowledged authorities in the field of vocational education. They are primarily centered on "issues which have confronted vocational educators for many years and which remain essentially unresolved as we enter the decade of the 1970's.

Vocational-technical Education: A Prospectus for Change. Edited by Carl J. Schaefer and Jacob J. Kaufman. Boston, Advisory Council on Education, Commonwealth of Massachusetts, 1968. 173 pp.

The major papers presented at a symposium, held in Boston Nov. 28-29, 1967. Partial topics discussed: Manpower needs, curriculum development, administration of vocational education programs.

The Vocational-technical Library Collection: a Resource for Practical Education and Training. Newark, N. J., Bro-Dart Foundation, 1970. 377 pp.

An annotated list of vocational-technical books and periodicals to serve vocational educators, librarians and counselors. Designed primarily to include sources for the high school through less than the baccalaureate level.

Ware, Fabian. *Educational Foundations of Trade and Industry.* New York, D. Appleton & Co., 1901. 293 pp.

Treats of the situation in England, Germany, France and America. Gives an adequate presentation of American school conditions with reference to the effect of American ideals and form of school organization upon industrial affairs.

Warmbrod, J. Robert. *Review and Synthesis of Research on the Economics of Vocational-technical Education.* Columbus, Ohio, Ohio State University, Center for Vocational and Technical Education, 1968. 53 pp.

Research reviewed is grouped under five headings: "Economics of Education"; "Benefits and Costs of Vocational Technical Education"; "Reports of Research: Public School Vocational-Technical Education"; "Reports of Research: Costs and Benefits of Manpower Training Programs"; "Other Indices of Economic Benefits".

Warren, Julius E. *Industrial Education in the Public Schools.* [Boston, Wright & Potter Printing Company, 1909.] 9 pp.

Reprinted from the 72d report of the Massachusetts board of education.

Warriner, Eugene Clarence. *Industrial and Vocational Training in the Public Schools.* Published by the State Superintendent of Public Instruction. (Lansing), 1909. 10 pp. (Michigan. Department of public instruction. Bulletin no. 2. 1909)

Washington, Booker T. ed. *Tuskegee and Its People: Their Ideals and Achievements.* New York, D. Appleton & Co., 1906. xiv, 354 pp.

Part I consists of papers by the directors of Tuskegee Institute, describing the work, etc. Part I is made up of autobiographies of graduates, who give interesting accounts of the results accomplished in later life.

Washington, Booker T. *Working with the Hands.* New York, Doubleday, Page & Co., 1904. xi, 246 pp.
Describes methods employed at the Tuskegee Institute to train skilled laborers. Emphasizes the value of industrial education for negroes.

Weaver, E. W. *The Vocational Adjustment of the Children of the Public Schools.* High School Teachers Association of New York City, (1910). 12 pp.

Weeks, Ruth Mary. *The People's School. A Study in Vocational Training.* Boston, New York (etc.), Houghton Mifflin Company (1912). 208 pp. (Riverside educational monographs, ed. by H. Suzallo)
    Bibliography: pp. 195-202.
    Contents. — 1. Foreword. 2. The hand of iron. 3. The public school. 4. A school for the plain man. 5. Trade education and the woman. 6. In the country. 7. Trade education and organized labor. 8. Trade education and socialism. 9. Foreign trade schools. 10. American experiments. 11. The type of trade school needed in the United States. 12. Choosing a vocation. 13. Conclusion. 14. Bibliography on elementary vocational education.

Weissman, Harold H., ed. *Employment and Educational Services in the Mobilization for Youth Experience.* New York, Association Press, 1969. 224 pp.
    This collection of papers is one of four volumes describing the programs offered by the Mobilization for Youth Project. Established in 1962 in New York City's Lower East Side,. MFY seeks to help combat juvenile delinquency and unemployment of low-income youths by providing them with the skills needed for employment and increasing employment opportunities for them, through training. These books should prove a great source of information and a sueful guide for vocational educators engaged in training programs for employed youths, particularly in large cities.

Wenrich, Ralph C. *Review and Synthesis of Research on the Administration of Vocational and Technical Education.* Columbus, Ohio, Ohio State University, Center for Vocational and Technical Education, 1970. 71 pp.
    A summary of significant research covering the period 1963 to 1968. Grouped under nine topics, the research covers such aspects as policy making, organizing for administration and program planning.

Wenrich, Ralph C. and J. William Wenrich. *Leadership in Administration of Vocational and Technical Education.* Columbus, Charles E. Merrill, 1974.

Western Drawing and Manual Training Association. *Proceedings . . . Chicago. Twelfth Annual Report, 1905.* [Chicago, 1905.] *206 pp.*
    Contains constitution of the association. Name was originally Western Drawing Teachers' Association, but changed at the above meeting. Papers by F. D. Cranshaw, C. S. Hammock, and others.

Western Drawing and Manual Training Association. *Proceedings . . . Chicago. Thirteenth Annual Report, 1906.* [Peoria, Ill., Press of J. W. Franks & Sons, 1906] 117 pp.

Contains reports of Committee on handicrafts in the public schools, pp. 69-87. Elizabeth E. Langley, chairman. Data based upon replies received from a questionnaire sent to public schools in various parts of the country. Report represents all the states except North Dakota, Arizona, Oklahoma, South Carolina, Mississippi, and Louisiana.

Western Drawing and Manual Training Association. *Proceedings . . . Indianapolis [Ind.] Fifteenth Annual Report, 1908.* 104 pp.
    Contains: 1. C. A. Bennett — A cycle of development, pp. 22-27. 2. W. O. Thompson — The place of manual arts in the school, pp. 28-33. 3. W. L. Bryan — Moral education through art and manual training, pp. 34. 4. Mary S. Snow — The place of domestic economy in the curriculum, pp. 40-44. 5. Elizabeth Rinehart — The relation of domestic science to the future welfare of society, pp. 45-49. 6. J. F. Barker — Manual training in high schools, pp. 58-61. 7. E. G. Allen — The place of woodworking in the high school, pp. 62-65. 8. F. L. Burnham — The need of the power to visualize in the manual arts, pp. 66-72. 9. Report of committee on college entrance credits, pp. 73-79.

Western Drawing and Manual Training Association. *Proceedings . . . Saint Louis. Sixteenth Annual Report, 1909.* [Bloomington, Ill., Pantagraph Ptg. and Sta. Co., 1910] 208 pp.
    Contains: 1. E. D. Day — The socio-economic value of domestic art in the education of future home makers, pp. 87-92. 2. C. M. Gibbs — Preparation necessary for a teacher of domestic arts, pp. 93-100. 3. K. F. Steiger — The place of the study of clothing in the life of a girl, pp. 101-3. 4. C. M. Gibbs — Household arts in the grades, pp. 105-8. 5. C. M. Woodward — History and influence of the manual training movement, pp. 122-30. 6. C. F. Perry — Trade teaching in the public schools pp. 131-42. 7. Florence Ellis — The manual arts in the primary grades, pp. 158-59.

Western Drawing and Manual Training Association. *Proceedings . . . Minneapolis. Seventeenth Annual Report, 1910.* [Oak Park, Ill., Oak Leaves Company, 1910] 239 pp.
    Contains: 1. H. N. Winchell — Problems involved in the introduction of the industrial arts in the elementary schools, pp. 36-42. 2. L. A. Bacon — Correlation of art and manual training in grade schools, pp. 43-44. 3. H. Wood — The correlation of art and manual training in high schools pp. 45-51. 4. O. L. McMurry — Bookbinding in grade schools, pp. 52-55. 5. W. Sargent — Fine and industrial art in public education, pp. 56-62. 6. R. W. Selvidge — Industrial education from viewpoint of organized labor, pp. 63-74. 7. E. M. Chruch — Relative values of subjects in school courses of study, pp. 76-80. 8. A. F. Payne — The Correlation of metal work and design in the grammar and high school, pp. 90-94. 9. D. Upton — Is manual training worth while?, pp. 95-100. 10. Mary S. Snow — Correlation of household arts with other subjects of the curriculum, p. 107-10. 11. A. P. Norton — Domestic science in public schools in relation to the pure food law, pp. 111-15. 12. C. A. Bennett — Some suggestive features of industrial Education in Germany, pp. 147-56.

Whipple, Guy M., ed. *Vocational Guidance and Vocational Education for the Industries.* (National Society for the Study of Education, 23rd Yearbook, Part II). Bloomington, Indiana, Public School Publications, 1924.

Valuable historical resource on schools and industrial contexts in first quarter of 20th century.

Winslow, Charles H. *Report on the Relations of European Industrial Schools to Labor.* Boston, Wright & Potter Printing Co., 1908. 22 pp.

(Massachusetts. Commission on industrial education. Bulletin no. 10)

Wirth, Arthur G. *Education in the Technological Society: The Vocational Studies Controversy in the Early Twentieth Century.* Scranton, Intext Educational Publishers, 1972.

The origins of vocational training in the 19th century, and a study of educational policy in the first two decades of the 20th century.

Wirtz, Willard. *The Boundless Resource: A Prospectus for an Education-Work Policy.* Washington, New Republic Books, 1975.

Develops the concept of a "community work council" as a possible means of providing a job for every person and a person for every job.

Wisconsin. Commission upon the Plans for the Extension of Industrial and Agricultural Training. *Advance Sheets. . .* Madison, Wis., Democrat Printing Company, State Printer, 1911. vii, 135 pp.

C. P. Cary, chairman.

This commission, appointed by the Governor of Wisconsin in 1909, to investigate industrial and agricultural education and formulate plans upon which to base legislative action, submitted its report on January 10, 1911. Among other measures it recommended continuation schools, with compulsory attendance of children from 14 to 16 years of age already engaged in industry, supplemented by trade and evening schools. It advised the modernization and extension of outgrown apprentice laws and their adaptation to the requirements of proposed industrial schools.

Wolfbein, Seymour L. *Education and Training for Full Employment.* New York, Columbia University Press, 1967. 264 pp.

A review of the education and training efforts of the 1960's. The author presents also a wide number of "principles" concerning the education and training process itself, and the social and economic consequences of using such a process.

Women's Educational and Industrial Union, Boston, Mass. *Thirty-third Annual Report . . . for the Year 1910-1911.* Boston, Mass., 1912. 76 pp.

Woodward, Calvin M. *The Manual Training School.* Boston, D. C. Heath, 1887.

Major source on manual training by a leader in the field. See also Woodward's *Manual Training in Education* (1890).

Woolman, Mary Schenck. *The Making of a Trade School.* Boston, Whitcomb & Barrows, 1910. 101 pp.
    Bibliography: p. 341.
    An account of the history, organization, and work of the Manhattan trade school for girls, New York City.
    See also *Teachers College Record,* 10:275-341, September 1909.

Wright, Carroll D. *The Apprenticeship System in Its Relation to Industrial Education.* Washington, Government Printing office, 1908. 116 pp. (U.S. Bureau of education. Bulletin no. 6, 1908)
    List of references: p. 87-92.
    Describes certain ways in which the desired combination of schooling and apprenticeship may be effected, as exhibited by experience in a few of our leading industries.

York, Edwin G. *A Compilation of Resource Lists for Vocational Educators: An Annotated Bibliography of Bibliographies in Vocational Education, 1960-1969.* Trenton, N. J., Bureau of Occupational Research Development, Department of Education, 1969.
    A register of 579 annotated entries on resources for all phases of vocational education.

Young Men's Christian Associations. Educational Department. *Apprentice Schools* . . . (New York, Young Men's Christian Association Press, 1908?) (4) pp.
    Reprint from Information and suggestions.

II. ARTICLES IN PERIODICALS

Adams, J. B. "The Working Girl from the Elementary School in New York." *Charities and The Commons* 19: 1617-23, February 22, 1908.
A study of 78 girls who left school before completing the elementary grades. Throws light on the advantages of vocational education.

Addicott, James E. "Definitions Pertaining to Industrial Arts." In *National Education Association of the United States. Journal of Proceedings and Addresses,* 1909, pp. 599-606.

Adler, Eleanor H. and Marshall, Serena G. "Self-support for the Handicapped." *Survey* 24: 180-85, April 30, 1910. illus.
Industrial education of cripples.

"Administrative Problems in Vocational Education." *American Vocational Journal* 44(Jan., 1969): 41-56.
A review of the research on administrative problems in vocational education, divided into sections on national and state leadership, the local administrator, cost/benefit analysis, plant and facilities and other phases. A complete bibliography of all research studies is given at the end of the article.

Adrian, H. A. "Equal Opportunity for All Children." *Western Journal of Education* 13: 305-12, June 1908.
A plea for each child's education to be fitted to his ability and bent of inclination.

"Adult Education in East St. Louis." *Public Aid in Illinois* 32 (May 1969): 1-5.
A description of the Adult Education School at 3105 Missouri Avenue in East St. Louis, operating on a full-time basis to provide training for welfare and public aid recipients in order that they may acquire basic education and job skills. Information on courses and schedules are included as well as some encouraging results.

Agan, R. J. "Total and Interdisciplinary Programs of Vocational Education." *High School Journal* 52(Feb. 1969): 241-246.

A description of the pilot program, now in its third year in Paola, Kansas under the leadership of the Kansas State University College of Education. It consists of a junior year program, followed by a senior year of actual occupational experience for students. For a brief description of the beginning of this pilot program see the article by R. J. Agan in the *American Vocational Journal*, v. 42, dec. 1967: 28-29.

"Alabama's New Trade School." *Progressive School Journal* 1: 9-10, July 1911.

Bill passed by Legislature, appropriating $50,000 for the Alabama school of trades and industries at Ragland, Ala., for white boys.

Albany, N. Y. Board of Education. "The Albany Vocational School." In its *Annual Report,* 1909, pp. 66-80. illus.

Programme: p. 81-82.

Albee, Helen Rickey. "Profitable Philanthropy." *Review of Reviews* 22: 57-60, July 1900. illus.

Teaching handicrafts in country districts.

Albertson, Ralph. "The Decay of Apprenticeship and Corporation Schools." *Charities and the Commons* 19: 814-20, October 5, 1907.

Shows how the modern specialization of industry has brought about a disintegration of the trades.

"Along with this disintegration and the loss of the old system of apprenticeship training, other great industrial changes have taken place calling for skill of other kinds — for skilled foremen, superintendents, and workers in the skilled sections of the factories that have supplanted the old tradesmen, and also for skill in the new arts and trades created by recent science and invention."

Advocates industrial education in schools rather than in factories. Article illustrated with graphic statistics.

Alden, Vernon R., and John A. Hodges. "When Classrooms Fail." *Teachers College Record* 66(January 1965): 305-309.

The purpose and objectives of the Job Corps established by the Economic Opportunity Act, a brief summary of the curriculum of the Job Corps camps, and the "challenge" to schoolmen are the topics discussed in this article.

Aldrich, F. R. "Industrial Éducation in the Early 19th Century." *Elementary School Teacher* 13: 478-485, 1913.

Valuable overview of programs and developments.

Alexander, Magnus W. "The Apprenticeship System of the General Electric Company at West Lynn, Massachusetts." *American Academy of Political and Social Science. Annals* 33: 141-50, January 1909.

Describes the origin, the progress and effect of the Lynn system.

In order to get the best results this company organized "a special depart-ment—training rooms—devoted entirely to the preliminary practical training of the apprentices. It appointed a superintendent of apprentices . . . and placed him in direct charge of the training rooms. Furthermore, it made an arrangement whereby such instructive commercial work could be transferred from the factory into the training rooms from time to time as the development of the apprentices might require." /Finally, classrooms were established in the factory in which the boys might obtain mental training in the related sciences, etc.

The author declares the apprenticeship system of the General Electric company to be perhaps the best exemplification of the efficacy of this prin-ciple. Similar systems have since been organized by other manufacturing establishments, and the same scheme has been adopted by trade schools found-ed in recent years.

Alexander, Magnus W. "The Factory as a Continuation School." In *New York State Teachers' Association. Proceedings, 1909.* Albany, University of the State of New York, 1910. pp. 281-92 (Education department. Bulletin no. 483, November 15, 1910)
    The educational work of the General Electric Company, Lynn, Mass.

Alexander, Magnus W. "Industrial Training from the Standpoint of the Manufacturer. In *American Institute of Instruction. Proceedings* [*1906*]. Boston, 1906. pp. 373-88.
    The education given by the apprenticeship system of the General Electric Company, West Lynn, Mass., and the needs in the public schools.

Alexander, Magnus W. "The Needs of Industrial Education from the Stand-point of the Manufacturer." *Social Education Quarterly* 1: 196-201, June 1907.

Allen, Charles R. "Some Experiences in the Development of a Type of In-termediate Industrial School under the Massachusetts Law." In *National Society for the Promotion of Industrial Education. Proceedings of the Third Annual Meeting.* 1909, pp. 163-72. (Its Bulletin no. 10)

Allen, Frederick J. "The Vocation Bureau and the Boston School System."- *National Municipal Review* 2: 108-10, January 1913.

Allinson, Francis G. "The Cultural and the Vocational in the College Curriculum. *Education* 32: 284-92, January 1912.
    Emphasis laid upon the fact that culture does not necessarily exclude vocational training, while the latter may include culture.

American Federation of Labor. "Present Industrial Educational Enact-ments." In its *Industrial Education*. Washington, D.C., 1910. pp. 49-55.
    A review of state laws.

Anderson, R. D. "A Rationale for Area Vocational Education Centers." *Agricultural Education Magazine* 41 (Feb. 1969): 181, 184.

The author emphasizes the value of job-skill training and enumerates the advantages of the area center over that of the single school program.

Andrews, Benjamin R. "The Schools of Household and Industrial Arts, Teachers College." *Columbia University Quarterly* 12: 397-407, September 1910. illus.

Andrews, E. Benjamin. "Industrial Education in a Prairie State." *Social Education Quarterly* 1:156-74, June 1907.
  Address, Social education congress, December 1, 1906.
  Also in *Southern Educational Review*, 3:137-54, December 1906-January 1907; and under title, "Western Industrial Education." In *School Journal*, 74: 11-13, 43, January 5, 12, 1907.
  Describes situation in Nebraska.

Armstrong Association, Philadelphia. Educational Committee. "Report. Industrial Opportunities for Negroes in Philadelphia." *Southern Workman* 40: 419-42, July 1911. tables.
  Opportunities for industrial education, pp. 421-28.

Arnett, L. D. "Educational Outlook Based on Occupations." *Pedagogical Seminary* 12: 334-38, September 1905.
  A statistical study based upon the returns of the census of 1900.

Arnold, Sarah Louise. "The Sargent Industrial School; a Successful Experiment in Industrial Training." *Survey* 24: 32-39, April 2, 1910.
  School is located at Matteawan, N.Y. Founded and developed by Mrs. Winthrop Sargent in 1878. Central purpose of school is "to provide essential instruction in the arts and industries belonging to home making." Gives programme of classes, etc.

Arnold, Sarah Louise. "Training of Teachers for Trade Schools." *Journal of Education* 73: 570, May 25, 1911.

Arnold, Walter K., and Russell K. Britton. "Fifty Years of Progress in Trade and Industrial Education." *American Vocational Journal* 31: 83-90,104, December, 1956.
  A review of programs with historical source materials.

Arnold, Walter M. "All-age, All-job Program." *American Education* 1(December 1964-January 1965): 8-11.
  An official of the U.S. Office of Education discusses what he believes a "balanced program of vocational education" should be and cites instances of such programs now in existence in North Carolina, Pennsylvania, and other States.

Arnold, Walter M. "Area Vocational Education Programs." *School Life* 42(January 1960): 16-21.

"The nature and activities of the programs receiving Federal aid under title VIII of the National Defense Education Act."

Arnold, Walter M. "Changing Patterns in Vocational Education." *Education* 85(December 1964): 206-10.

A discussion of "the aims, provisions, and results of the Manpower Development and Training Act of 1962 and of the Vocational Education Act of 1963 in relation to current needs."

Arnold, Walter M. "Meeting Manpower Needs Through Technical Education." *American Vocational Journal* 37(December 1962): 8-11.

A report on the technical training programs made possible through the provisions of Title VIII of the National Defense Education Act.

Arnold, Walter M. "Reappraisals Called for in Financing Vocational Programs." *American Vocational Journal* 44(April 1969): 26-28.

How the 1968 Amendments to VOA of 1963 impose on the state boards for vocational education "new legal requirements that will call for an entirely new look at funding policies."

Arnold, Walter M. "Vocational Education-Its Role Today." *Theory into Practice* 3 (December 1964): 163-166.

The Assistant Commissioner of Education for Vocational and Technical Education, U. S. Office of Education, cites some of the urgent needs for vocational education today and discusses "six salient features" of the Vocational Education Act of 1963.

Arnold, Walter M. "Vocational Guidance and Vocational Education; the Common Goal." *Vocational Guidance Quarterly* 16 (Sept. 1967): 2-6.

The former Assistant Commissioner for Vocational and Technical Education of U.S.O.E., points out the provisions of the Vocational Education Act of 1963 in regard to guidance services. He also outlines plans and national programs geared to make vocational education more productive.

Arnold, Walter M. "Washington Report." *Industrial Arts and Vocational Education* 56 (Nov. 1967 –).

A regular feature of this journal, giving concise and timely information on Federal legislation regarding vocational education and other current trends in the field.

Arnold, Walter M. "What the Vocational Education Act Implies for Local School Agencies." *Industrial Arts and Vocational Education* 54 (May 1965): 23-25.

Pertinent information for educators at "the grass-roots level" by the Assistant Commissioner for Vocational and Technical Education, U.S. Office of Education.

Arnold, Walter M. and James F. McNamara. "A Systems Approach to State-local Program Planning in Vocational Education." *Socio-economic Planning Sciences: an International Journal* 5 (Jun. 1971): 231-53.

"The results of a study which developed a model to illustrate how educational planners might better utilize socio-economic data to improve the information base for decision-making and program planning in vocational education." Although originally developed for Pennsylvania, the study provides a model useful in any region or planning area.

Arnstein, George E. "Vocational Education" *National Association of Secondary-School Principals Bulletin* 48 (November 1964): 56-72.

The author believes "vocational education, by design, budget, and legislation, has been separated from the main current of American education." In discussing means of making vocational education more effective, Mr. Arnstein also includes remarks on the Report of the Panel of Consultants on Vocational Education. (See entry U.S. Panel of Consultants on Vocational Education. "Education for a Changing World of Work." Report of the Panel of Consultants on Vocational Education. Washington, U.S. Government Printing Office, 1963.)

Ash, L. C. "Trade and Industrial Education; an Effective Program." *Education* 85 (December 1964): 211-216.

"The significant role that trade and industrial education plays in preparing potential dropouts for various kinds ˙of useful and satisfying vocations in the years ahead."

Ash, William C. "The Philadelphia Trades School." *American Academy of Political and Social Science. Annals* 33: 85-88, January 1909.

Ash, William C. "Solving of the Skilled Mechanic Problem by the Public Trade School." *Pennsylvania School Journal* 59: 549-53, May 1911.

Investigation of industrial and trades education in 60 cities.

"Automation and Youth." *The American Child* 42 (March 1960): 24 pp.

A collection of articles by Jerome Rosow, Walter Reuther, and others on the effects of automation on the training and the employment of youth in this decade.

"Automation: Outlook for Youth. *The American Child* 44 (November 1962): 15 pp.

Four brief but pertinent articles are included in this issue: View from Washington by Seymeur Wolfbein; Automation: Training for What? by Louise Knapp; The School Story by T. Stanley Warburton; The Controversy Ahead by William Gomberg.

Avritch, Richard T. "Vocational Education: a Continuing Problem." *Journal of Education* 148 (October 1965): 35-42.

"The author attempts a critical analysis of the Vocational Education Act of 1963 . . . traces the history of vocational education, exposes various negative attitudes toward it."

Bachmura, Frank T. "The Manpower Development and Training Act of 1962—Its Significance for Rural Areas." *Journal of Farm Economics* 45(February 1963): 61-72.
A discussion of the magnitude of farm unemployment and the opportunity for organized rural effort for communities and for individuals in rural areas.

Bacon, Mary Applewhite. "Industrial Education in the South." *Harper's Monthly Magazine* 107: 659-67, October 1903. illus.

Bader, Paul. "Die aufgabe der Schule bei der Berufswahl und Stellenvermittlung der Jugendlichen." *Archiv für Pädagogik* 1: 129-38, December 1912.
Describes current attempts at vocational guidance in connection with German schools.

Bailey, Henry Turner. "Elementary Schools as a Factor in Industrial Education." *Manual Training Magazine* 11: 297-301, April 1910.

Bailey, Henry Turner. "The Industrial Educational Movement and the Elementary School." In *New Jersey State Teachers' Association. Annual Report and Proceedings* 1907. pp. 119-31.
"Industrial education . . . will furnish all the opportunities we need in the public school for laying broad and deep the foundation of industrial efficiency."

Bain, A. Watson. "Preparation in the Elementary School for Industrial and Domestic Life." *Elementary School Teacher* 9: 167-77, December 1908.
"The course of study suggested is frankly and primarily planned as a training for vocation; but it would be a preparation for avocation as well."

Baker, James. "[Technical Education] in Russian Poland." In his *Report on Technical and Commercial Education in East Prussia, Poland, Galicia, Silesia, and Bohemia.* London, Wyman and Sons, 1900. pp. 22-28.

Balcomb, Ernest Elwell. "Encouraging Practical Education. The Work of the National Committee on Agricultural Education." *American School Board Journal* 43: 7,42, July 1911.
Dolliver-Davis bill; girls' industrial school exhibits, etc.

Baldwin, William Alpheus. "Industrial-social Education for the Primary and Grammar School Grades." In *Eastern Manual Training Association. Proceedings,* 1904. Philadelphia, Pa., Published by the Association, 1905. pp. 104-12.

Balfour, Graham. "Continuation Schools." In *Imperial Education Conference. Report,* 1911. London, Printed by Eyre and Spottiswoode, 1911. pp. 183-95.
Discussion: p. 195-201.

Barker, James F. "The Cleveland Technical High School." In *North Central Association of Colleges and Secondary Schools. Proceedings,* 1910. Chicago, published by the association, 1910. pp. 35-44.
Promotions quarterly.

Barlow, Melvin L. "The Enemy Unseen." *American Vocational Journal* 34(January 1959): 10-13.
A prominent vocational educator believes that the first phase of vocational education has been successful in that "making a living" type of training has been achieved. However, this attitude has within it the "enemy unseen," for vocational education of this kind has no responsibility for, or relationship to, the general goals of education. It blinds us to the vast resources of the program, placing it in the "rut leading to oblivion."

Barlow, Melvin L. "Impact of a World of Missiles, Rockets, and Satellites on Vocational Education." *Teachers College Journal* 31(January 1960): 100-4.
The author believes that the real impact of technological change upon our vocational education programs is to be found in the sociological problems this impact has created. One solution lies in easing up "on the death grip we have upon some of our earlier principles and convictions . . . and permit ourselves and our programs to be influenced by other environments."

Barlow, Melvin L. "Just Try to Find a Job without It." *American Education* 4(Dec. 1967): 8-9.
The importance of training for job skills as discussed by the Staff Director of U.S.O.E's Advisory Council on Vocational Education.

Barlow, Melvin L., ed. "Listen! The School Board Speaks." *American Vocational Journal* 45(Oct. 1970): 13-64.
Entire issue of 13 articles on opinion of various board presidents, as they write of vocational education policy and commitment.

Barlow, Melvin L. "200 Years of Vocational Education, 1776-1976."- *American Vocational Journal* 51: May, 1976.
A special Bicentennial issue devoted to the history of vocational education in the United States. Issue features a five-section article by Melvin L. Barlow on the principles, techniques, and legislation in vocational education.

Barlow, Melvin L. "Vocational Education as a Social Movement." *American Vocational Journal* 44 (Apr. 1969): 30-32.
The inter-action between the social changes in our society and the changes in vocational training: each continue to motivate action on the part of the other.

Barlow, Melvin L. "Why National Review?" *American Vocational Journal* 42(Dec. 1967): 10-11.
Why periodic review of the status of American vocational education is necessary if it is to be meaningful to our American society.

Barnes, J. Ward. "Continuation Center for Adult Education in Eldorado." *Public Aid in Illinois* 32(May 1965): 6-10.

How this center came into being and the programs conducted for uneducated and unemployed adults in Eldorado, Ill. Those attending are receiving welfare aid.

Barney, Edgar S. "Industrial Training of Boys." *American Education* 13: 257-60, February 1910.

"Our only solution to the problem [of skilled labor] is to turn to the schools and introduce in them thorough practical courses leading to a vocation, courses which . . . will lead to industrial intelligence."

Barney, Edgar S. "Intermediate Industrial Schools." In *National Society for the Promotion of Industrial Education. Proceedings of the Third Annual Meeting,* 1909. pp. 185-95. (Its Bulletin no. 10)

Discussion: pp. 195-204.

Chiefly regarding the Hebrew Technical Institute for Boys; virtually the same article as in National Education Association of the United States. Journal of Proceedings and Addresses, 1908. pp. 793-98.

Barrows, Alice Prentice. "The Dangers and Possibilities of Vocational Guidance." *Child Labor Bulletin* 1: 46-54, June 1912.

The writer says: "Is there any reason why we should not profit by the mistakes of England? Can not we prevent the state here from finding itself committed to the questionable duty of finding work for children who are not prepared for it?"

Barrows, Alice Prentice. "Report of the Vocational Guidance Survey." In *New York City. Department of Education. 14th Annual Report, July 31, 1912.* New York [1913] pp. 385-97. (Appendix G.)

The Vocational Guidance Survey was organized under the auspices of a joint committee of the Junior League and the Public Education Association. The work upon which this report is founded was started on September 18, 1911. The field investigation stopped on June 11, 1912. The final report is in preparation. The Vocational Guidance Survey has now become the Vocational Education Survey, a department of the Public Education Association.

The survey was organized to find answers, if possible, to the following questions: 1. Why do children leave school in large numbers as soon as they are fourteen? 2. What becomes of them? 3. Will vocational guidance aid them?

The investigation was based on an intensive study of a small group, supported by comparison with a larger group. The large group was made up of the 19,672 children who took employment certificates in Manhattan in 1911. The intensive work was done in Public Schools 8, 95, 41, and 3 in District 9, and Public Schools 76, 74, and 82 in District 13.

Three investigators interviewed children who applied for working papers from September, 1911, to June, 1912. The children were first interviewed in school; then the investigator visited their homes before they left school, and again at the end of two to five months to find out what had happened to them in their work. One thousand five hundred and fifty-seven visits were made to this group and 327 records secured. The total number of cases dealt with was 695. The total number of visits was 2,203. From these children and their families information was secured as to why they left school, the income of the family, the plans for work, and experience in work.

Economic pressure was found to be least potent and the least frequent cause for children leaving school to go to work. Need for training in the trades is very important. Children should not be blindly guided into jobs. Miss Barrows thinks that there are no jobs for children under 16 that they ought to take.

Baxter, J. D. "Job Retraining Problem Grows; How Should It Be Handled?" *Iron Age* 189 (February 1, 1962): 65-67.

A training specialist from the General Electric Co. states the reasons why he believes that retraining is a job for industry and points out what is needed to accomplish this retraining.

Beaumont, J. A. "Broadened Scope of Vocational Education." *American Vocational Journal* 44 (Apr. 1969): 19-20+.

An explanation of how the new Congressional direction and increased authorization for vocational education through the Vocational Education Amendments of 1968 provide "the impetus that could change the course of all education, forcing it to focus more directly on the needs of youth and adults in our society."

Bechtel, Helen. "A Sampling of School Dropout Projects in Texas." *Texas Journal of Secondary Education* 18 (Spring 1965): 13-19.

Brief summary of projects carried out by various Texas school systems and communities for school dropouts. These programs consist of special classes, vocational courses geared to local employment needs, part-time jobs, and study centers.

Bennett, Charles A. "The Manual Arts: To What Extent Shall They Be Influenced by the Recent Movement Toward Industrial Education." In *North Central Association of Colleges and Secondary Schools. Proceedings,* 1907. Urbana, Illinois, Published by the Association, 1907. pp. 38-49.

Discussion: pp. 50-54.

Also in *Manual Training Magazine,* 8: 189-95, July 1907.

"Our public schools . . . have not met the demands of industry . . . so that there is now a national demand for skilled workers in the industries and there is no adequate means of supplying this demand."

Bennett, Charles A. "Outline of a High School Course in Metal-Working." *Manual Training Magazine* 9: 335-39, April 1908.

Bennett, Charles A. "Visiting Manual Training Schools in Europe." I, II, III, IV, V. *Manual Training Magazine* 11: 1-26, 109-34, 214-36, 345-65, 440-55, October, December 1909, February, April, June 1910.

1. London. 2. Oxford and Birmingham. 3. Leicester and Sheffield. 4. Manchester and Leeds. 5. Glasgow and Edinburgh.

Berry, Martha. "Uplifting Backwoods Boys in the South." *World's Work* 8: 4986-92, July 1904. illus.
    Reprinted. New York, 1904. 16 p.
    Describes the Berry Industrial School, near Rome, Ga.

Birge, E. A. "Should Industrial and Literary Schools be Combined or Encouraged to Separate?" In *North Central Association of Colleges and Secondary Schools. Proceedings* [1901] Ann Arbor, Ann Arbor Printing Company, 1901. pp. 51-55.
    Discussion: pp. 55-61.

Bishop, E. C. "Industrial and Agricultural Education." In *Iowa State Teachers' Association. Proceedings, 1910.* pp. 80-86.
    "Give the child all through his course the right kind, quality, and quantity of industrial training interwoven and interdependent upon his language, mathematics, history, science, and home life. . . . The school should serve the time, the place, and the people. The application of the school must vary as the conditions, the needs, and the desires of the people change."

Bixler, Richard C. "Vocational Live-in." *American Education* 5 (Mar. 1969): 7-9.
    A description of the Ohio Mahoning Valley Vocational School which provides living quarters for its students as well as occupational training.

Bizzel, W. B. "The Progress of Industrial Education in Colleges for Women in the Southern States." In *Southern Educational Association. Journal of Proceedings and Addresses,* 1911. pp. 556-58.

Blair, R. "Girls' Schools." In *Imperial Education Conference. Report, 1911.* London, Printed by Eyre and Spottiswoode, 1911. pp. 166-74. tables. appendices A-C (ii)
    In Great Britain.

Bloomfield, Meyer. "Vocational Guidance." In *National Education Association of the United States. Journal of Proceedings and Addresses, 1912.* pp. 431-36.
    Shows what has been accomplished in Boston. Reviews the situation throughout the country. Emphasizes the fact that thousands of children drop out of school, through no economic pressure, to go to work as soon as the law permits. See also Survey, 30: 183-88, May 3, 1913.

Bolger, James. "New Look in Vocational Education." *Business Education World* 45 (September 1964): 13-16; (October 1964): 28-30+; (November 1964): 26-29; (December 1964): 18-21.
    The editor of *Business Education World* has written four articles on vocational education "new look" with subtitles as follows: "The First 100

Years in Vocational Education;" "The Forces That Demand Education for Employability;" "Provisions of the Vocational Education Act of 1963;" "Business Education and the Vocational Education Act of 1963."

Bonnell, Clarence. "The First Week at the Beginning of the School Year in the High School Woodworking Shop." *Manual Training Magazine* 13: 401-23, June 1912.

Suggests to those of limited experience some practical expedients, which, used in a shop where space and light and the instructor's time are all limited, have proved to be helpful.

Bonser, Federick G. ."Vocational Work below the High School in Its Bearing on the Growing Ideal Interests of Children." In *Illinois State Teachers' Association. Journal of Proceedings, 1908.* Springfield, Ill., Illinois State Journal Co., 1909. pp. 153-58.

Bookwalter, Alfred G. "Continuation Work-Education for the Industrial Workers." *Charities and The Commons* 19: 856-61, October 5, 1907.

Discusses the various types of continuation schools — correspondence; Y.M.C.A.; private, etc.

See also Boston Public Schools. Circular of information relating to evening and continuation schools. Boston, 1912. pp. 57-65.

Boone, Cheshire Lowton. "A Course of Study in Manual Training — VII, VIII. *Manual Training Magazine* 11: 46-58, 410-17, October 1909, June 1910.

Boone, Cheshire Lowton. "Pottery Craft in Schools. I. Equipment; II. Building Processes; III. Design." *School Arts Book* 9: 118-26, 329-40, 925-34, October, December 1909, May 1910.

Boston, Mass. "Committee on Vocational Direction. Report." In *Boston Public Schools. Annual Report of the Superintendent, July 1910.* pp. 147-51. (Appendix G)

Chairman, George A. Tyzzer.

See also Annual Report of the Superintendent, December 1911.

Bottoms, Gene. "State Level Management for Career Education." *American Vocational Journal* 47 (Mar. 1972): 89-92.

The author, coordinating editor of this issue of the journal believes that effective implementation of career education lies in "revision of the educational management system" and that "one important level of that system is the state department of education." In this article this theme is developed and discussed.

Bottoms, James E. and E. Swain. "Effects of Program Development on Area Vocational-technical School Enrollment." *Vocational Guidance Quarterly* 15 (Jun. 1967): 267-272.

Description of a state-wide project in the state of Georgia designed to bring together in greater number the young men and women in the state and the facilities of the state's vocational-technical schools. Funded under the Vocational Education Act of 1963, the project was designed for a three-year period.

Bowen, C. R. "The Paradoxes of Abundance." *National Association of Secondary-School Principals Bulletin* 48 (November 1964): 3-15.

A review of the technological revolution upon the U.S. economy and employment, where the "new jobs" will most likely come, and the possibilities that might be accomplished by providing the right kind of education for an abundant society with its great segments of poverty.

Bowlby, Roger L. and William. A. Schriver. "Nonwage Benefits of Vocational Training: Employability and Mobility." *Industrial and Labor Relations Review* 23(Jul. 1970): 500-509.

Results of a study of two groups: one had received Tennessee Area Vocational-Technical School training and the other had received no training beyond high school.

Braddock, Clayton. "Vo-ed is for the Majority." *Southern Education Report* 2 (June 1967): 2-11.

An examination of four types of schools offering vocational programs: comprehensive high schools, technical high schools, area vocational-technical schools and community colleges.

Brademas, John. "View from Capitol Hill." *Grade Teacher* 85 (Nov. 1967): 12+.

A: U.S. Congressman from Indiana gives his view on the weaknesses of our present vocational education programs, and discusses proposed legislation to overcome these inadequacies.

Brandon, Edgar Ewing. "Commercial Education" [in Latin America]. In his *Latin-American Universities and Special Schools.* Washington, Government Printing Office, 1913. pp. 94-103. (U.S. Bureau of Education. Bulletin no. 30, 1912)

Brandon, G.L., ed. "Vocational Education Curriculum." *American Vocational Journal* 44 (Mar. 1969): 41-56.

A review of significant research in the field of vocational education curriculum. A bibliography of the studies reviewed is given with additional studies not included in the review.

Brazziel, William F. "Basic Education in Manpower Retraining Programs." *Adult Leadership* 13 (November 1964): 145-146.

The author is the Director of General Education, Norfolk Division, Virginia State College. In this article he describes the retraining program in the Norfolk Division, a program designed to raise the basic skill levels of youths and adults.

Brett, George, P. "The Need of Commercial Education." *Independent* 72: 728-30, April 4, 1912.

The author says that "for the children of our cities, about 90 per cent of whom leave school at about the age of 14 and enter business, commercial education is vitally necessary."

Briggs, L. D. "Support from the Top: Major Areas of Responsibility for Professional Development in Vocational Education." *American Vocational Journal* 46: 42-44, November, 1971.

Review of federal legislation for vocational education.

Brooklyn Teachers' Association. "Report of Sub-Committee on School Incentives." In its *Report of the President, 1908-9*. Brooklyn, N.Y., 1909. pp. 25-37.

"The utmost development of the capabilities of every individual child means more in the aggregate to the national wealth than does the proper development of our material resources."

Brooks, L. B. "Norfolk State College Experiment in Training the Hard-core Unemployed." *Phi Delta Kappan* 46 (November 1964): 111-116.

An account of a project to retrain unemployed adults, financed by grants from the U.S. Office of Education, Cooperative Research Division, and the Office of Manpower, Automation and Training of the U.S. Department of Labor. Conclusion: ". . . that proper training can work miracles in the lives of men formerly without hope."

Brooks, Stratton Duluth. "Vocational Guidance." *School Review* 19: 42-50, January 1911.

The work of the Boston Vocation Bureau and Public Schools Vocation Direction Committee, the High School of Commerce, and Trade School for Girls.

Brown, James Stanley. "Commercial and Industrial High Schools Versus Commercial and Industrial Courses in High Schools." In *North Central Association of Colleges and Secondary Schools. Proceedings, 1908*. Chicago, Published by the Association, 1908. pp. 136-43.

Brown, James Stanley and others. "The Place of Vocational Subjects in the High School Curriculum." In *National Society for the Scientific Study of Education. Fourth Yearbook*. Bloomington, Illinois, Pantagraph Printing and Stationery Company, 1905. pt. 2: 9-52.

Brown, John Franklin. "Vocational Training [in the high school]." In his The American High School. New York, The Macmillan Company, 1909. pp. 369-73.

Brown, Roy D. "Grooming Unemployables for Productive Life." *American Vocational Journal* 45 (Mar. 1970): 53-55.

The author describes "hard-hitting techniques" used in the MDTA program at the Sikeston, Missouri Public Schools, aimed particularly at the unmotivated student.

Brownell, S. M. "School Dropouts and Unemployed Youth." *American Journal of Public Health* 52 (September 1962): 1401-1406.
   Solving the problem of young people in rural areas who drop out of school and have little chance of employment.

Bryan, W. J. S. "College Entrance Credits for Vocational Subjects." In *National Society for the Scientific Study of Education. Sixth year-book.* Chicago, University of Chicago Press, 1907. pt. I: 57-63.

[Buffalo, N. Y. Vocation Bureau]. *American School Board Journal* 42: 20, May 1911.

Bulkley, William L. "An Evening Industrial School for Adults." *Southern Workman* 35: 540-44, October 1906.
   Negroes, in New York City.

Burkett, L. A. and others. "Vocational and Technical Education: Issues, Developments, Principals' Views." *National Association of Secondary-School Principals Bulletin* 47 (November 1963): 150-160.
   Three articles by Lowell A. Burkett, Merle E. Strong, and Orlin D. Trapp on the relationship of the public secondary school and vocational-technical education programs as they now exist.

Burkett, Lowell A. "Access to a Future." *American Education* 5 (Mar. 1969): 2-3.
   An assessment of the Vocational Education Amendments of 1968 and their implications for students, educators and the schools.

Burkett, Lowell A. "Latest Word from Washington." *American Vocational Journal* 51: 13-14, January, 1976.
   Discussion of Education Amendments of 1975 and pending federal legislation for vocational education (amendments of Vocational Education Acts of 1963 and 1968).

Burkett, Lowell A. "Vocational Education at the Crossroads." *American Vocational Journal* 43 (Feb. 1968): 13-15.
   In an address to the General Assembly of the 61st Annual Vocational Convention, the executive director of the AVA deplores the lack of Federal leadership in vocational education and points out the new directions AVA will take to strengthen and expand its role in working with state vocational associations.

Burks, J. D. "Democracy in Education." *Elementary School Teacher* 8: 130-42, November 1907.
   An argument for the introduction of vocational training into the public schools. Shows that the loss of pupils in the upper elementary grades is due to the ill-adaptation of our educational organization. Concludes that adequate

provision for vocational training, beginning at about the sixth year of school, would tend to prolong the school life and increase the vocational efficiency of the great mass of children.

Also in *National Education Association of the United States. Journal of Addresses and Proceedings.* 1907. pp. 787-96, with different title.

Burks, Jesse Dismukes. "Can the School Life of Pupils be Prolonged by an Adequate Provision for Industrial Training in the Upper Grammar Grades?" In *National Education Association of the United States. Journal of Proceedings and Addresses,* 1907. pp. 787-96.

Also in *Elementary School Teacher,* 8: 130-42, November 1907. Title: Democracy in Education.

"A rational system of secondary education must provide not only for the training of special capacities but for making children conscious of the special capacities that they individually possess."

Burks, Jesse Dismukes. "Getting Our Bearings on Industrial Education." In *National Education Association of the United States. Journal of Proceedings and Addresses,* 1909. pp. 291-96.

Also in *Elementary School Teacher,* 9: 445-54, May 1909.

"The question is whether human beings who differ widely in native gifts and acquired tendencies shall be forced to pursue a single conventional course of training, or have the privilege of choosing a course that will equip them not only for the worthy use of their leisure, but for the intelligent pursuit of their vocations."

Burnham, Frederic Lynden. "Industrial Education in the Public Schools." In *Massachusetts. Board of Education. Annual Report, 1906-7.* Boston, Wright & Potter Printing Co., 1908. pp. 253-64. (Appendix D)

Burnham, Frederic Lynden. "Supervision and the Teaching of the Manual Arts in the High School. Report." In *Massachusetts. Board of Education. Annual Report,* 1907-08. Boston, Wright & Potter Printing Co., 1908. pp. 267-96. (Appendix D)

Burrows, S. M. "Industrial Schools and School Gardens in Ceylon." In *Great Britain. Board of Education. Special Reports on Educational Subjects.* London, Wyman & Sons, 1905. v. 14 pp. 341-62. (Appendix 7)

Burruss, Julian A. "The Industrial Factor in Public Education in the South." In *Southern Educational Association. Journal of Proceedings and Addresses, 1907.* pp. 244-57.

Also in *Southern Educational Review,* 5: 163-75, October-November 1908.

Burt, Samuel M. "If I Were a Member of a Vocational Education Committee." *Industrial Arts and Vocational Education* 57 (Feb. 1968): 30-31.

The essentials of what is desired and expected by a community representative on a vocational school advisory committee, when he voluntarily gives his time to such an organization.

Burt, Samuel M. "Initiating Vocational and Technical Programs." *American Vocational Journal* 42 (May 1967): 22-23.

This article is based on the author's study entitled "Industry and Vocational Technical Education." Here he describes "how to eliminate the gamble and speed up the process" in initiating new vocational programs.

Butler, Elizabeth Beardsled. "Training in Salesmanship." In her Saleswomen in Mercantile Stores, Baltimore, 1909. New York, Charities Publication Committee, 1912. pp. 159-73.

Appendix B. — What the schools can do to train girls for work in department stores, by Mrs. Lucinda W. Prince, pp. 187-93. Appendix C. — Salesmanship classes in the store of Hale Brothers, San Francisco, pp. 200-5.

Butler, Louis C. "Interest Aids in Grade Joiner." *Manual Training Magazine* 9: 417-21, June 1908.

Butler, Nicholas Murray. "Vocational Preparation as a Social Problem." *Educational Review* 45: 289-97, March 1913.

Address before the educational committee of the Commercial Club, of Chicago, Ill., December 14, 1912. Writer says: "To use existing industries, whether they be those of the farm, those of the shop, or those of the factory, as schools of apprenticeship, observation and training while the formal instruction goes on side by side for the one or two year's period provided — this is the essential point in the whole matter."

Butterfield, Howard F. and Burch, E. G. "What Normal Schools Should Do to Train Teachers to Teach Vocational Subjects in the Elementary Schools . . ." In *North Dakota Educational Association. Proceedings, 1908-1909.* Bismarck, N.D., Tribune, State Printers and Binders, 1909. pp. 133-40.

Byerly, Carl L. "Vocational Education Act 1963 Holds Unusual Implications for Large Cities." *School Shop* 23 (April 1964): 40-41.

The assistant superintendent of the Detroit Public Schools, Mr. Byerly tells in this article of the changes that can be expected in the large cities' training programs as a result of the Vocational Education Act, 1963.

[California. Commission on Industrial Education]." A Tentative Industrial Education Bill." *Sierra Educational News* 6: 26-30, October 1910.

Chairman, Col. Harris Weinstock.

Call, Arthur Deerin. "The Specialized or Vocational vs. the Composite High School." In *National Education Association of the United States. Journal of Proceedings and Addresses, 1912.* pp. 174-80.

Also in *American School Board Journal,* 45: 8-9, October 1912.

Campbell, Charles F. F. "Experiment Station for the Trade Training of the Blind." *Boston, Charities and The Commons* 15: 635-40, February 3, 1906.

Campbell, P. G. "Vocational Subjects Offered in High Schools?" *The Balance Sheet* 51 (Dec. 1969): 164-67.

A summary of arguments for and against vocational education in the American public high school, taken from the works of current educational writers.

Campbell, W. H. "The Value of Industrial Training in the Elementary Schools." *Educational Bi-monthly* 3: 285-98, April 1909.

Cardozier, V. R. "Vocational Education and Federal Control." *American School Board Journal* 150 (April 1965): 30-32.

A discussion of the new State requirements for implementing the Vocational Education Act of 1963 by a former specialist in the Vocational Education Division of the Office of Education.

(Career Education) "Education for Career Development: Symposium." *Educational Leadership 30*: 203-205, December, 1972.

"Career Education: Equipping Students for the World of Work." *College and University Business* 51 (Dec. 1971): 39-50. Same: *Nation's Schools* 88 (Dec. 1971): 35-48.

"What has traditionally been known as vocational education is now becoming career education, and this special section explores the educational changes at the secondary and post-secondary levels necessary to make this transition." Includes interview with U.S. Commissioner of Education, Sidney P. Marland, Jr.

Carman, George N. "Co-operation of School and Shop in Promoting Industrial Efficiency." *School Review* 18: 108-14, February 1910.

Carman, George N. "Promotion of Industrial Education by Means of Public High Schools." *Western Journal of Education (Ypsilanti)* 2: 1-12, January 1909.

Enlargement of paper read at the National Society for the Promotion of Industrial Education, Atlanta, 1908, under title: "Promotion of Industrial Education by Means of Trade Schools."

Carruth, David C. "Programming Multi-district Cooperation in Vocational Education." *School Shop* 28 (Oct. 1968): 45-47.

How New York State's creation of a system of agencies, named Board of Cooperative Educational Services (BOCES) has helped to build special centers for job-entry skills. Included also is a description of the multi-occupational program operating with Federal funds, under BOCES auspices, located in upper Erie County, New York.

Casartelli, L. C. "Industrial Education in Catholic Missions." In *Great Britain. Board of Education. Special Reports on Educational Subjects.* v. 14. pp. 251-320.

Discusses work done in various parts of Africa, India, Ceylon, North Borneo, and America.

Cavanaugh, Donald. "Industry's Needs and the Vocational School." *School Shop* 23 (March 1964): 17-19.

An engineer from the mechanical industries discusses the needs of his particular field and what the vocational schools are doing to supply the trained manpower to fill these needs.

Chamberlain, Arthur H. "The Vocational Middle School." *Manual Training Magazine* 12: 105-13, December, 1910.

Chamberlain, Neil W. "Job Obsolescence; Challenge and Opportunity." *Educational Record* 44(January 1963): 26-32.

Contents: The casualties of automation (the unskilled worker); the stultifying effects of technological unemployment (the plight of the unskilled older worker); continuing education as a modern substitute for experience (new concepts of formal education are needed); company programs (what management must do for manpower training to extend the working capacity of its personnel.)

Chancellor, William E. "The Genuine Democracy of the Unique School System of Buffalo." *American School Board Journal* 46: 9-14, 53-55, March 1913.

The city of Buffalo, N.Y., has 10,000 mechanics working in iron and in steel and 5,000 printers. A remarkable work is being accomplished by the public schools in vocational training, emphasis being put upon the particular trades in vogue in the city.

Chaplain, Alexandria. "Manual and Industrial Instruction in the Public School." *Virginia Journal of Education* 5: 256-59, March 1912.

The author points out that manual and industrial instruction in the public schools is an educational, economic, and social necessity.

Charlton, Charles H. "The School at Interlaken (Laporte, Ind.)." *Survey* 25: 377-84, December 3, 1910.

Chase, Edward T. "Learning to Be Unemployable." *Harpers Magazine* 226 (April 1963): 33-40.

An article critical of the vocational education programs the author claims are "fantastically biased in favor of farming and home economics" and teaching skills that are obsolete, including trade and industrial education. "We need to launch a program of practical training for real jobs in a vast national effort" is one of the solutions proposed by Mr. Chase.

Cheney, Howell. "The Educational Needs of the Larger Towns and Cities." In *Connecticut. Board of Education. Report*. Hartford, Published by the State, 1909. pp. 547-60.

"The industrial training can not be the predominating discipline until about a sixth grade is reached. Even then it should be . . . designed especially for those . . . who . . . go (no) further with a general intellectual course."

Chicago. Board of Education. "Continuation Schools." In its *Report, 1909.* -

pp. 86-90.

"The superintendent reports that in his opinion the work of the continuation schools will not be successful unless the merchants, the manufacturers, and the workingmen of the city lend their assistance. Schools of this kind must be thoroughly practical." p. 87.

[Chicago. Farragut Continuation Schools.] *School News* 23: 203-204, January 1910.

Childs, G. B. "Is the Work Ethic Realistic in an Age of Automation?" *Phi Delta Kappan* 46(April 1962): 370-75.

In the age of automation the author believes that "our educational system must prepare people to live in a world in which work will not hold the central position it has held in the past."

Christine, E. R. "What Education is Good?" *Clearing House* 42(Sept. 1967): 19-22.

Because of the large number of school dropouts as well as the large number of students not going on to college, the author believes that meaningful programs in secondary vocational education is more vital than ever.

Cincinnati. (Board of Education.) "Continuation Schools." In its *Annual Report,* 1909. pp. 65-68; 1910. pp. 70-74. table.

Clague, Ewan. "The Occupational Outlook." *National Association of Secondary-School Principals Bulletin* 48(November 1964): 37-44.

The author is Commissioner of the Bureau of Labor Statistics, U.S. Department of Labor. In this article, he outlines the manpower requirements of these labor categories: the white-collar worker, the blue-collar worker, the service workers, and those in farm occupations. His analysis indicates "the most rapidly growing occupations are generally those that require the most education and training."

Clark, Ida Hood. "Manual Arts in Open Air Schools." *School Arts Work* 9:1045-51, June 1910. illus.

For tuberculous children of London schools.

Clark, J. J. "The Correspondence School: Its Relation to Technical Education and Some of Its Results." *Science* 24: 327-34.

Exposition of methods employed and results obtained.

Cleveland, O. Board of Education. "The Cleveland Technical High School." In its *Annual Report, 1907.* pp. 84-99. plans., illus.

Course of study, boys, p. 98; course of study, girls, p. 99. On the four-quarter plan; four years' work in three years.

Coe, B. D. "Vocational Education in the High School; Area Vocational Schools and Centers." *Theory Into Practice* 3 (December 1964): 171-174.

Contents: The new demands for vocational education, "the typical student in secondary school vocational programs, the present vocational education program in the secondary school, with the county high schools of New Jersey as an example."

Coe, Burr D. "What is Quality Vocational Education?" *American Vocational Journal* 43 (Feb. 1968): 16-17.
A brief summary of the 14 principles that should characterize worthwhile vocational education.

Cohen, David K., and Marvin Lazerson. "Education and the Corporate Order." *Socialist Revolution* 2: 47-72, March/April, 1972.
Vocational education in the framework of American educational change.

Cohen, Sol. "The Industrial Education Movement, 1906-17." *American Quarterly* 20: 95-110, Spring, 1968.
Explores the connections between the industrial education movement, child labor, and the compulsory education movement.

Coleman, James S. "A Future without Jobs." *Nation* **196 (May 25, 1963):** 440-443.
The author discusses various solutions to the problem of unemployment, particularly job training for out-of-school youth, and changes in our educational structure to keep more people in school for a longer period of time.

"The Coming Crisis: Youth without Work." *The American Federationist,* **70** (April 1963): 8-15.
The economic outlook for the unemployed youth, and what dangers large scale unemployment of this segment of the population hold for American society. This article also discusses the problems of job opportunities for young people who have dropped out of school and what types of training and help they need.

Commons, John R. "Constructive Investigation and the Industrial Commission of Wisconsin." *Survey* 29: 440-48, January 4, 1913.
A survey of the activities of the Commission in various social fields. Industrial and vocational education considered. The December 21, 1912, number of the Survey contains a tabulated statement of the classified duties of the Commission.

Conant, James B. "Vocational Education and the National Need." *American Vocational Journal* 35 (January 1960): 15-19.
An address delivered at the American Vocational Association convention, December 7, 1959, in Chicago, in which the present status of vocational education programs in the comprehensive high school is discussed. Recommendations for more effective programs in the future are also given.

Connelly, C.B. "Manual Training as a Preparation for a Scientific or

Engineering Course." *Pennsylvania School Journal* 56: 139-41, September 1907.

Cook, George B. "The Agricultural and Industrial Educational Movement in the South." In *Conference for Education in the South. Proceedings,* 1909. pp. 69-84.

Cook, W. A. "Vocational Training for the Indians." *Vocational Education* 2: 289-98, March 1913.

Cooley, Edwin G. "The Continuation School." *American School Board Journal* 45: 11-59, August 1912.

Shows the need of a new type of school in our educational system — the vocational continuation school.

Cooley, Edwin G. "Pre-apprenticeship Schools of London." *Vocational Education* 1: 174-83, January 1912.

Describes the day, evening, and part-time vocational schools of London.

Cooley, Edwin G. "The Scottish System of Continuation Schools." *Vocational Education* 1: 225-42, March 1912.

Shows the thoroughness with which the Scotch have undertaken the work of vocational education.

Cooley, Edwin G. "Training of Vocational Teachers in Germany." In *U.S. Bureau of Education. Report of the Commissioner for the Year 1911.* v. 1. Washington, Government Printing Office, 1912. pp. 389-417. chapter xi.

Describes the training given to teachers of vocational schools of middle and lower rank, including the continuation schools, special trade schools, commercial schools, vocational schools for women etc.

Cooley, Edwin Grant. "The Adjustment of the School System to the Changed Conditions of the Twentieth Century." In *National Education Association of the United States. Journal of Proceedings and Addresses, 1909.* pp. 404-10

Discussion: p. 410-15. Also in *Educational Bi-monthly,* 4: 1-11, October 1, 1909.

Cooley, Edwin Grant. "The Need for Vocational Schools." *Educational Review* 44: 433-50, December 1912.

A report to the Educational Committee of the Commercial Club of Chicago.

"It is," says the writer, "plainly impossible to provide in the present system of elementary and secondary schools the instruction recommended. Separate schools are necessary whose equipment, corps of teachers, and board of administration must be in the closest possible relation to the occupation."

Cooley, Edwin Grant. "The Problem of Establishing Vocational Schools." *School and Home Education* 32: 214-19, February 1913.

"If self-preservation through the training of the character of the future citizen is the justification for spending public money for schools, the state must enter the entire field of vocational education, and must provide for all — the artisan, the professional man, the farmer, and the merchant."

Writer says that such schools should be "separate, independent, compulsory day schools, supported by special taxes, carried on usually in special buildings." They should be administered by special boards of practical men and women, and taught by men trained in the vocations. There should be the closest possible co-operation between the school and the factory, etc.

Copa, George H. "Policy Positions Affecting Vocational Education." *Educational Forum,* Vol. 40 (January 1976), pp. 169-178.

A critique of a sample of major documents which develop policy positions for vocational education: Special Task Force to the Secretary of Health, Education, and Welfare, *Work in America* (Cambridge: MIT Press, 1972); "Policy Issues and Analytical Problems in Evaluating Vocational Education," Final Report, Parts I and II(Washington: National Planning Association, Center For Priority Analysis, 1972); Garth L. Mangum and John Walsh, *A Decade of Manpower Development and Training* (Salt Lake City: Olympus Publishing Co., 1973).

Corazzini, Arthur J. "The Decision to Invest in Vocational Education: an Analysis of Costs and Benefits." *Journal of Human Resources* 3 (Supplement 1968): 88-120.

A case study of vocational education Worcester, Mass. Some of the conclusions indicate that such a program was only "marginally profitable" and that "cheaper ways need to be found to keep people in school and to provide them with the skills necessary for employment."

Cordasco, Francesco. "The Federal Challenge and Peril to the American School." *School & Society* 94: 263-265, Summer, 1966.

A review of federal educational statutes, noting that they are "critically an attestation of the forfeiture of the prerogatives of American educational leadership," with special reference to the Vocational Education Act of 1963.

Corey, John. "North Carolina's New System of Vocational and Technical Education." *Phi Delta Kappan* 46 (April 1965): 383-387.

An account of vocational-technical education in North Carolina since 1957. Programs in the secondary school and the community junior college are stressed.

Cosand, Joseph P. "OE on Career Education." *Change, the Magazine of Higher Learning* 4 (Jun. 1972): 7, 60-61.

An official of the U.S. Office of Education explains the programs of the Office in regard to post-secondary vocational education.

Costello, Mary, "Education for Jobs." *Editorial Research Reports* (Nov. 3, No. 17, 1971): 845-62.

Contents: Education and changing job market; Academic vs occupational instruction; New directions in career education (includes "Federal Testing of Proposals in Career Education")

Coster, J.K. and L.A. Ihnen. "Program Evaluation." *Review of Educational Research* 38 (Oct. 1968): 417-433.

In reviewing the research done on program evaluation since October 1962, the authors divide their summaries under two headings: the product of vocational, technical and practical arts education (particularly follow-up studies) and cost-benefit analysis of vocational and technical education.

"Craftmanship for Crippled Chilren. A Home School Where They Are Taught to Be Skilled Workers and Are made Happy and Independent." *Craftsman* 9: 663-74, February 1906.

Free industrial home-school, New York.

Crane, William I. "A Plea for the Education of the Hand." In *Eastern Manual Training Association. Proceedings, 1901.* Cleveland, O., The Evangelical Association, 1902. pp. 27-39. diagr.

Crawshaw, Fred Duane. "Manual Training in the Franklin School. [Peoria, Ill.]" In *Western Drawing and Manual Training Association. Report, 1905.* pp. 86-100.

Discussion: pp. 101-28. Clay-work, sewing, tool-work, etc., in the grades.

Crawshaw, Fred D. "What Can the High School Do Better to Help the Industries?" *Manual Training Magazine* 13: 193-204, February 1912.

This article deals with "the high-school boy in the training he may get in the high school manual arts department to give him either the cultural values which have been accredited to manual training or the vocational values which it is believed the public high school manual arts should have."

Crooks, Nellie. "The Content of a College Course in Textiles for the Training of Teachers, and Its Application in the Lower Schools." *Journal of Home Economics,* 3: 222-28, June 1911. illus.

Cross, C. W. "Practical Results from a Modern Apprenticeship System." *Railway Club of Pittsburgh. Official Proceedings. September 25, 1908.* v. 7 no. 8, pp. 281-86.

Bibliography: p. 286-88.

Croswell, J. G. "The One Thing Needful." *Educational Review* 37: 142-59, February 1909.

"If our schools create this vocational atmosphere even in the cultural studies, great improvements must follow . . . . Under no vocational ideal of school instruction could the absurd proposition maintain itself that every child, in every public school, must study every subject."

Cruikshank, Lewis M. "Manual Training and Industrial Education in Pennsylvania." *Manual Training Magazine* 12: 440-45, June 1911.

Chronological table showing sequence in Pennsylvania's school industrial work, p. 441-42.

"This has been, perhaps, the most difficult state in the Union in which to educate the people to the value of hand training in their schools."

Cruikshank, Lewis M. "Needed Legislation in Pennsylvania for the Promotion of Manual Industrial Education." *Pennsylvania School Journal* 59: 141-45, September 1910.

Cubberley, Ellwood P. "Does the Present Trend toward Vocational Education Threaten Liberal Culture?" *School Review* 19: 454-65, September 1911.
Contends that the common man desires "an education for his children which shall be vocational and liberal in the same sense that the old classical training was and still is vocational and liberal for the few." Shows how the secondary school can realize the new ideal in education.

Cushman, L. S. "Governmental Co-operation in Industrial Education." *Elementary School Teacher* 8: 603-7, June 1908.

Dakin, W.S. "Vocational Education for Men in Service." *Vocational Education* 2: 89-109, November 1912.
"Summarizes the efforts which have been put forth by numerous corporations and other large employers of labor to supply deficiencies in public education."

Daniel, Roland B. "The Secondary Industrial School, Columbus, Georgia." *Vocational Education* 2: 119-38, November 1912.
See also article by C. B. Gibson in American Academy of Political and Social Science. *Annals,* 33: 42-49, January 1909.

Daugherty, James S. "The Illinois State Reformatory School of Sheet-metal Work." *Vocational Education (Peoria)* 1: 22-32, September 1911. illus.

Davenport, Eugene. "Industrial Education a Phase of the Problem of Universal Education." In *National Education Association of the United States. Journal of Proceedings and Addresses, 1909.* pp. 277-88.
Advocates combining the vocational and the nonvocational in the high schools. Says: "If members of the several vocations are to be educated separately the education will not only be hopelessly narrow and needlessly expensive, but, what is even worse, our people will be educated in groups separately, without knowledge of or sympathy with each other, producing a stratification of our people that is not only detrimental to society but dangerous if not fatal to democratic institutions."

Davis, Benjamin Marshall. "The Present Status of Manual Training in its Relation to Industrial Education in Rural Schools." *Manual Training Magazine* 11: 456-61, June 1910. illus.

Davis, Benjamin Marshall. "Shall Teachers Be Prepared to Give Instruction

in Elementary Agriculture?" *Western Journal of Education* 11: 5-15, May 1906.

[The Davis Bill for Secondary Education in Agriculture, Mechanic Arts, and Home Economics]." *Western Journal of Education* 13: 321-25, June 1908.
Gives full text of the bill.
Introduced in House of Representatives early in 1908 by Hon. C.R. Davis, of Minnesota. The object of the bill was the raising of a per capita tax of 10 cents to establish and maintain industrial and agricultural high schools, one-half of the proceeds to be appropriated for industrial high schools in the cities and one-half for agricultural high schools in the rural districts.

Davis, Jesse B. "Vocational and Moral Guidance through English Composition." *English Journal* 1: 457-65, October 1912.

Davis, Jesse B. "Vocational Guidance. A Function of the Public School and Its Application to the Commercial Department." In *Journal of the Michigan Schoolmasters' Club. 46th Meeting,* Held in Ann Arbor, March 29-April 1, 1911. Ann Arbor, Mich., Published by the Club (1911) pp. 119-28.
Author made a study of 531 boys in the high school of Grand Rapids, Mich. Gives outlines of a course of study and discusses the function of the vocation bureau. He says: "The commercial course should be the largest department of the modern high school."

Davis, Jesse B. "Vocational Guidance in the High School and its Application to the Church and Sunday School." *Religious Education* 7: 110-18, April 1912.
A system of vocational guidance in use in the Central High School of Grand Rapids, Mich.

Dawson, Kenneth E., and Lowell A. Burkett. "A Conversation on Industrial Arts and Vocational Education." *NEA Journal* 54 (November 1965): 25-28.
Officials of the American Industrial Arts Association and the American Vocational Association respectively answer questions put to them by members of the *NEA Journal staff.* The significance of industrial arts and vocational technical education is duscussed.

Dean, Arthur D. "Functions of a State Board of Education in the Establishment of Forms of Special Education." *Pennsylvania School Journal* 59'; 315-19, January 1911.

Dean, Arthur D. "Principles and Methods to Be Pursued in Organizing Trade Schools." In *Massachusetts. Bureau of Labor. Bulletin no. 43, September 1906.* pp. 313-22.

Dean, Arthur D. "Relation of Manual Training in the Public Schools to Industrial Education and Efficiency." *Craftsman* 14: 74-81.
Essay awarded the first prize in the "Craftsman" competition on this subject.

Dean, Arthur D. "Trade Schools—Private Initiative Creates Public Enterprise." In *Citizens' Trade School Convention. Proceedings and Addresses, 1907* [Indianapolis, Winona Technical Institute] pp. 44-53.

Dean, Arthur D. "Vital Needs of Evening Schools for Industrial Workers." *Machinery* 13: 244-46, January 1907.
    Calls attention to the necessity for improved methods in organizing and conducting evening industrial schools.

Dearborn, Lillian and Pierce, Louisa. "[Bibliography of Manual Arts]." In *Year-book of the Council of Supervisors of the Manual Arts, 1907.* Seventh Annual Meeting, New York, 7-8, February 1908. pp. 139-65.

De Garmo, Charles, "Training for Industrial Efficiency in the High School." In *New York [City] High School Teachers' Association. Year-book, 1906-1907.* pp. 21-30.

De Laguna, Theodore. "Vocational Studies for College Entrance Requirements." In *National Society for the Scientific Study of Education. Sixth year-book.* Chicago, University of Chicago press, 1907. pt. I: 36-49.

Denbigh, John H. "Some Problems of the Secondary School." In *New York and Vicinity. Schoolmasters' Association. Annual Report, 1908-1909.* pp. 7-17.
    Discussion: pp. 17-20
    "Total neglect of either the vocational or social aims must equally surely result in failure to adapt the school to the real needs of a community."

Dennis, J. S. "The Development of Industrial Training through Mission." In his Christian Missions and Social Progress. New York, Revell, 1906. 3. pp. 95-127.
    Missionary work in this field all over the world briefly narrated.

Des Marais, Philip H. "New Developments in Occupational Training and Vocational Education." *Balance Sheet* 46 (September 1964):|21-23.
    An official of the U.S. Department of Health, Education, and Welfare gives a brief review here of the Federal programs which provide aid to vocational training.

De Vore, Paul W. "Preparing People for the World of Work." *Journal of Industrial Arts* 29 (Mar-Apr 1970): 22-28.
    The text of a speech delivered at the 1970 Convention of the American Association of School Administrators. The theme of this address is that because of pressing social and psychological factors operating outside of the school a reassessment of vocational education is necessary.

Dewey, John. "Culture and Industry in Education." In *Eastern Art Teachers' Association and Eastern Manual Training Association. Proceedings of the*

Joint Convention, 1906. [Asbury Park, New Jersey, Kinmonth Art Press) [c1906] pp. 21-30.
   Also in *Educational Bi-monthly,* 1:1-9. October 1906.

Dick, Arthur A. "The Case for the Self-Contained Technical-vocational High School." *Industrial Arts and Vocational Education,* 54 (May 1965): 26-29.
   A discussion of the merits of the vocational-technical high school as opposed to the comprehensive high school offering vocational education as one of its many courses.

Dickerman, H. E. "Implications of Automation for Vocational Education. *NEA Journal* 45 (December 1956): 564-565.
   An outline of the provisions that vocational education will have to make to keep pace with the manpower needs of our growing economy.

Dickinson, William W. "Unemployed Young People and Federal Training Programs." *Welfare in Review* 10 (Jan.-Feb., 1972): 13-24.
   A review of Federally supported training programs as the Job Corps, Community Job Corps Centers, Public Service Career Programs, Manpower Development and Training Programs and the Apprenticeship Training Program. The author comes to the conclusion that a true evaluation of these training programs is unavailable although they "should show precise results and permit comparability of program outcomes."

Dillon, Charles. "The Money Value of Training for the Trades." *World's Work* 22: 14756-58, August 1911.
   Writer calculates that "a boy taught under the apprenticeship system earns $29,000 in a life-time; a trade school boy earns $40,000; a technical graduate earns $65,900."

"Disadvantaged Children and the World of Work." *The American Child* 40 (November 1958): 24 pp.
   A presentation of the problems of a great segment of American youth. Articles are devoted to the school dropout, the "uneducables," migrant children, children of low-income farm families, minority youth, and juvenile delinquents.

Dodd, A.E. "Hand Work Training for the Normal Student." In *Eastern Manual Training Association. Proceedings, 1908.* [Springfield, Mass., The F. A. Bassette Company) pp. 42-48.

Dodd, Alvin E. "Better Grammar Grade Provision for the Vocational Needs of Those Likely to Enter Industrial Pursuits." *Manual Training Magazine* 11: 97-107, December 1909.

Dodd, Alvin, E. "Vocational Consciousness in Manual Training." *Manual Training Magazine* 13: 329-38, April 1912.
   Argues that manual training is the natural basis upon which to build up a large and important section of vocational work.

Dodge, James M. "The Money Value of Technical Training." *American Society of Mechanical Engineers* 25: 40-48.
Comparison made of the earning capacity of men trained in the shop and those trained in school.

Donnelly, Samuel B. "The Problem of Industrial Education in Large Cities." *Schoolmasters' Association of New York and Vicinity. Monthly Report* 15: 58-63, March and April 1908.
Discussion: p. 64-66.

Donovan, John C., "Implications of Manpower Training for American Education." *Phi Delta Kappan* 46 (April 1965): 366-369.
A summary of the aims, achievements, and potential of the manpower development and training program and related Federal efforts are given here by the former manpower administrator in the U.S. Department of Labor.

Dooley, C. R. "Solving of the Skilled Mechanic Problem by Schools Furnished by Manufacturers." *Pennsylvania School Journal* 59: 553-57, May 1911.
Describes the educational system of the Westinghouse Electrical and Manufacturing Company, for its employees. During the four years' apprenticeship the training costs the boy nothing, and he receives in wages nearly $1,600.00.

Dooley, Channing R. "Evening School." In *National Society for the Promotion of Industrial Education. Proceedings of the Third Annual Meeting, 1909.* pp. 126-33. (its Bulletin no. 10)

Dooley, William H. "Practical Education for Industrial Workers." *Educational Review* 38: 261-72, October 1909.
Lawrence Industrial School.

Dorr, Rheta, Childe. "Keeping the Children in School." *Hampton's Magazine* 27: 55-66, July 1911.
Extracts, reprinted in *Pittsburgh School Bulletin,* 5: 5-9, October 1911. The School of William Wirt, Gary, Ind.

Downing, Augustus S. "The Meaning of Industrial Education to the Elementary Schools." In *National Education Association of the United States. Journal of Proceedings and Addresses, 1909.* pp. 380-85.
Discusses the use of study; vocational education, etc.

Draper, Andrew Sloan. "The Adaptation of the Schools to Industry and Efficiency." In *National Education Association of the United States. Journal of Proceedings and Addresses, 1908.* pp. 65-78.
Reprinted. "We cannot escape the fact that the elementary schools are wasting time, and that the lack of balance in the educational system is menacing the balance of the country. . . . The demand that the programs of the schools shall be more rational and the work of the teachers shall fit children for definite duties with more exactness, is heard on every side."

Draper, Andrew S. "The Essential Groundwork of Industrial Training." In *New York (State) Education Department, Addresses and Papers by Andrew S. Draper* . . . 1909-1910. Albany, N. Y. pp. 85-100.

Draper, Andrew Sloan. "From Manual Training to Technical and Trades Schools." *Educational Review*, 35: 401-11, April 1908.
    The writer contends that "the rational equilibrium between the exclusively intellectual and the decidedly industrial interests of the country must be restored and can hardly be restored without" the trades and technical schools.

Draper, Andrew S. "Our Children, Our Schools, and Our Industries." In *New York State Teachers' Association. Proceedings, 1907.* Albany, University of the State of New York, 1908. pp. 32-78. (Education Department. Bulletin no. 424, May 1908)
    Reprinted. A strong showing of the utter inadequacy of American facilities for trade and industrial education, as compared especially with Germany.

Draper, Dale C. "Vocational Education and the Comprehensive School.' *National Association of Secondary School Principals Bulletin*, 51 (May 1967): 107-120.
    A paper prepared and given at the 51st annual convention of the National Association of Secondary School Principals. The author believes that "potentially 100 percent of high school students could benefit from vocationally oriented education."

"Dropouts: Number One Challenge to America's Schools." *The American Child* 43 (March 1961): 20 pp.
    "This issue of *The American Child* tells why (the dropout) is the number one challenge facing our schools and reports on four experimental programs developing techniques to meet the challenge."

Drouet, Pierre. "The Case for More Systematic Evaluation of Vocational Training Programs." *International Labour Review,* 102 (Oct. 1970): 355-375.
    Evaluation should be something more than a mere post mortem, and should make it possible to improve current or planned vocational training programs financed by national or international technical co-operation agencies."

Drouet, Pierre. "Economic Criteria Governing the Choice of Vocational Training Systems" *International Labour Review* 98 (Sept. 1968): 193-223.
    This article seeks to provide the reader with a systematic approach to selecting one training system over the other when new or additional investments are to be made. The training systems evaluated are: 1) full-time vocational training at a school; 2) Day-release courses; 3) Block-release courses; 4) Sandwich courses; 5) Evening classes; 6) Vocational training of adults.

Dudley, Arthur J. "Automation and Education." *Industrial Arts and Vocational Education* 52 (April 1963): 38-40, 55.

"A detailed analysis of automation and what it implies for education, generally and industrial education, specifically."

Duffy, Frank. "Industrial Education and What Labor Unions Are Doing to Promote It." *Vocational Education* 2: 28-35, September 1912.

This article is by the General Secretary of the United Brotherhood of Carpenters and Joiners. "His extended knowledge and experience, as well as official position, enable Mr.Duffy to speak with authority on this question."

Duncan, R. K. "Temporary Industrial Fellowships at Kansas University" *North American Review* 185: 54-62, May 1907.

Established by commercial houses.

Duncanson, D., editor. "Educational Programs for Non-college-bound Youth." *Teachers College Journal* 36 (November 1964): 61-76.

The subject "Educational programs for non-college-bound youth" was the one adopted as the theme for the Third Annual Educational Development Council Spring Workshop at Indiana State College, April 2-3, 1964. This article contains four of the addresses delivered at this meeting: Bynum, Alvis S., "Too many, too soon: a commentary on the problems of youth, school, and work;" Beymer, Lawrence, "Nonsense and horse sense about dropouts;" Frantz, Welby M., "Education and industry: mutual-aid program;" Kozelka, Robert F., "Resolved: cooperative education is best."

Dutton, Samuel Train. "The Relation of Education to Vocation." *Educational Review* 12: 335-47.

Treats of the narrow bounds of early school education; development of commercial prosperity; schools backward in recognizing the scientific trend of the times. Discusses the deficiency in manual training; trade schools, etc.

Dutton, Samuel Train and Snedden, David (Samuel). "Administration of Evening and Continuation Schools." In their *The Administration of Public Education in the United Sates*. New York, The Macmillan Company, 1908. pp. 480-91.

References: p. 491.

Dutton, Samuel Train. and Snedden, David (Samuel). "Administration of Vocational Education." In their *The Adminstration of Public Education in the United States*. New York, The Macmillan Company, 1908. pp.

References: pp. 424-25.

Eastern Manual Training Association. Committee on Handwork for Girls. "Report." In its *Proceedings, 1905*. Philadelphia, Pa., Published by the Association, 1906. pp. 82-90.

Domestic science, laundry work, cookery, etc.

Eaton, Joseph J. "The Manila Trade School." *American Academy of Political*

and Social Science. Annals 33: 89-96, January 1909.
    Reorganized, 1905.

Eddy L. W. "Meeting the Challenge for Technical Education at the High School Level." *Industrial Arts and Vocational Education* (April 1963): 18-19.
    Some "guarding principles and operating procedures" necessary for successfully training technicians at the high school level.

"Education and Automation: the Coming World of Work and Leisure." *National Asssociation of Secondary-School Principals Bulletin* 48 (November 1964): 3-110.
    Entire issue devoted to the relationship of education and automation. Pertinent articles listed here are analyzed under individual authors. General contents of issue: "The Nation, the Economy and Employment;" "Education, the School and the Student."

"Education for Work and Family Living." *Review of Educational Research* 18 (June 1947): 210-250.
    A review of the literature for the 3-year period October 1944 to October 1947, covering these topics: Education for work movement; home and family life education; industrial education; business education; agricultural education.

Ekberg, Dennis and C. Ury. "Education for What?"—a Report on an M.D.T.A. Program." *Journal of Negro Education* 37 (Winter 1968): 15-22.
    An evaluation of the success of two Manpower Development and Training Act (MDTA) programs carried out in Oakland, California and each lasting for a period of 30 weeks. According to the authors, the difficulties encountered were mainly the fault of the "program's assumption that white middle-class values of work, honesty, the importance of time and individual responsibility can be transmitted to the Negroes of the ghetto."

Ellington, John R. "Jobs for Youth: a Critical Problem for the 60s." *State Government* 34 (Spring 1961): 118-123.
    The author believes that one of our most serious social problems is the unemployment of our youth, who are unable to get jobs because of inadequate vocational training.

Elson, William H. "Intermediate Industrial Schools." In *National Society for the Promotion of Industrial Education. Proceedings of the Third Annual Meeting, 1909.* pp. 172-79. (Its Bulletin no. 10)
    Discussion: pp. 195-204.

Elson, William H. "The Technical High School of Cleveland." *School Review* 16: 353-59, June 1908.

Elson, William H. and Bachman, F.P. "Different Courses for Elementary Schools." *Educational Review* 39: 357-64, April 1910.
    Work in Cleveland, Ohio.

Eno, R. H. "Oregon's Program of Vocational Education Leadership Development. *Business Education Forum* 22 (Mar. 1968): 23-24.

A summary of activities of a unique leadership intern program conducted by the Oregon State Department of Education, Oregon State University and the university's Division of Continuing Education.

Erwin, Kate. "New Careers." *American Education* 4 (May 1968): 20-22.

A description of the New Careers program in Winston-Salem, North Carolina. One of 39 such training centers in the U.S., New Careers prepares low income groups for skilled jobs relating to human services.

Essex, M.W. "Education for Jobs; Recommendations of the Advisory Council on Vocational Education." *American Vocational Journal* 43 (Mar. 1968): 37-40.

Twenty-six recommendations are listed here, with brief explanations of each. Over one half of the recommendations concern the Vocational Education Act of 1963.

Evans, Rupert N. "Cooperative Programs: Advantages, Disadvantages and Factors in Development." *American Vocational Journal* 44 (May 1969): 19-22+.

The Dean of the College of Education of the University of Illinois presents his definition of cooperative work programs, and some of the obstacles encountered in this form of vocational education.

Evans, Rupert, N. "Industry and the Content of Industrial Education." *School Shop* 21 (April 1962): 29-31, 110.

Who shall determine the contents of courses for effective vocational-industrial education? The author believes that such decisions should be composed of a team, equally represented by the local school administration and industrial economists, psychologists, labor-management specialists, and others from industry.

Evans, Rupert N. "The Secondary School and Occupational Preparation." *National Association of Secondary School Principals Bulletin* 53 (Feb. 1969): 23-40. (Same condensed in *Education Digest* 34 (May 1969): 20-23.

The author is the Dean of the College of Education at the University of Illinois. He believes that "for a large portion of its student body, the school makes no conscious effort to prepare for the transition from school to employment," but only prepares students for more school. As an alternative he suggests work-study courses, eliminating obsolescence in the vocational education curriculum and creating placement facilities for students in the schools, so that they may be able to get employment more easily.

Evans, Rupert. N. "Training Time and Placement Time in Vocational and Technical Education." *American Vocational Journal* 45 (Mar. 1970): 16, 18.

A discussion of the desirability of providing the same length of vocational education programs for the able student and the slow learner. The question of spacing training programs, rather than graduating all in the same class is also reviewed.

Fant, J.C. "A New Feature in School Work." *Mississippi Educational Advance* 2: 12-14, March 1913.

At McComb, Miss., the superintendent of schools has perfected an arrangement with the master-mechanic of Illinois R.R. Co.'s building and repair shops by which boys may take their high school course with extended practical work in the shops. The arrangement is founded upon the plan of having two boys act as a unit, so that while one is in school the other is in shop, and vice versa. For their shop work the boys are paid, each making from $15 to $18 per month.

Faulkner, T.L. "We Must Serve Those Being Neglected." *Agricultural Education Magazine* 41 (Sept. 1968): 57, 59.

An official of Alabama's State Department of Education describes those who are "the neglected", youths from low income families. The ways and means of helping these students are briefly described.

"Federal Funds: Short-term Institutes Held for Vocational Educators." *American Education* 6 (Apr. 1970): 35-36.

Charts showing schedules of short-term multiple institutes for professional personnel in vocational and technical education, held from January through October 1970 and serving more than 2,000 participants.

Fee, Ira B. "Business Course for High Schools of Smaller Cities." *American School Board Journal* 45: 15, October, 1912.

Feirer, Albert J. "The Future Role of Vocational-technical Education in Our Society." *Industrial Arts and Vocational Education* 53 (May 1964): 23-26, 67-68, 70.

An outline of the problems to be faced in vocational education for the 1960's, the accomplishments of some States in preparing for the new challenges ahead in training youth and adults for the world of work.

Feldman, M. J. "Why Manpower Training Should Be a Public Mission." *American Vocational Journal* 42 (Nov. 1967): 26-28.

Reasons why public education should have the responsibility for "pre-employment or pre-college" programs in manpower development, and why vocational education should become a part of each level of public education, "either to prepare for further education or to provide a greater number of terminal skills" useful for employment.

Feldman, Marvin. "Vocational Education in a New Comprehensive System." *Today's Education* 58 (Nov. 1969): 47-48.

The author, an official of the Ford Foundation, believes that "the idea behind comprehensive education is to make vocational education the principal feature of a new system, not merely fit it into the existing system."

Fellows, Doug, M. "How Industry Sees Technical Education." *Industrial and Vocational Education* 58 (Sept. 1969): TE9-TE16.

Guidelines for the training of technicians from the Director of the Ward Technical Institute, University of Hartford, Conn.

Felmley, David. "The Normal Schools and Vocational Education." *Western Journal of Education (Ypsilanti)* 4: 154-60, April 1911.
    Same article in *Educational Bi-monthly*, 5: 395-401, June 1911 (a little differently paragraphed and with different title)

Ferguson, James. "Industrial Education in High Schools." *Sierra Educational News* 5: 28-35, November 1909.

Fernandez, G. "Project: Vocational Education." *Journal of Secondary Education* 40 (February 1965): 65-68.
    Description of the organization and accomplishments of a "community classroom" vocational program designed for high school seniors in the Cupertino High School, Cupertino, Calif., during the 1964-65 academic year.

Fibel, Lewis R. "At the Two-year Community-junior College: What is Technical Education?" *Industrial Arts and Vocational Education* 58 (Sept. 1969): TE13-TE15.
    The author presents the functions of the junior college in regard to technical education, the analytical approach in forming the curriculum, how changes in our society have contributed to the growth of education.

Finch, B. "Summaries of Current Vocational Education Acts." *School Shop* 24 (June 1965): 17-19.
    A useful and timely summary of the eight vocational education acts now in operation, giving appropriations for fiscal 1965, use of funds, administrative requirements, etc.

Fitch, Sir Joshua G. "Hand Work and Head Work." In his *Educational Aims.* pp. 145-76.
    Psychological basis, educational influence and limitations to the value of manual training. Gives accounts of some celebrated technical schools.

Fitchburg, Mass. "Manual Arts [School.]" In its *Annual Report* (1908): 28-30 (1909): 56-63.
    "First of its kind in America"; for grammar grade boys and girls.

Fitchburg, Mass. School Committee. "Industrial Training. In its *Annual Report* (1908): 19-28.
    A co-operative industrial course introduced into the high school. A distinctively new and untried feature of high school work. The basis of the plan is the alternating of shop work and school work. The course is of four year's duration. The first year is spent wholly in school, and during the other three years the boys alternate weekly between school and shop.
    See also *Annual Report* 1909. pp. 35-45.

Fitchburg, Mass. School Committee. "Industrial Training. In its *Annual Report* (1909): 35-45.
    Also in North Central Association of Colleges and Secondary Schools. *Proceedings, 1910.* Chicago, Published by the Association, 1910. pp. 45-58.
    Questions submitted to members of the class, regarding reasons for

taking the course, and its practical benefits to them. Answers: pp. 46-52. Manufacturers' opinions: pp. 54-55. Report of W. B. Hunter.

Fleege, Urban H. "Job Training — by Schools or Industry?" *School and Society* 90 (Summer 1962): 263-264.
    Should the American public school be responsible for job-preparation to ease the unemployment of youth and adults? The author favors on-the-job training by industry, leaving for the schools the important role of educating the mind, imagination, emotions, and creative impulses of the human person.

Fletcher, W. I. "The Duty of Normal Schools to Provide Literary Training." *Southern Educational Review* 4: 149-57, October-November 1907.

Flexner, Mary. "A Plea for Vocational Training." *Survey* 22: 650-55, August 7, 1909.
    Based on a study of 1,000 children who left school to work.

Foos, Charles S. "Industrial Education and Manual Training." In *Reading, Pa. Board of Education. Bi-ennial Report, 1907-1909.* pp. 514-50. illus.
    Detailed information from one hundred cities, pp. 525-50.

Foos, Charles S. "[Report on Vocational Training]." In *Reading Pa. Board of School Controller. Minutes, 1909.* pp. 34-72.
    Also in *Reading, Pa. Board of Education. Bi-ennial Report, 1907-1909.* Reading, Pa., Eagle Book and Job Press, 1909. pp. 514-50.
    Answers to questionnaire from 100 cities: p. 525-50.

Forbes, George M. "Organization and Administration of Industrial Schools." *American School Board Journal* 46: 11-13, 50-51, January 1913.
    The subject is dealt with in the concrete, i.e., by following an actual experience covering four years in the city of Rochester, N.Y., in the introduction of industrial education.
    See also *Vocational Education,* 2: 278-88, March 1913.

Forbush, William Byron. "Vocational Training and Guidance." In his *The Coming Generation.* New York and London, D. Appleton and Company, 1912. pp. 136-50.
    A brief but good review of the subject. Contains graphic statistics of the German system of industrial education. References: p. 150.

Forkner, Hamden L. "Vocational Business Education under the Vocational Education Act of 1963." *Balance Sheet* 45 (February 1964): 256-258.
    An analysis of the Vocational Education Act of 1963 for those in the field of business education, giving specific information as to how this legislation may be utilized at State and local levels.

Franklin, George A. "Do Industrial Courses Promise Substantial Returns in

Efficiency." In *Minnesota Educational Association. Journal of Proceedings and Addresses, 1909.* [Minneapolis, Minn., Syndicate Printing Company] pp. 63-66.
    Statistics of 62 schools.
    Discussion: pp. 67-68.

Freedman, Marcia. "Vocational Training." *The American Child* 42 (November 1960): 9-12.
    The problems of high school youth unable to go on to higher training are discussed here. How can they become employable, since much of the present high school vocational education programs are "at a fairly low skill level?"

Freeman, Sarah J. "The Educational Value of Bookbinding." *Kindergarten-primary Magazine* 20: 156-58, 210-11, 243-45, January-March 1908.

"[Freeport (Ill.) Half-time Factory Co-operative Work for High Schools]" *American Educational Review* 30: 520-21, August 1909.

Frost, Joseph M. "Industrial Training in High Schools." In *National Education Association of the United States. Journal of Proceedings and Addresses, 1909.* pp. 317-19.

Fullan, M. Thomas. "Advantages of the Trade School over the Apprenticeship System." In *Southern Educational Association. Journal of Proceedings and Addresses, 1908. pp.* 541-50.

Fullan M. Thomas. "Industrial Education in the New Rural School" In *Alabama Educational Association. Official Proceedings, 1910.* pp. 140-48.

Fuller, Edgar. "Report from Washington: Schools Assigned Responsibilities and Funds in Manpower Development and Training Act." *Nation's Schools* 69 (May 1962): 106, 108.
    How the provisions of the Manpower Development and Training Act of 1962 will effect vocational education, what is expected by way of reducing unemployment resulting from automation and technological changes.

Fulwider, L. A. "A Co-operative School and Shop Course." In *Illinois State Teachers' Association. Journal of Proceedings, 1909.* Springfield, Ill., Illinois State Journal, State Printers, 1910. pp. 179-87.
    Course of study: pp. 183-84.

Furney, Oakley. "Education with an Aim to Service." *Vocational Review 2:* 299-317, March 1913.
    Describes work of the Albany (N.Y.) vocational schools. Illustrated.

Gaylor, G. W. "Elimination and Vocational Training." *Psychological Clinic* 6: 69-73, May 15, 1912.

Gibboney, R. A. "Social Context and Vocational Education." *School and Society* 97 (January 1969): 28-31.
An assessment of vocational education at the secondary level. The author believes that the vocational educator is "isolated" from other specialists in our schools, but still holds a unique position. He is able to "point out to citizens and legislators that the necessary investment in programs directed at the root causes of poverty and unemployment."

Gibbs, Charlotte M. "Preparation Necessary for a Teacher of Domestic Arts."
In *Western Drawing and Manual Training Association. Proceedings, 1909.* pp. 93-100.

Gibson, Carleton B. "The Need of Industrial Education in the South." In *Conference for Education in the South. Proceedings, 1912.* pp. 70-81.

Gibson, Carleton B. "Recent Tendencies toward Industrial Education in Europe and America." In *Southern Educational Association. Journal of Proceedings and Addresses, 1908.* pp. 157-66.
Also in *Southern Educational Review,* 6:275-84, February-March 1909.

Gibson, Carleton B. "Technical Education for the South" In *Southern Commercial Congress. Proceedings, Third Annual Convention, Atlanta, Ga., March 1911.* pp. 369-83.

Gilbert, Charles B. "The Motor Activities in Expression." *Educational Foundations* 20: 7-23, September 1908.
A suggestion that manual training and physical culture be recast along the lines of the expression of thought and feeling.

Gillette, John Morris. "The Sociological Warrant for Vocational Education." *American Journal of Sociology* 14: 219-32, September 1908.

Gillie, Angelo C. "Search for a Statewide Framework: Occupational Education in Pennsylvania." *Junior College Journal* 40 (Apr. 1970): 15-19.
The author believes that the major centers for postsecondary vocational education in Pennsylvania may be the junior colleges. Future plans for higher education in that state mark the junior colleges as instrumental in unifying most programs now offered in occupational education.

Gillie, Angelo C. "Women in Vocational Education: Symposium." *American Vocational Journal* 49: 34-46, November 1974.

Glover, Katherine. "Working for an Education in a Southern School." *Craftsman* 15: 707-17, March 1909. illus.
Berry Industrial School.

Golden, John. "The Educational Need from the Viewpoint of Organized Labor." *Journal of Education* 70: 91-92, July 22, 1909.

Golden, John. "Importance of Industrial Education to the Workingman." *Social Education Quarterly* 1: 191 95, June 1907.

Golden, John. "Position of Labor Unions Regarding Industrial Education." In *American Academy of Political and Social Science. Annals* 33: 185-87, January 1909.

Golden, John. "State Legislation for Industrial Education, and Organized Workingmen." In *National Society for the Promotion of Industrial Education. Proceedings*[*1909*] pp. 133-38.

Goldsmith, Evelyn May. "Schools for Crippled Children Abroad." In *U.S. Bureau of Education. Report of the Commissioner, for the Year 1909.* Washington, Government Printing Office, 1909. v. 1, pp. 503-11.
    Reprinted.

Goodwin, Edward J. "The Present Status of Public Education." In *New York (State) University Convocation, 1908.* Albany, University of the State of New York, 1909. pp. 75-89. (Education Department. Bulletin no. 443, March 15, 1909).
    Discussion: p. 89-99.
    "The differentiation . . . at the beginning of the seventh school year should be threefold. It should provide (1) shopwork, (2) suitable instruction in business subjects and (3) foreign language study."

Gordon, M. M. Ogilvie. "Juvenile Employment Bureaus." *Contemporary Review* 99: 723-32, June 1911.
    Describes Edinburgh, Scotland, system.

Gorst, Harold E. "An Educational Revolution." *North American Review* 189: 372-85, March 1909.
    Advocates vocational training.

Great Britain. Board of Education. "[Technical and Industrial Education in Russia]." In its *Education in Russia.* London, Wyman and Sons, 1909. pp. 136-39, 200-204, 460-504. (Special reports on educational subjects. v. 23)

Grede, John F. "Trends in Occupational Education: Illinois." *Junior College Journal* 40 (Apr. 1970): 20-26.
    A summary of the plans underway for new occupational programs in Illinois' junior colleges. The expansion and coordination of established programs are also discussed.

Green, Edith. "People, Jobs and Federal Priorities." *Compact* 4 (Aug. 1970): 4.
    Congresswoman Edith Green believes that our manpower needs should be given greater priority by greater emphasis on vocational-technical education.

Greene, Bert I. "A New Concept of the High School." *School Shop* 24 (April 1965): 46-48, 108.

The author believes that the present concept of the high school is outmoded, and he gives his reasons for this belief and states ". . . we are about to enter a new phase of education and that the Vocational Education Act of 1963 will show us the way." He proves this argument by an examination of the provisions of the act, and the possibilities it has for reconstructing the American High School.

Gregory, R. J. and J. Gordon. "Vocational Education; Relationships with Special Education and Vocational Rehabilitation." *High School Journal* 52 (Feb. 1969): 247-253.

An examination of the historical background that has produced certain attitudes toward vocational education and how these attitudes still persist today. Means by which vocational education can be more vital in preparing individuals to become more productive are discussed.

Grote, C. Nelson. "Towards Fulfilling a Total Obligation." *Industrial Arts and Vocational Education* 58 (May 1969): 28-29.

According to the author teaching "saleable skills" to a person is not enough. The student must be helped to relate his job responsibilities to that of his life as a "social being".

Grubb, W. Norton and Marvin Lazerson. "Rally Round the Workplace: Continuities and Fallacies in Career Education." *Harvard Education Review* 45: 451-474, Fall, 1975.

Challenges contentions that career education can help ease unemployment, and calls into question the basic assumptions of career education.

Gustafson, Lewis. "A New Task for the Public Schools." *Vocational Education* 1: 145-58, January 1912.

A statement of some of the fundamental principles which must control the development of vocational education.

Hadden, S. M. "The Place of Normal Schools in Vocational Training." *Western Journal of Education (Ypsilanti)* 3: 412-19, November 1910.

Haddon, A. M. and W. J. Jacobs. "Men's Job Corps: A Total Program of Human Renewal." *Audiovisual Instruction* 13 (Feb. 1968): 141-143.

What the Job Corps has done to fulfill its original goals, that of increasing the employability of its enrollees and providing them with the tools for good citizenship. The author notes in particular the reading and speech courses offered to enhance job skill levels.

Hall, Frank Haven. "The Ethical Value of Vocational Instruction in Secondary Schools. In *National Education Association of the United States. Journal of Proceedings and Addresses, 1909.* pp. 492-97.

Hall, G. Stanley. "Industrial Education." In his *Educational Problems.* vol.

1. New York and London, D. Appleton and Company, 1911. pp. 540-710.
"Next to moral education . . . industrial training is by general consent the greatest and most urgent problem confronting the American people."
An interesting study written in the author's characteristic style. Discusses the present tragic wastage of pubescents; a proposed substitute for manual training; vocational and trade schools, etc. Running bibliographical references.

Hamilton, Samuel. "Plea for Industrial Education. In *Pennsylvania State Educational Association. Department of City and Borough Superintendents. Proceedings, 1910.* pp. 31-40.
  Historical: pp. 38-39.
  Also in *Pennsylvania School Journal,* 58: 501-10, May 1910.

Hamlin, H. M. "All Students Benefit from Education for Work." *Nation's Schools* 64 (August 1959): 47-49.
  The author is professor of agricultural education, University of Illinois. In this article he discusses the means by which all school activities and subjects can contribute to vocational education, and help students "face up to vocational alternatives" in choosing a life's work.

Hamlin, H. M. "New Designs in Vocational and Practical Arts Education. Part I: The South." *American Vocational Journal* 39(December 1964): 12-15.
  This report is the first section of a national report on new designs in vocational, technical and practical arts education, and vocational guidance, being prepared by a subcommittee of the American Vocational Association.

Hamlin, Herbert M. "Education to Serve Occupational Ends: Vocational Education Diverse in Content and Essential to Economic Growth Has Taken a Giant Step. *Monthly Labor Review* 91(Mar., 1968): 49-54.
  Entire issue contains articles on "Labor in the South". This article describes the great progress made in the 1960's in the South's public school vocational education programs.

Hamlin, Herbert M. "What is Evaluation?" *American Vocational Journal* 42(May 1967): 19-22.
  The evaluation of occupational education from the citizen's viewpoint and procedures to be used for lay groups at the local and state level.

Hammel, William Charles Adam. "Industrial Education in the Public Schools." In *North Carolina Association of City Public School Superintendents and Principals. Proceedings and Addresses, 1909.* Raleigh, Edwards & Boughton Printing Co., 1909. pp. 39-53.
  Reprinted.

Haney, James Parton. "Manual Training as a Preventive of Truancy. *Educaton* 27: 634-41, June 1907.

Haney, James Parton, "The National Society for the Promotion of Industrial Education." *Manual Training Magazine* 11: 27-35, October 1909.
    A brief review of the activities of the National Society.

Haney, James Parton. "Vocational Work for the Elementary Schools." *Educational Review* 34: 335-46, November 1907.
    Considers the necessity of offering some form of vocational training in the elementary school. and recommends that for certain schools a modified form of the course of study be arranged to permit vocational training in the seventh and eighth years.

Hansen, Gary B. "Training Ideas from Britain." *Manpower.* 3(Nov. 1971): 19-23.
    "National system of vocational training carried out on an industry-by-industry basis under the direction of specially created industrial training boards."

Hanus, Paul Henry. "Industrial Continuation Schools for Boys and Girls from Fourteen to Sixteen Years of Age." In *New York State Teachers' Association. Proceedings, 1906.* pp. 31-34.
    Schools in Switzerland, Germany, and France. Cities the grave need for similar schools in the United States.

Hanus, Paul Henry, "Industrial Education in Massachusetts." In *New York (State) University Convocation. Proceedings, 1907.* Albany, University of the State of New York, 1908. pp. 137-55. (Education department. Bulletin, no. 422, March 1908)
    Discussion: pp. 155-60.

Hanus, Paul Henry. "Vocational Education." In *New Jersey State Teachers' Association. Annual Report and Proceedings, 1907.* pp. 78-89.
    The need of industrial schools to supplement the public schools, offering a course of four years; with evening instruction for men and women already engaged in the trades.

Harcourt, Charles. (Forbes-Lindsay, Charles Harcourt) "Reform for the Truant Boy in Industrial Training and Farming." *Craftsman* 15: 436-46, January 1909.

Harrington, Gordon M. "Vocational Education Moving in Diverse Directions." *Nation's schools,* 60(July 1957): 45-48.
    "The observations made here summarize the results of a survey made in 1953 of the State director of vocational education in each State and Territory. . . . Inferrences about trends are based on the opinions of the State level officials who are responsible for vocational programs in the schools."

Harris, Caroline E. "The Los Angeles Polytechnic High School." *Manual Training Magazine* 7: 150-55, April 1906. plans.

Harris, James H. "Wage Earning among Grammar Grade Boys." *American School Board Journal* 45: 13, November 1912.

An effort to discover how many boys in the Dubuque (Iowa) elementary schools were earning money in out-of-school employments.

Harris, Norman C. "Redoubled Efforts and Dimly Seen Goals." *Phi Delta Kappan* 46 (April 1965): 360-365.

The author is professor of the Technical Education Center for the Study of Higher Education, University of Michigan. He states what he believes are the "hard questions" to be asked in administering the "fivefold expansion in vocational education funds" so that the program may prove successful.

Harrisburg, Pa. School Board. "Special Committee to Investigate the Matter of Introducing Sewing into the Schools. Report." In its *Annual Report, 1909.* Harrisburg, Pa., Star Printing Company, 1909. pp. 101-16.

Questionnaire sent out to 120 largest cities in the United States, pp. 114-16; tabulated replies, pp. 111-13.

Harvey, Lorenzo Dow. "Manual Training in the Grades." *Elementary School Teacher* 7: 390-407, March 1907.

Harvey, Lorenzo Dow. "The Need, Scope, and Character of Industrial Education in the Public School System." In *National Education Association of the United States. Journal of Proceedings and Addresses, 1909.* pp. 49-70.

Discusses the demand for industrial education. Author contends that manual training may be so organized as to have a distinct value for industrial efficiency without loss of cultural value. Shows the basis for reorganization of manual training courses for industrial ends.

Harvey, Lorenzo Dow. "A School for Home Makers." In *U.S. Bureau of Education. Report of the Commissioner for the Year 1911.* 1, Chap. viii, pp. 313-29.

Describes work at the Stout School for Teachers of Domestic Science and Art, Menomonie, Wis. Outlines course of study.

Hatch, Henry D. "Some Observations on Scottish Public Educational Provisions for Promoting the Life Careers of Pupils Leaving School" *Educational Bi-monthly* 7: 203-21, February 1913.

Shows the work of the juvenile branch of the Board of trade labour exchange in the school board offices, Edinburgh.

Hatch, Luther A. "Manual Training in the Practice School at the De Kalb Normal." *Manual Training Magazine* 3: 201-10, July 1902.

Hatch, Luther A. "Out-door Industrial Work for Rural Schools." *Manual Training Magazine* 6: 75-81, January 1904.

Hatch, William E. "Industrial Education in Massachusetts." *Educational Review* 40: 369-74, November 1910.

Heath, Howard R. "Manual Training in the Primary Schools of Victoria, Australia." *Manual Training Magazine* 14: 151-56, December 1912.

Illustrated. There are at present about thirty-five centers in Victoria, the center system being in vogue in the cities and large towns. In addition to the above, from 50 60 rural school sar receiving the instruction from the ordinary teachers.

"Hebrew Technical Institute, New York City." In *Ontario. Department of Education . . . Toronto, 1911.* pp.211-16.

Gives curriculum.

Hedges, William. "A Year of Prevocational Work." *Educational Bi-monthly* 7: 191-202, February 1913.

Describes work of the Jackson School, Chicago.

Heeter, S. L. "Economy of Time and Energy in Treating the Course of Study." *Educational Foundations* 20: 24-32, September 1908.

"We must decrease the school hours so far as formal studies in the grammar schools are concerned for certain boys and girls forced . . .to go early to work, but increase the time correspondingly for such pupils to be given to industrial training and commercial subjects; . . . ending possibly in a closely articulated elementary system of apprenticeship between the grammar schools and leading industrial enterprises."

Hein, Leon F. A. "The Cost of Materials for Manual Training in the Elementary Grades." *Manual Training Magazine* 14: 129-37, December 1912.

A questionnaire was sent to 41 supervisors in 15 states and the District of Columbia. Writer tabulates the results obtained.

Heller, Walter W. "Men, Money and Materials." *Educational Record* 44 (January 1963): 12-16.

This noted economist outlines the advantages to be reaped in investing "money and materials" on education to provide skilled manpower. He also lists eight "policy guides" for further investments in education and training to insure the achievement of greater skills from workers.

Henschel, H. "Hauswirtschaftliche Schulanlagen." *Das Schulhaus* 14: 479-87, Heft 11, 1912.

Describes domestic science equipment in a German school. Well illustrated by photographs.

Herrick, Cheesman A. "Vocational Subjects for College Entrance Requirements." In *National Society for the Scientific Study of Education. Sixth Year-book.* Chicago, University of Chicago Press, 1907. pt. I: 7-15.

Herrick, Cheesman A. and others. "The Proper Place in American Education for Instruction in Commercial and Industrial Subjects." In *Association of Colleges and Preparatory Schools of the Middle States and Maryland. Proceedings, 1905.* pp. 11-36.

Hicks, W. E. "Industrial Education in Secondary Schools." *School Science and Mathematics* 6: 736-44, December 1906.

Higgins, Milton P. "Plan of a "Half-time" School." *American Society of Mechanical Engineers* 21: 646-78.

One of the first papers to indicate a feasible plan whereby boys could attend school part of a day and work in a factory the remainder of the working day.

Hildreth, Helen R. "Four Months in a Girls' Trade School." *Vocational Education* 1: 305-15, May 1912.

Describes school at New Britain, Conn. Answers many perplexing questions that frequently arise among those interested in definite plans looking to the opening of courses for girls.

Hines, J. J. "Industry Needs High School Graduates." *American School Board Journal* 149 (October 1964): 13-14.

Results of a survey made by three vocational education teachers in an Illinois community of 40,000 population. These teachers interviewed the personnel managers of 20 companies "to determine what terminal high school graduates should be taking to qualify for employment."

Hirsch, E. G. "Moral Aspects of Industrial Education." *Educational Review* 35: 448-54, May 1908.

Hitchcock, James. "The New Vocationalism." In *On Learning and Change* (New Rochelle, New York: *Change Magazine,* 1973), pp, 91-103.

The new vocationalism and its implications for higher education.

Holbrook, Heber. "Manual Training in Its Relation to Civilization." In *Eastern Manual Training Association. Proceedings, 1912.* Allegheny, Pa., John C. Park, Printer, 1903. pp. 27-50.

Holt, Elizabeth G. "Negro Industrial Training in the Public Schools of Augusta, Ga." *Journal of Home Economics* 4: 315-23, October 1912.

Horn, Francis H. "Liberal Education Reexamined." *Harvard Educational Review* 26 (No. 4, 1956): 303-314.

Originally given as a speech at the Andiron Club of New York City, December 16, 1955, this article by Dr. Horn of the Pratt Institute states three complaints against the attitude of the spokesmen for liberal education. One of these complaints is their failure to recognize the importance of both liberal and vocational education in our present day society.

Hover, J. Milton. "The Problem of the Village High School." *Western Journal of Education (Ypsilanti)* 4: 253-64, June 1911.

The course and scheme of work of the Friends' academy, Bloomingdale, Ind., domestic science and agriculture.

Howe, Charles B. "The Future of the Manual Training High School in Vocational Education." *Manual Training Magazine* 14: 105-14, December 1912.

Author says that "the manual training high school of the future must be a vocational school, pure and simple, as all high schools are now and probably will be in the future. The immediate educational problem of the manual training school is the determination of its particular vocational function."

Howe, Harold, 2d. "Education and Social Reconstruction." *Educational Leadership* 25 (Jan. 1968): 321-323.

The former U.S. Commissioner of Education considers two recommendations made by the President's Commission on Law Enforcement and Administration of Justice in its report on Juvenile Delinquency and Crime. These two recommendations are 1) secondary vocational programs to equip the non-college bound student with marketable skills and 2) new types of retraining programs for teachers, guidance counselors and other school staff to aid in the "social reconstruction" of students.

Howe, Harold, 2d. "The Human Side of Vocational Education." *School Shop* 25 (April 1966): 2.

A guest editorial by the U.S. Commissioner of Education in which he points out the "interesting changes in program and facilities" of the Vocational Education Act of 1963.

Huffman, Harry. "Cooperative Vocational Education: Unique among Learn and Work Programs." *American Vocational Journal* 44(May 1969): 16-18.

How cooperative education programs differ from other vocational education plans, and the factors that must be present to insure success.

Hunt, Eugene H. and R. W. Jefferson. "Developing Professionalism in Vocational Education." *Business Education World* 49(Mar. 1969): 11 + .

The authors deplore the lack of research and experimentation at the local level by vocational educators. They list the reasons commonly given for such want of "creativity and innovation at the grass-roots level", and take issue with each of these reasons.

Hunter, W. B. "The Fitchburg Plan." In *National Society for the Promotion of Industrial Education. Fourth Annual Convention. Proceedings.* New York City, Society for the Promotion of Industrial Education, January 1911. pp. 93-108. (Its Bulletin no. 13, pt. III).

Hunter, W. B. "The Fitchburg Plan of Industrial Education." *School Review* 18: 166-73, March 1910.

Hurt, Mary L. "Educating for the World of Work: a Team Approach." *Educational Leadership* 22 (January 1965): 221-225.

An outline of ways and means to expand academic and vocational education programs under the Vocational Education Act of 1963.

Hutchinson, T. Herbert. "Vocational Guidance." *Association Seminar* 20: 427-52, June 1912; 21: 9-27, 46-60, October, November 1912; 21: 84-101, December 1912; 128-47, January 1913.
  Bibliography: p. 145-47.
  Gives evidence of the necessity of training for efficiency, and points out the need and importance of vocational guidance.
  Pt. 3 deals with the history of vocational guidance.

Hylla, E. "Die Verwicklichung der Arbeitschulideen in Elementarunterricht." *Pädagogische Warte* 20: 13-18, January 1, 1913.
  Urges that teachers consider carefully the vocational school idea as a special field of opportunity in the elementary schools.

"Imperative Needs of Youth." *National Association of Secondary-School Principals Bulletin* 31 (March 1947): 3-144.
  A discussion of 10 needs of youth, all of which have implications for industrial training. Emphasis is particularly placed on the need for developing salable skills.

Indiana. Department of Public Instruction. "Industrial Education." In *24th Biennial Report of the State Superintendent of Public Instruction for the School Years Ending July 31, 1907, and July 31, 1908.* Indianapolis, 1908. pp. 417-26.
  Contains account of the development of industrial education in the public schools of Indiana.

Indiana. State Superintendent of Public Instruction. "Manual and Industrial Training and Agriculture." In his *Biennial Report, 1905-1906.* Indianapolis, Wm. B. Burford, 1906. pp. 355-430. illus.
  Chiefly the work of the Bluffton, Ind., schools.

"Industrial Arts and/or Vocational Education." *TIP (Theory into Practice)* 9(Dec. 1970): 277-312.
  Entire issue of eight articles devoted to what impact vocational education should have on industrial arts. Partial contents of note: "How to live with change and not be corrupted by money" by Rupert N. Evans; "Occupational education: a means of focusing industrial arts" by Robert Swanson and others.

"Industrial Education." *School Review* 15: 375-99, May 1907.
  Symposium by C. H. Thurber, H. J. Skeffington, and C. W. Hubbard at Harvard teachers' association. Second paper discusses the attitude of the trade-union and workingman. Third paper outlines effective industrial schools for a small factory community.

"Industrial Education. Endowed Trade School Offers New Opportunity in Boston." *Pennsylvania School Journal* 60: 162-64, October 1911.
  Describes the New Wentworth institute, Boston, Mass.

"Industrial Education. General Outline." In *A Cyclopedia of Education,* ed. by Paul Monroe . . . v. 3. New York, The Macmillan Company, 1912. pp. 425-44.

A condensed but excellent review of the whole field of industrial education in the United States, England, Germany, and France. Bibliographical references only to the most important and accessible titles given, p. 443-44.

"Industrial Training in the Philippine School of Arts and Trades and the Iloilo Trades School." *Philippine Education* 6: 12-16, February 1910.

"Influence of Industrial Arts and Science upon Rural and City Home Life." In *National Education Association of the United States. Journal of Proceedings and Addresses, 1909.* pp. 636-43.

Contents. — (A) From the standpoint of domestic science [by] Mrs. Ellen H. Richards. — (B) From the standpoint of economic interests [by] A. Salisbury.

Ittner, Anthony. "The History of Trade Schools." In *Citizens' Trade School Convention. Proceedings and Addresses, 1907.* [Indianapolis, Winona Technical Institute] pp. 37-44.

Iversen, Robert W. "Peace Corps Training: Lessons of the First Year." *Educational Record* 44(January 1963): 17-25.

A description of the Peace Corps educational training for particular skills that might be applied to other types of vocational education. Among the "lessons" learned from this system: " . . . Highly motivated students can absorb a great deal in a relatively short time. Some training programs have, in fact, compressed the equivalent of a year of college into 12 weeks."

Jackson, Edwin R. "How Forestry Can Help the Manual Training Teacher." *Manual Training Magazine* 14: 138-50, December 1912.

"The chief importance of forestry in its relation to manual training lies in the opportunity it affords to awaken the student to a sense of his duty as a citizen to help in the great work of eliminating waste from our industrial world, to broaden his mind until he sees himself not alone but as a part of a great social system composed of individuals like himself, but each one dependent upon the other."

Jacobson, Paul B., ed. "Youth at Work; a Manual Containing Descriptions of a Number of Selected National Youth Administration Projects for in-and-out-of-school Youth." *National Youth Administration of Secondary School Principals Bulletin* 25(May 1941): 3-197.

An entire issue devoted to the work programs under the NYA. Includes information on programs for out-of-school youth which enabled them to work and still receive training through the schools to make them more productive on the job.

James, Edmund J. "Commercial Education." In *Education in the United States.* A Series of Monographs, ed. by Nicholas Murray Butler. New York [etc.] American Book Company, 1910. pp. 655-703.

Shows the evolution of commercial education in this country, beginning with business colleges, etc., to the introduction of commercial subjects into the public high schools. Gives courses of study and statistics of schools.

James, Edmund J. "Public Trade Schools and Technical High Schools." In *National Association of State Universities. Transactions and Proceedings, 1908.* Bangor, Maine, Bangor Co-operative Printing Co. pp. 309-19.

James, Edmund Janes. "Vocational Training and Its Future." *Vocational Education (Peoria)* 1: 1-9, September 1911.
"Business men can do an immense amount to stimulate and help this development, greatly to the benefit not only of the young fellows who are going into business, but, above all, to the community."

Jennings, J. F. "Emerging Issues in Vocational Education." *American Vocational Journal* 50: 29-32, September, 1975.

Jinks, John H. "Manual Training at Hampton Institute and Its Relation to the Trades." *Manual Training Magazine* 9: 200-10, February 1908. illus.
Also in *Southern Workman,* 37: 217-27, April 908.

Jinks, John H. "The Training in Hand Work of Teachers for Rural Schools." *Southern Workman* 37: 343-50, June 1908.
At Hampton Normal and Agricultural Institute, Hampton, Va.

Johnson, B. Lamar. "Guideline and Trends in Postsecondary Vocational-Technical Education." *Phi Delta Kappan* 46(April 1965): 376-380.
Eight trends in junior college organization and education are discussed to point out the value of the junior college as an effective institution for vocational-technical training.

Johnson, Ben W. "Industrial Education in the Elementary School." *School Exchange* 4: 338-46, March, 1910.
An argument for division of the work, after the sixth grade, into work of intermediate character with elective courses leading to trade or vocational schools or back to high school or out into industry.

Johnston, Charles Hughes. "The Social Significance of Various Movements for Industrial Education." *Educational Review* 37: 160-80, February 1909.
A review of the problem of industrial education, based chiefly on Continuation schools in England and elsewhere, ed. by M. E. Sadler, and the writings of various American specialists. Author says: "The opinion of many is that to protect industrial training from extreme measures, the safest way is not to house it in independent school plants, but have it organically affiliated with the present system."

Johnston, George M. "Industrial Opportunities of Our Schools." *Ohio Teacher* 32: 453-56, May 1912.
Deals particularly with the situation in Cincinnati, O.

Jones, Paul O. "We Train Dropouts." *Industrial Arts and Vocational Education* 54(June 1965): 26,43-44.
The author is the Assistant Superintendent of Vocational Education and Training, U. S. Bureau of Prisons. He describes here the training program given school dropouts in Federal correctional institutions.

Jones, Richard A. "Eight Guidelines for Planning a Vocational Technical Education School." *American Vocational Journal* 44(Jan. 1969): 36-40.
Among the guidelines discussed are space requirements related to educational goals, character of the school, site selection and physical facilities.

Jones, Thomas Jesse. "Relation of Industrial Education to the Economic Progress of the South." *Southern Workman* 38: 139-44, March 1909.
Reprinted.
The relation of the industrial training of Negroes to southern prosperity. Illustrated with graphic statistics.

Jordon, G. Gunby. "Material and Moral Benefits of Industrial Education." In *National Society for the Promotion of Industrial Education. Proceedings, Second Annual Meeting.* New York City, National Society for the Promotion of Industrial Education, June 1909. pp. 122-33. (Its Bulletin no. 9)

Kane, Thomas Franklin. "The Maintenance of the College of Liberal Arts in a State University in Competition with Professional and Technical Colleges in the Same Institution." In *National Association of State Universities. Transactions and Proceedings, 1910.* Hamilton, Ohio, Republican Publishing Company [1910] pp. 120-39.
Discussion: pp. 139-54.

Kaufman, Jacob J. "Occupational Training Needs for Youth." *Journal of Human Resources* 3(Supplement 1968): 121-140.
An assessment of factors that show how vocational education does not seem to be meeting the needs of youth in our society. A few of the recommendations suggested are: that vocational education must "expand its offerings, make them attractive, understand the culture and problems of Negro youth, adjust to servicing lower ability students."

Kaufman, Jacob J. and Anne F. Brown. "Manpower Supply and Demand. *Review of Educational Research* 35 (Oct. 1968): 326-345.
A review of the research published since October 1962 on manpower requirements, labor force projections as they relate to vocational training and related subjects.

Kaufman, Jacob J. and Morgan V. Lewis. "The Potential of Vocational Education." *National Association of Secondary School Principals Bulletin* 53 (Feb. 1969): 1-22.
The author believes that "vocational education has the potential for making the school experience relevant". However, much must be ac-

complished before this is realized, and this includes replacing old styles of administration, designing and testing new types of programs.

Kaufman, Jacob J. and C. J. Schaefer. "Is U. S. Vocational Education Measuring up to the Need?" *School Shop,* 27 (Sept. 1967): 45-47 + .
A condensation of the report "The Role of the Secondary Schools in the preparation of youth for Employment".

Kaufman, Jacob V. "The Role of Vocational Education in the Transition from School to Work," in Arnold Weber, *et al.,* eds. *Public-Private Manpower Policies.* University of Wisconsin, 1969.
A general conceptual assessment with summaries and critical review of the literature.

Kehew, M. M., ed. "The Movement for Industrial Education." *Charities and The Commons* 19: 803-64, October 5, 1907.
A survey of present opportunities and immediate and future needs in the vocational training of American boys and girls.
Contents. — H. S. Pritchett — A national society for the promotion of industrial education. S.M. Kingsbury — What is ahead for the untrained child in industry? Ralph Albertson — Decay of apprenticeship. P.H. Hanus — Industrial education in Massachusetts. C. F. Warner — Industrial training in the public schools. C.R. Richards — Private trade schools for boys. M.S. Woolman — Private trade schools for girls. F.M. Marshall — The public school and the girl wage-earner. R. A.Woods — Industrial education from the social worker's standpoint. A.G. Bookwalter — Continuation work.

Keith, Charles W. "Capstone Curriculum for Two-year Technicians: a Second Chance for Advanced Study." *American Vocational Journal* 45 (Mar. 1970): 29-30.
The problems encountered by graduates of the two-year technical schools who wish to go on for a B.A. degree. The author suggests various approaches in solving the problem.

Keith, John A. H. "Industrial Education for Wisconsin Boys and Girls." *Wisconsin Journal of Education* 44: 65-69, March 1912.

Kelley, Mrs. Florence. "Part-time Schools." *Child Labor Bulletin* 1: 106-12, June 1912.
"We can not give to young girls and boys eight hours of stupefying work and then save them for an intelligent citizenship by adding evening school work to that. It can not conceivably be sufficiently recreational."

Kemp, Barbara H. "Where Vocational Education Is a Special Need." *American Vocational Journal* 42 (Nov. 1967): 24-25, 52.
A program specialist at USOE describes generally vocational education activities for the exceptional and culturally disadvantaged student and explains how these activities may be improved.

Kemp, Barbara H. "The Youth We Haven't Served." *American Vocational Journal* 40 (October 1965): 24-26.

"What can vocational educators do to compensate for long years of neglect?" This article suggests eight lines of action.

Kent, Ernest B. "The Elementary Curriculum and the Industries." *Education* 30: 582-90, May 1910.

Kent, Ernest B. "Elementary School and Industrial Occupations."- *Elementary School Teacher* 9: 178-85, December 1908.

Presents a plan for developing "vocational choice" by the pupil of the elementary school—with a scheme for using school shops for special vocational classes.

Keppel, Francis. "Big-city School: Problems and Prospects; New Vigor in the Urban High Schools." *PTA Magazine* 59 (March 1965): 4-6.

The former U.S. Commissioner of Education presents an "agenda for reform" in revitalizing the high schools in our big cities. On this "agenda" are suggestions for better training opportunities for jobs.

Keppel, Francis. "Vocational Education: A Promise for Tomorrows." *American Vocational Journal* 39 (February 1964): 15-18.

An address by the U.S. Commissioner of Education at the 57th Annual Vocational Convention in Atlantic City, N.J., December 9, 1963. In this address Mr. Keppel emphasizes the importance of State planning as indicated in the proposals of the Vocational Education Act of 1963.

Kern, Olly Jasper. "Manual Training in the Country School." In his *Among Country Schools.* Boston [etc.] Ginn & Company [1906] pp. 309-41.

Kern, Olly Jasper. "What Form of Industrial Training Is Most Practical and Best Suited to the Country Child." *Elementary School Teacher* 7: 323-28, February 1907.

Kerschensteiner, Georg. "The Fundamental Principles of Continuation Schools." In his *Three Lectures on Vocational Training* . . . Published by the Commercial Club of Chicago, 1911. pp. 1-16.

Also in *School Review,* 19: 162-77, March 1911.

Kerschensteiner, Georg. "The School of the Future a School of Manual Work." Tr. by T. C. Horsfall. *School and Home Education* 31: 278-86, March 1912.

Address given to Swiss teachers at Zurich. The writer believes "that character can not be developed by teaching in words alone, but that training in the actual doing of things must accompany knowledge getting."

Kilpatrick, Van Evrie. "Department of Elementary School Problems: Vocational Training in the Elementary School." *Education* 30: 448-53, March 1910.

Kimmins, C. W. "Trade Schools in London." *Elementary School Teacher* 10: 209-19, January 1910.

King, Charles A. "Pre-vocational Training." *Education* 33: 105-8, October 1912.
Argues that a system of vocational instruction should include training of both sexes, and makes provision for students between 14 and 16 years of age.

King, Charles A. "Vocational Training in the Public Schools." *Education* 31: 657-62, June 1911.

Kingsbury, Susan M. "What Is Ahead for the Untrained Child in Industry?" *Charities and The Commons* 19: 808-13, October 5, 1907.
Data based on an investigation for the Massachusetts commission on industrial and technical education, 1906. Illustrated by interesting graphic statistics.

Kirby, C. Valentine. "Craftsmanship as a Preventive of Crime." *Craftsman* 8: 171-80, May 1905.

Kliever, Douglas E. "The Vocational Education Act of 1963." *School Life* 46: 3-12, March/April, 1964.
Offers background and specifics of the Vocational Education Act of 1963.

Knoebel, R. M. "Post-secondary Occupational Education; Phenomenon of this Generation." *American Vocational Journal* 43 (Apr. 1968): 15-18.
"In this overview, the author points up issues and problems, and the immense potential for occupational education at the post-secondary level."

Knox, George Platt. "How Should the School System Contribute to an Intelligent Choice of Vocation on the Part of the Pupil?" In *National Education Association of the United States. Journal of Proceedings and Addresses, 1912.* pp. 417-25.
Urges the value of preparation. This preparation should both precede and follow the choice of vocation.

Koehn, Emil A. "The State Leadership Role In Vocational Education." *American Vocational Journal* 45 (Oct. 1970): 17-19, 82-83.
The author believes that there does exist a comprehensive manpower policy at both the state and national levels and that state boards of vocational education should be involved in the formulation and implementation of this policy at both levels.

Kohler, Mary C., and Andre Fontaine. "The Job Situation." *Saturday Evening Post* 235 (March 24, 1962): 58, 61-62.
One of the fundamental reasons why youth cannot find work is to be found in the breakdown of the apprentice system and total lack of training for work which might be available to them.

Kolberg, William H. "Upgrading the Working Poor." *Manpower* 1 (no. 10, Nov. 1969): 24-27.

The term "upgrading" refers to a program of occupational training, conducted to advance the employed to jobs with higher skills and higher pay. In a discussion of upgrading the author states up to now, most programs of this nature have been directed to training the unemployed for entry-level jobs. What is needed now is a type of training that combines work and education and should be available to older workers as well as youths.

Kraft, Richard H. "Vocational Technical Training and Technological Change." *Educational Technology* 9 (Jul. 1969): 12-18.

Reasons why vocational-technical training should be geared to meet manpower needs and technological changes in our society. The author also discusses the gap between "the academic world on the one hand and the vocational world on the other", a gap that he believes is reflected in many other phases of the American social order.

Kreuz, M. L. "Innovators Move to Meet Local Problems." *American Vocational Journal* 44 (Feb. 1969): 62-65.

Brief sketches of the papers delivered at the Secondary Department session at the 62nd Annual Vocational Education Convention. Innovations in vocational training given at various high school levels are described.

Kreuzpointner, Paul. "Constructive Industrial Education." *American Machinist* 33: 343-44, August 25, 1910.

By the chairman of Industrial Education Committee, American Foundrymen's Association.

Kreuzpointner, Paul. "Industrial Education." *Journal of Education (Boston)* 74: 594-95, December 7, 1911.

Adverse to the purely commercial aspect of the subject.

Kreuzpointner, Paul. "Industrial Education." *Educational Foundations* 23: 400-8, 626-32, March and June 1912.

Gives the aims of industrial education and the nature of the subjects to be taught. Deals also with the continuation, trade, and evening schools.

Kreuzpointner, Paul. "The New Standard of the Present Day Industrial Education in Europe." *American School Board Journal*, 43: 15-17, September 1911.

"We have as a new standard in the present system of industrial education in Europe, a growing power of the state over the organization of such schools, the extension of the compulsory feature of attendance at industrial schools, under eighteen years of age, and a vast increase of expenditures by the state and the municipalities over former years — for the education of the masses of industrial workers."

Kugler, Harold L. Self Examination for Public Education; What We Can Learn from the Job Corps?" *American Vocational Journal* 42 (Nov. 1967): 32-34.

The author dispells the "myths" which he believes are held by public school educators in regard to the Job Corps. He points out why the public school system in the U.S. could not adequately provide the type of training needed by the typical Job Corps enrollee.

Kult, Dennis and others. "Characteristics of Successful and Dropout MDTA Trainees." *Journal of Employment Counseling* 6 (Dec. 1969): 186-191.
This study centers on one program of MDTA training as an example of how this type of program functions to meet the needs of those at low educational levels.

Lane, Robert H. "Our Inefficient **Grammar** Schools." *Western Journal of Education* 13: 259-69, May 1908.
A statistical consideration to prove that children in American schools should be fitted to earn a livelihood.

Lane, Winthrop D. "Broadening Industrial Education." *Survey* **29**: 321-23, December 14, 1912.
Treats of the different types of industrial education. Says: "Distinction should be made between what are called prevocational and vocational instruction. One of the proposed means of securing greater harmony between the public school system and the actual environment of life is the making over of the elementary curriculum to include, side by side with reading, writing, and arithemetic, training in manual dexterity, in the purposes and use of tools, and perhaps in some of the elementary processes which may be found to underlie modern trades."
Discusses also the work of the sixth annual meeting of the National Society for the Promotion of Industrial Education.

Lane, Winthrop D. "Education and Work: a Twilight Zone." *Survey* **29**: 225-28, November 23, 1912.
Describes the work of the second National Conference on Vocational Guidance, New York City, October 1912.

Lang, Ossian H. "The Educational Outlook." *Forum* 38: 106-15, July-September 1906.
Treats of the relation of the public school system to industrial education.

Langley, Euphrosyne. "Constructive Activities as an Essential and Important Factor in the Elementary School Course." *Elementary School Teacher* 9: 32-37, September 1908.
Advocates handwork in the elementary school, from the kindergarten up.

Langworthy, C. F. "Status of the Training of Teachers of Home Economics in the United States, 1907. In *Lake Placid Conference on Home Economics. Proceedings, 1907.* Lake Placid Club, Essex Co., N.Y., 1907. pp. 55-77.
Institutions offering courses, pp. 72-77; state normal schools, pp. 62-63.

Lapp, John A. "The Present Tendencies in Vocational Education." *Journal of*

Education 76: 683-84, December 26, 1912.

"The movement began in Massachusetts with separate schools under separate boards, both state and local. That has been changed to permit either a separate school or a school as an integral part of the regular school system. Wisconsin has adopted the separate school idea, and such a plan is proposed in Illinois; the states of New York, New Jersey, Ohio, and Maine make the work a part of the school system. Indiana follows the latter group."

Larson, M. E. "Philosophy Education Forgot; Concepts for the Education of the Noncollege Bound." *American Vocational Journal* 43 (Mar. 1968): 22-23.

How best to provide quality education for the youth who will not go on to college. The author believes that this means "providing enough time in vocational courses for adequate preparation."

Larsson, Gustaf. "Industrial Education in Secondary Schools." In *American Institute of Instruction. Proceedings [1906]*. Boston, Massachusetts, 1906. pp. 389-95.

"Let the present manual training high schools be converted into vocational schools for children over 17 years of age, and establish a manual training laboratory in every high school building as an organic part of the school curriculum."

Lautner, John E. "Industrial Continuation Schools of Munich." *Western Journal of Education (Ypsilanti)* 3 : 385-1, November 1910.

Lautner, John E. "State Industrial Education in Massachusetts." *Western Journal of Education (Ypsilanti)* 3 : 97-118, March 1910.

Course of study: pp. 112-13.

Law, G. "Area School: Getting the Most for the Education Dollar." *School Shop* 23 (April 1964): 57-60.

A description of the Lewis Wilson Technological Center, Huntington, N.Y. Useful as a study of an area vocational school's founding and development.

"The Lawrence, Mass., Industrial School." *Journal of Education* 68: 483-84, October 5, 1908.

Opened, 1907.

The first free engineering laboratory in the country.

Lawson, John B. "Vocational Preparedness for a Technical Age." *American Vocational Journal* 38 (September 1963): 10-12.

The author is vice president of the Philco Corporation. He believes that "we must take a good hard look at our vocational preparedness programs" and uses California as an example in planning for ways to meet the vocational needs of that State. This planning Mr. Lawson terms "Master Plan for Vocational Education," and he describes the possible impact on education and labor if it were to materialize.

Leavitt, Frank M. "The Cleveland Elementary Industrial School." *Vocational Education (Peoria)* 1 : 10-21, September 1911. illus.

Leavitt, Frank M. "The Continuation School'; Cincinnati's Examples," *Vocational Education* 2 : 218-34, January 1913.
A comprehensive review of the work accomplished in Cincinnati, Ohio. Author says these schools "furnish the best illustrations of this type of educational effort to be found in the country." The schools can be grouped. for purpose of study, as "evening schools," "voluntary continuation schools" and "compulsory continuation schools."

Leavitt, Frank M. "The Independent Industrial School of Newton, Massachusetts." *Vocational Education* 1 : 243-57, March 1912.
Treats of the general organization, methods, and results of the Independent industrial school. An exposition of some of the possibilities under the Massachusetts law.

Leavitt, Frank M. "Industrial Education in the Elementary Schools." *Manual Training Magazine* 9 : 377-84, June 1908.
For school training rather than education through private business interests.

Leavitt, Frank M. "The Need, Purpose, and Possibilities of Industrial Education in the Elementary School." *Elementary School Teacher* 13 : 80-90, October 1912.
Contends that elementary industrial work will be most effective when conducted under the direction of the manual training authorities.

Leavitt, Frank M. "The Relation of the Movement for Vocational and Industrial Training to the Secondary Schools." *School Review* 19 : 85-95, February 1911.

Leavitt, Frank M. "The Relation of the Present Movement for Vocational Education to the Teaching of the Mechanic Arts." *Elementary School Teacher* 12 : 158-68, December 1911.
Shows the value of "pre-apprentice" or "pre-vocational" work in the schools.

Leavitt, Frank Mitchell. "Some Sociological Phases of the Movement for Industrial Education." *American Journal of Sociology* 18 : 352-60, November 1912.
Emphasizes the fact that the industrial education movement is bound to have a profound effect on the whole system of popular education. Discusses vocational education in all its phases.

Leavitt, Frank M. "Vocational Education in the Boston Public Schools." *Vocational Education* 1 : 316-31, May 1912.
"A comprehensive and readable presentation of the remarkable provision made for vocational opportunities for all the children by a large city school system."

Leavitt, Frank M. "Vocational Purpose in the Manual Training High School, Indianapolis, Indiana." *Vocational Education* 2: 36-52, September 1912.

"A discriminating discussion of the way in which one progressive community is attempting to secure the maximum of service from its high school."

Lee, A. M. "Status of Vocational Education in the United States." *Journal of Research and Development in Education* 7: 18-28, Spring, 1974.

Lee, Allen, and Herbert M. Hamlin. "Organization and Administration of Vocational Education. *Review of Educational Research* 38 (Oct. 1968): 395-404.

A criticism of the research done in the organization and administration of vocational education, 1962-1968. Areas considered are policy and planning, personnel, finance and facilities.

Lee, Joseph. "The Boy Who Goes to Work." *Educational Review* 38: 325-43. November 1909.

The child should not be permitted to go into any occupation "that does not include education toward his ultimate efficiency."

Leshner, Saul S., and George S. Synderman. "Helping Unemployed Youth — a Community Approach." *Children* 8 (November-December 1961): 213-217.

The authors state their views on the needs of the school dropouts, and what services and training the community can provide to aid their future.

Lewis, E. E. "The Present Status of Vocational Subjects in the High Schools of California." *Manual Training Magazine* 14: 229-34, February 1913.

Data secured by H.C. Greenwood. Returns obtained from 165 different high schools in California.

Lewis, E. E. "Studies in Vocational Guidance." *School and Home Education* 32: 135-38, 212-14, 247-51, December 1912; February, March 1913.

A study of the employment found by 4,386 children who left the schools of St. Louis and took employment certificates.

Lexis, W. H. R. A. vi. "Technical High Schools." vii. "High Schools for Special Subjects." viii. "Middle and Lower Professional Schools. In his *General View of the History and Organization of Public Education in the German Empire;* tr. by G.J. Tamson. Berlin, A. Asher & Co., 1904. pp. 114-82.

Lieberthal, M. "Labor: Neglected Source of Support." *American Vocational Journal* 42 (Dec. 1967): 49-52.

Suggestions of ways to influence labor unions and the labor movement so that their support will help to bring about a vast expansion in vocational education.

Lindsay, Samuel McCune. "New Duties and Opportunities for the Public Schools." *Social Education Quarterly.* 1: 79-92, March 1907.

Industrial education and child labor.

Little, J. Kenneth. "The Wisconsin Research Center for Vocational-technical Education." *Phi Delta Kappan* 46 (April 1965): 412-413.

In October 1964, the University of Wisconsin, with the assistance of a Ford Foundation grant, established the Center for Research and Development in Vocational-Technical Education and Training. A brief description of its objectives and activities is given in this article.

Liveright, A. A. "Lifelong Education." *National Association of Secondary School Principals Bulletin* 48 (November 1964): 99-110.

The author is the director of the Center for the Study of Liberal Education for Adults at Boston University, Brookline, Mass. He outlines the important needs of adult education today. Partial contents: Educating non-technologists about technology and preparing for continuing and accelerating change in jobs and professions.

Lockette, Rutherford E. "Implications for Industrial Arts Education: Education for a Changing World of Work." *American Vocational Journal* 39 (April 1964): 26-27.

A professor of industrial education of the Trenton (N.J.) State College outlines four programs for industrial arts education at the senior high school and adult level. He believes that such programs would make vocational education available to a larger number of youths who would profit from such training.

Lodge, Thornton H. "Vocational Subjects in the Secondary School." *Educational Review*. 39: 333-41, April 1910.

Logan, W. B. "Vocational Education Facts and Misconceptions." *Theory into Practice* 3 (December 1964): 161-162.

The author states that "in spite of the favorable record established by vocational education in 50-plus years since its inception, there are still misconceptions in the field." Among these misconceptions there are eight outstanding ones, some of which are that Federal funds bring Federal control, vocational education is limited to learning a narrow skill, that vocational education is for students of low ability, and that high school vocational education students will not be able to enter college.

"[London Schools] Employment Bureaus . . . " In *Brooklyn Teachers' Association. Report, 1908-1909.* pp. 35-37.

"A Look at Vocational Education in Appalachia." *Appalachia* 3 (Aug. 1970): 1-8.

A description of vocational educational development in four Appalachia states. Includes charts of statistics on funds spent through June 30, 1970, enrollment of students, status of 1969 graduates of Appalachian facilities.

Loomis, William P., and Louise Moore. "Occupational Education in the Schools." *Annals of the American Academy of Political and Social Science* 302 (November 1955): 68-73.

"Most of the activities covered in this report concerning placement and follow-up are based upon operations of the schools in the field of trade and industrial education, which includes training for employment in manufacturing, construction, technical, and service occupations."

Lord, Everett W. "Vocational Direction, or the Boy and His Job." In *National Child Labor Committee. Proceedings of 6th Annual Conference, Boston, January 13-16, 1910.* New York, 1910. pp. 73-85.
    "Boys find themselves in their vocations as the result of custom, heredity, propinquity, or accident far oftener than through deliberate and conscious choice." Advocates vocational guidance.

Lovejoy, Owen R. "Will Trade Training Solve the Child-Labor Problem?" *North American Review* 191: 773-84, June 1910.

Lowens, Milton. "Needed: Vocational Institutes!" *High Points* 45 (November 1963): 65-76.
    The author gives his reasons why he believes the vocational high schools of New York City "are obsolete and should be replaced without delay." He includes suggestions for modern programs more in keeping with current needs and believes that vocational institutes are the answer to combat obsolescence in vocational high schools.

Lugg, Charles H. "What Shall the High School Do?" *South Dakota Educator* 26: 12-14, January 1913.
    Discusses the advisability of introducing the industrial courses into the small high schools.

McAndrew, William. "High Schools for All of Us." *Educational Bimonthly* 4: 207-21, February 1910.
    "School shops we must have if we would serve the 90 per cent whose lives will have to do with industries, but the education of the mere shop can not but be degenerating and stupefying. Higher things . . . must be taught . . . You can do it better if your trade and commercial students are mingled with your purely academic classes. . . . All high school education will be better done if done in the same school."

McAndrew, William. "Industrial Education from a Public School Man's Point of View." *Educational Review.* 35: 109-28, February 1908.
    Argues for introduction of industrial education into the public school system.

McBride, Paul W. "The Co-Op Industrial Education Experiment, 1900-1917." *History of Education Quarterly* 14: 209-221, Summer, 1974.
    Study of public schools which cooperated closely with local industry in the formulation, control, and staffing of industrial education programs.

McClusky, Howard Y. "General Education and Work Experience." *Review of Educational Research* 14 (October 1944): 289-300.

A review of the literature covering a 3-year period, October 1941 to October 1944, on the subject of student employment as a part of the general education curricula. Includes evaluation of research on such programs as the National Youth Administration and the Civilian Conservation Corps.

McCollum, Sylvia G. "Vocational Programs outside the Public School System. *American Vocational Journal* 44 (Feb. 1969): 66-67.
A summary of the talks given at the 62nd annual Vocational Education Convention, in a department meeting of Special and Related Programs. Training programs such as those found in the Job Corps and the U.S. Rehabilitation Service are briefly described.

McCourt, Okey E. "Programed Instruction in Vocational-Technical Training." *American Vocational Journal* 40 (January 1965): 17-18.
How automated instruction was initiated in the Sussex County (Delaware) area vocational school and a brief assessment of its effectiveness.

McDaniel, C. H. "The Hammond Plan. What One City Is Trying to Do." *American School Board Journal* 45: 13-14, December 1912.
Shows what has been accomplished in adopting the school work of the Hammond (Ind.) public schools to the industrial needs of the community.

McElroy, James. F. "The Most Urgent Need of Our Educational System Is an Adequate Provision for the Vocational Needs of Children Destined for Industrial and Domestic Pursuits." In *National Education Association of the United States. Department of Superintendence. Journal of Proceedings and Addresses, 1908.* pp. 48-52.

McGahey, C. R. "The Young American Workman as Seen by a Shop Superintendent." *Engineering Magazine* 35: 384-86, June 1908.
Recommends trade schools as a remedy for defective home and union training.

McGlauflin, Isabelle. "Vocational Training for Girls." *Education* 31: 523-26, April 1911.

McIntire, Ezra Elmer. "Formulating of New Educational Aims for Secondary Schools." In *Minnesota Educational Association. Journal of Proceedings and Addresses, 1909.* [Minneapolis, Minn., Syndicate Printing Company] pp. 73-82.

McKay, Roberta V. "Job Training Program in Urban Poverty Areas. *Monthly Labor Review* 94 (Aug. 1971): 36-41.
"A special survey shows that one in six poverty area residents in six major U.S. cities received vocational training, most through school programs". This article discusses this special survey on the value of vocational training as it relates to the urban poor.

McKeever, William W. "Vocational Education Unsuited for the Socially Disadvantaged." *Clearing House* 44 (Sept. 1969): 43-44.

A brief but well documented refutation of current theories concerning vocational training as a "panacea" for disadvantaged youth.

McLure, William P. "The Challenge of Vocational and Technical Education." *Phi Delta Kappan* 43 (February 1962): 212-217.

This article is the result of a comprehensive study made on vocational education in Illinois. The subject of vocational education is treated here from a national viewpoint, re-defining it from the needs of the high school level, and placing the teaching of vocational education in a more comprehensive school. The author also suggests the "fundamental policy decision" that must be made by each State to make its vocational training programs more effective.

McLure, William P. "Future of Vocational and Technical Education." *American Vocational Journal* 36 (March 1961): 7-9. Also in *National Association of Secondary School Principals Bulletin* 35 (February 1961): 7-12.

A professor of education at the University of Illinois discusses the demands now being made on our high schools. He believes that the future task for vocational education is one of close cooperation between the educational institution and fields of occupational employment.

MacNary, Egbert E. "Printing in a Manual Training Shop." *Manual Training Magazine* 10: 41-49 October 1908.

Magnus, Philip. "Industrial Education in England." In Roberts. *Education in the Nineteenth Century.* New York, Macmillan, 1901. pp. 140-170.

Magruder, William T. "The Cosmopolitan High School Curriculums from the Standpoint of Colleges of Engineering." In *National Education Association of the United States. Journal of Proceedings and Addresses, 1908.* pp. 599-605.

Mahal, L. Kenneth and Roy E. Olson. "An Architect's Approach to Vocational School Planning." *American Vocational Journal* 44 (Jan. 1969): 31-35.

An article useful for those who are planning to build an area vocational school. Describes, by way of example, the steps taken by the St. Paul Minnesota Technical-Vocational Institute, in its initial research, the coordination of programs offered and facilities, consideration given to future enrollments.

Main, Josiah. "Agriculture in Secondary Schools." In *New Jersey State Teachers' Association. Annual Report and Proceedings, 1907.* pp. 65-77.

"The high school teacher should have had a rural training . . . in a good agricultural college."

Malia, D. H. "More on an Age-old Controversy." *Journal of Industrial Arts Education* 28 (Nov. 1968): 18-20.

The author believes that "vocational education must overturn its present image". He suggests the means for doing this, by beginning with present structural regulations that hamper the curriculum.

Mandel, Henry. "Fundamental Considerations in Vocational Program Planning." *American School and University* 34 (1962-63): G-5-G-10.

Basic information on setting up a vocational-technical program in a typical American community. Includes advice on equipment, tools, and supplies, space requirements, and how much to spend.

"Manhattan Trade School for Girls (New York City) Placement Bureau." *Teachers College Record* 10: 291-95, September 1909.

Organized, October 1908.

Mann, C. R. "Industrial and Technical Training in the Secondary Schools and Its Bearing on College-entrance Requirements." *School Review* 16: 425-38, September 1908.

A justification of the introduction of industrial and technical training into the high schools, and the consequent changes required in college entrance requirements.

Manny, Frank A. "A German Contribution to Education for Vocation and Citizenship." *School Review* 16: 154-61, March 1908.

"Manpower Development and Training Act: The 1963 Amendments." *School Life* 46 (March-April 1964): 12-16.

A discussion of the need for changes in the MDTA program to make it more effective. Information on the eligibility requirements under the amendments is also given.

"Manpower Development: Vo-ed for the Disadvantaged." *American Vocational Journal* 45 (Sept. 1970): 41-56.

One of this journal's regular features "Research Visibility". This issue consists of abstracts of recent research on manpower development, training the disadvantaged, training disadvantaged youth.

Margoschis, A. "Memorandum on Technical Education in Southern India." In *Great Britain. Board of Education. Special Reports on Educational Subjects.* London, Wyman & Sons, 1905, v. 14. pp. 337-40.

Markus, Henry F. "A Scheme for Grading in Manual Training." *Manual Training Magazine* 13: 450-51, June 1912.

"The use of this scheme of grading makes a monthly grade in manual training possible, which sometimes proves a great stimulus to work."

Marland, Sidney P., Jr. America's Need for Career Education." *Occupational Outlook Quarterly* 16 (Summer 1972): 2-4.

The U.S. Commissioner of Education presents the outline of a model program that integrates career orientation into the basic academic curriculum from kindergarten through high school.

Marland, Sidney, P., Jr. "Career Education: Every Student Headed for a Goal." *American Vocational Journal* 47 (Mar. 1972): 34-36 + .
An assessment of career education, and the role of the U.S. Office of Education in achieving the goals of such training, as described by the U.S. Commissioner of Education.

Marland, Sidney P., Jr. "Commissioner of Education Speaks out in Support of Vocational Youth Groups." *American Vocational Journal* 46 (Sept. 1971): 22-23.
"The U.S. Office is interested on two counts" says Dr. Marland — "its desire to strengthen the quality of vocational education and its concern for the development of well-rounded youth."

Marland, Sidney P., Jr. "Education for More than One Career." *World* 1 (Jul. 18, 1972): 46-49.
The U.S. Commissioner of Education outlines the role of the Office of Education in career education. He states: "basically, my Office sees career education as the companion to academic preparation at every grade level, from kindergarten through graduate school."

Marland, Sidney P., Jr. "Marland on Career Education." *American Education* 7 (Nov. 1971): 25-28.
Answers to questions frequently asked, posed to the U.S. Commissioner of Education by the editors of *American Education.*

Marsh, Kathleen. "Cooking, Sewing and Bench Work in the Rural School" *Atlantic Educational Journal* 8: 175-76, January 1913.
Describes the industrial work accomplished in the one-room rural school in Peru, Mass.

Marshall, Florencé M. "The Industrial Training of Women." *American Academy of Political and Social Science. Annals* 33: 119-26, January 1909.
Shows the necessity of industrial education for women. Says: "Not only are unskilled girl workers stunted in their growth physically and intellectually, but circumstances which make this possible too often result in a still more serious situation. The closed door of opportunity ahead, the wage usually too small to furnish the bare necessities of life, and the apathy resulting from monotonous labor prevent the cultivation of any ethical sense and tend to make girls careless and reckless regarding their moral standards."

Marshall, Florence M. "Manhattan Trade School for Girls." In *New York City. Department of Education. Fourteenth Annual Report . . . July 31, 1912.* pp. 341-53.
Among other items of interest, contains statistics of the earning capacity of graduates — 1910-11. "The majority of the girls trained by the school

remain at their trade, while it is common knowledge that untrained girls drift from one occupation to another."

Marshall, Florence M. "The Public School and the Girl Wage Earner." *Charities and The Commons* 19: 848-51, October 5, 1907.
　　Emphasizes the advantages of trade schools. Advocates the introduction of trade instruction into the public school system. Shows by means of graphic statistics the minimum and maximum wages of girls (from 14 to 20 years of age) without and with training.

Martin, W. Howard. "Dropouts and Agricultural Education." *Education* 85 (December 1964): 217-220.
　　How the provisions of the Vocational Education Act of 1963 provide for more flexibility in vocational agriculture and what can be done to adapt programs in agriculture for pupils "unsuited to formal schooling."

Mason, Louis, D. "School-work Programs: the Vocational Education Act in Action." *Clearing House* 42 (Jan. 1968): 294-296.
　　The implementation of a successful school-work program at Oshkosh (Wisconsin) High School, made possible by Federal funds under VEA of 1963.

Massachusetts. Board of Education. "Independent Industrial Schools." In its *Annual Report, January 1910.* pp. 137-53.
　　Schools by name. Conditions in 16 cities and towns.

Massachusetts. Commission on Industrial and Technical Education. "What the Value of the Years from Fourteen to Sixteen Might Be to Boys." In its *Report . . . April 1906.* pp. 57-69. chart.
　　To girls: pp. 70-84.
　　Summary: pp. 85-93.
　　Wages, tables: pp. 68-69, for boys; pp. 82-84, for girls.

Massachusetts. Commission on Industrial Education. "[A List of Massachusetts Evening Trade Schools]." Boston, Wright & Potter Printing Co., 1908. pp. 51-57. illus. (Bulletin no. 9)

Matheson, K. G. "Some Thoughts Concerning the Effect of Technical Education upon the Prosperity of the South." In *Georgia Educational Association. Proceedings and Addresses, 1910.* Macon, Georgia, Anderson Printing Co., 1910. pp. 59-69.
　　"Our exhaustless resources can never be fully developed until the best technical, industrial, and agricultural education possible is put within the reach of every Southern boy and girl."

Matthews, H. A. "Tomorrow Is Now in Educating for 21st Century Manpower Needs." *American Education* 3(Jun. 1967): 21-22.
　　A discussion of the purpose and aims of modern vocational education.

Mattoon, J. C. "The Common Schools from an Industrial Standpoint." in *Southern Educational Association. Journal of Proceedings and Addresses, 1908.* pp. 530-40.

Maughan, Elizabeth. "A Domestic Science Course in Schools for the Deaf." In *American Instructors of the Deaf. Proceedings, 1908.* Washington, Government Printing Office, 1909. pp. 1108-11.
    Schedule: pp. 110.
    Also in *American Annals of the Deaf,* 53: 352-58, September 1908.

Maurer, Wallace M., and Warren M. Maurer. "The Failure of Vocational Education." *School and Society* 86 (April 12, 1958): 169-170.
    Written during the "post-Sputnik" re-evaluation of our educational system, the authors point out the factors contributing to the failure of our vocational education programs to produce personnel "trained in the light of manpower needs." In addition the authors claim that "funds invested in such programs serve to continue their existence despite the adverse effects upon the individuals trained and the communities served."

Maxwell, G. E. "The Civic Value of Industrial Education for General Development." In *Minnesota Educational Association. Journal of Proceedings and Addresses, 1908.* [St. Paul, Minn., Press of Syndicate Printing Company]. pp. 270-75.

Mayer, Mary Josephine. "Vocational Training in Our Public Schools." *American Review of Reviews* 45: 449-56, April 1912.
    Argues that vocational training is not opposed to culture. Reviews the situation in this country.

Mays, Arthur B. "Fifty Years of Progress in Vocational and Practical Arts Education." *American Vocational Journal* 31: 29-38, 105, December, 1956.
    A review of programs with some historical source materials.

Mead, G. H. "Industrial Education, the Workingman and the School." *Elementary School Teacher* 9: 369-83, March 1909.
    "Two great facts stand out. One is that we are forced to reconstruct our whole apprenticeship training . . . The other is that apprenticeship provides an adequate and indeed almost the only adequate method of instructing children."

Meriam, J. L. "A Study in the Improvement of Public School Work." *Oberlin Alumni Magazine* 6: 85-90, December 1909.
    The training of teachers in the Practice schools of the University of Missouri, emphasizing studies in industrial activities.

Merrill, George Arthur. "Trade Schools and Trade Unions." In *National Education Association of the United States. Journal of Proceedings and Addresses, 1907.* pp. 1048-55.
    Reprinted in *Western Journal of Education,* 12: 501-509, October 1907.

Meyer, B. H. "The Preparation of Commercial Teachers for Work in the Public Schools." In *National Education Association of the United States. Journal of Proceedings and Addresses, 1902.* pp. 669-74.

Meyer, Ernest C. "Germany's Work in the Field of Trade Teaching." In *National Society for the Promotion of Industrial Education. Proceedings* [*1909*]. New York, 1910. pp. 156-63.

Meyer, Ernest C. "Literature on Industrial Education in Germany." In his *Industrial Education and Industrial Conditions in Germany.* Washington, Government Printing Office, 1905. pp. 145-47. (U.S. Department of Commerce and Labor. Bureau of Statistics. Special Consular Reports. v. 33).
Includes works in English and German.

Michigan. Superintendent of Public Instruction. "Industrial and Vocational Training in the Public Schools." In his *Annual Report, 1909-10.* Lansing, Michigan, Wynkoop-Hallenbeck-Crawford Co., 1910. pp. 14-25. (Bulletin no. 2)

Michigan, Superintendent of Public Instruction. "[Saginaw Trade School]" In his *Annual Report, 1909-10.* pp. 21-24.
Opened January 5, 1910.

Miles, H. E. "Work and Citizenship. The Wisconsin Experiment in Industrial Education." *Survey* 29: 682-85, February 15, 1913.
"By the Wisconsin law the local industrial schools are in the control of a committee consisting of two employers, two employees, and the city superintendent. This union of the social forces most interested becomes a new social leaven and is directly responsible for splendid results. It can not be said which is happiest and most devoted to the work, the employees, the parents, the employers, the school teachers, or the pupils."
Describes conditions in other states.
For a reply to this see Dewey, Joh. "Industrial Education and Democracy." *Survey,* 29: 870-71, 893, March 22, 1913.

Miller, F. E. "There Is a Need for Militancy in Adult Basic Education." *Adult Leadership* 17 (Jan. 1968): 68-70.
Essentials to be considered in reaching and training unemployed adults, particularly those with less than eight years of schooling. As an example, the author describes the Multi-Occupational Training Project of Philadelphia, a program founded jointly by the business community of the city and various departments of the U.S. Government.

Miller, Leslie W. "Vocational Training. The Philadelphia Textile School." *School Arts Book* 10: 501-11, January 1911. illus.

Miller, Wayne W. "Oklahoma's 21-year Experiment in Residential VE." *American Vocational Journal* 43 (Oct. 1968): 18-20.
In describing Oklahoma's two-year, post secondary vocational college,

the author believes that the major problem is in motivating students, parents, and high school teachers to "vocational thinking."

Miller, William T. "Vocation Teaching." *Atlantic Monthly* 104: 644-47, November 1909.

Milligan, L.E. "The Industrial Education of the Deaf, Blind, and Feeble-minded." In *National Education Association of the United States. Journal of Proceedings and Addresses, 1909.* pp. 885-89.
"All the trades taught have their educational value. Printing helps the pupil probably more than any other trade in gaining a command of language."

"Milwaukee School of Trades." In Ontario. *Department of Education Education for Industrial Purposes.* Toronto, 1911. pp. 198-203.
Gives curriculum.

Minear, Leon. P. "How Goes the Teamwork between Washington and the Vocational Educator?" A State-of-this-union Report. *School Shop* 28 (Dec. 1968): 31-33+.
A brief summary of current needs of vocational-technical education. Answers are given in response to questions on the role and relationship of government in regard to meeting the demands for occupational training.

Minear, Leon P. "A Piece of the Action." *American Education* 5 (Mar. 1969): 4-5.
The advantages of cooperative vocational education programs, the opportunities for establishing such programs under the Vocational Education Amendments of 1968.

Minear, Leon P. and others. "Blueprint for Vo-Tech Reform: Task Force on Vocational-Technical Education." *School Shop* 27 (Nov. 1967): 31-33.
"Priority targets" as set forth by the Task Force on Vocational-Technical Education, an organization created by the Education Commission for the States. The Task Force had as its initial purpose the designing of a "blueprint for action" by which state governments would be assisted in reviewing their educational objectives and resources, and if necessary help them to "make a clean break with the established educational structure."

Minear, Leon P. and others. "Changing the Context in Which Occupational Education Takes Place; Report by the Task Force on Vocational-Technical Education." *American Vocational Journal* 43 (Mar. 1968): 59-60.
The report discussed here contains a proposal for a Human Resources Council to be established in each state, followed by five principles for guiding these Councils.

Mobley, M. D., "Fifty Years of Progress in Vocational and Practical Arts Education." *American Vocational Journal* 31 (December 1956): 1-120.
Entire issue devoted to the progress made in vocational and practical arts

education for a fifty year period, including a history of Federal funds for vocational education.

Monaghan, J. C. "Vocational Training and the Manufacturer." *American School Board Journal* 39: 6-7, September 1909.

Monaghan, James C. "From the Standpoint of Economic and Manufacturing Interests, Should Special Trade Schools Be Established?" In *National Education Association of the United States. Journal of Proceedings and Addresses, 1909*. pp. 606-16.
Author says that manufacturers should organize and appoint experts to study the methods that have made Germany, Japan, and other countries so successful. Industrial and industrial-art education must take the place of the system of apprenticeship which has gone or is fast going. "The governments — state and national — show more or less interest. It remains only for the manufacturers to co-operate."

Monaghan, J. C. "Industrial Education in Germany." In *New York [State] University Convocation, 1900*. Albany, University of the State of New York. 1900. pp. 187-208. (Regents bulletin, no. 51, October 1900)
Discussion: pp. 208-12.

Moore, J. "How to Get Money for Vocational Education." *American Education* 4 (Dec. 1967): 10-11.
Basic information is given on the National Vocational Student Loan Program.

Morley, M. D. "Manpower . . . A Serious National Problem." *American Vocational Journal* 38 (May 1963): 8-10.
The executive secretary of the American Vocational Association explains why "more adequate and effective programs of vocational and technical education are needed" to provide work opportunities for "present and oncoming generations."

Morley, M. D. "Review of Federal Vocational-Education Legislatin, 1862-1963." *Theory Into Practice* 3 (December 1964): 167-170.
The author is the executive secretary of the American Vocational Association. A brief summary of Federal assistance to vocational education is given, and a more detailed report of the Manpower and Training Act of 1962 and the Vocational Education Act of 1963 is included.

Morley, M.D. "Vocational Education Outlook for the 60's." *American Vocational Journal* 35 (March 1960): 9-11. Also in *Overview* 1 (January 1960): 41-43.
A forecast of what can be expected in vocational education expansion for this decade by the executive secretary of AVA. Among Dr. Mobley's predictions are programs for adults, area programs embracing area vocational schools, comprehensive high schools with strong vocational and practical arts courses, especially in semirural areas and in large cities.

Morman, Robert R. "Automation, Dropouts, and Guidance." *National Association of Secondary-School Principals Bulletin* 48 (November 1964): 83-98.

Topics discussed in this article: Labor force projections and job changes within the next generation, providing effective vocational training for the out-of-school, unemployed youth, how vocational guidance will have to change to meet the demands of counseling in an automated age.

Morrison, G. B. "The Present Status and Future of Manual Training in the High School." In *National Society for the Scientific Study of Education, Fourth Year-book. pt.* 2 pp. 18-37.

Discusses the origin, growth and present conditions of manual training. Deals with the relation between vocational and cultural studies.

Morrison, Henry C. "Vocational Training and Industrial Education." *Educational Review* 36: 242-54, October 1908.

"So far as industrial education seeks to be a more efficient means of social betterment, so far will it be welcome; . . . so far as it involves a tendency to stratify American society, it must be held to be contrary to the spirit of our institutions."

Morse, Charles H. "An International Industrial School Beginning at the Sixth School Year." In *National Education Association of the United States. Journal of Proceedings and Addresses, 1908.* pp. 173-76.

Also in *Journal of Education,* 67: 482-83, April 30, 1908.

Outlines course for boys intending to go into the trades. Discusses the difference between manual training and industrial education.

Moss, Jerome. "Universal Vocational Education: A Vital Element of Public Education." *Educational Forum* 28 (November 1963): 63-70.

Vocational education as a public responsibility and its place in the secondary-school program are two aspects discussed in this article.

Moulton, Leonard B. "A Course in Salesmanship." *School Review* 20: 56-59, January 1912.

Methods pursued in the Boston high school of commerce.

"Moving Pictures as an Aid to Teaching Trades." *Scientific American Supplement* 67, 76, January 30, 1909.

Mowry, Duane. "Vocational or Cultural Education–Which? The Amherst Idea." *Education* 32: 373-76, February 1912.

Declares that specialization in education is one of the necessities in this work-a-day world, but we should not forget that mere specialization is not the whole of the education field. Commends the Amherst idea.

Münsterberg, Hugo. "The College and the Household Sciences." *Good Housekeeping* 56: 40-48, January 1913.

Advocates household courses in colleges and universities, and shows the insistent demand for such instruction.

Munroe, James P. "The Educational Bearings of Manual Training." In *Reprinted Manual Training Association. Proceedings, 1903.* pp. 70-82.

Murray, Michael W. "The Study of Printing." *Manual Training Magazine* 9: 329-34, April 1908.

Murray, Michael W. "The Training of Teachers for Industrial Work." In *National Education Association of the United States. Journal of Proceedings and Addresses, 1910.* pp. 621-24.

Musselman, H. T. "The Work of the College of Industrial Arts." *Texas School Magazine* 15: 7-9, December 1912.
    Describes what is being done at the College of Industrial Arts at Denton, Texas.

Mussey, H. R. "Education and Pay of Head and Hand." *Educational Review* 42: 450-64, December 1911.
    Advocates vocational training and guidance.

Nabel, Eugene. "The Schools of Switzerland." *Educational Foundations* 23: 95-101, 180-84, 297-300, October, November 1911, January 1912.
    Contains a brief account of the Swiss societies for promoting commercial education.

National Association of the Deaf. Bureau of Industrial Statistics. "Report." In its *Proceedings, 1907.* Hampton, Va., Houston, Va., Houston Printing and Publishing House, pp. 48-62.

National Association of the Deaf. Committee on Industrial Status of the Deaf. "Report." In *World's Congress of the Deaf . . . Proceedings, 1904.* Fort Smith, Arkansas, Thrash-Sick Printing Co. pp. 190-228.
    Chairman, Warren Robinson.
    "A period of ten years in school appears to give the best average results. Below seven years insufficient in most cases."

National Association of Manufacturers of the United States of America. Committee on Industrial-Educaton. "Report . . . " *Twelfth Annual Convention, New York City, May 20-22, 1907. Proceedings.* pp. 110-38.
    Discusses the necessity for trade schools and the attitude of labor unions toward them. Describes some of the newer American technical schools.

National Education Association of the United States. Department of Business Education. *Journal of Proceedings and Addresses, 1912.* pp. 1031-93.
    Contains valuable papers on training in salesmanship; high school commercial courses; business organization, etc.

National Education Association of the United States. Department of Manual Training. Committee on the Place of Industries in Public Education. "Report . . . " In its *Journal of Proceedings and Addresses, 1910.* Published by the Association, 1910. pp. 652-59; 680-788.

Jesse D. Burks, chairman.

Contains: 1. Report of subcommittee on the place of industries in the elementary school, p. 680-710. 2. Report of subcommittee on intermediate industrial schools, p. 710-31. 3. Report of subcommittee on industrial and technical education in the secondary school, p. 731-66.

A selected bibliography on industrial education, p. 766-73.

Papers: p. 659-80; 774-83 (with discussion).

Reprinted as separate. The Association, 1910. 123 p. 8.

Prof. F. T. Carleton, speaking of the industrial factor in social progress says: "In the process of adjustment involved in passing from small-scale and unsystematic to large-scale and routinized industry, social and political institutions, including the public school system, must undergo fundamental modifications." He declares that a science of education must rest on "the basis of social and economic progress and demands. Until this basic truth is clearly recognized no science of education can be formulated."

National Education Association of the United States. Department of Manual Training and Art Education. *Journal of Proceedings and Addresses, 1912.* pp. 897-1000.

Contains 1: C. B. Connelley: Citizenship in industrial education, pp. 899-907. 2. W. T. Bawden: The relation of the elementary school to subsequent industrial education, pp. 907-12. 3. C. A. McMurry: The significance of the industrial arts in the schools, pp. 918-21. 4. F. M. Leavitt: Some sociological phases of the movement for industrial education, pp. 921-26. 5. F. D. Crawshaw: Needed changes in manual arts, pp. 932-42. 6. C. R. Dooley: The manufacturers' viewpoint of industrial education, pp. 952-54. 7. J. A. Pratt: Modern apprenticeship training, pp. 955-58.

National Education Association of the United States. National Council of Education, Committee on Industrial Education in Schools for Rural Communities. "Supplementary Report . . . July 8, 1907." In its *Journal of Proceedings and Addresses, 1907.* pp. 409-54. illus.

L. D. Harvey, chairman.

A more extended discussion than the first report. Summarizes the purposes and values of industrial education for the children in rural communities, etc. Describes three typical schools in New York State, Illinois, and Missouri; scope and character of preparation of teachers of industrial subjects in the different kinds of schools investigated, and the conditions under which this preparation can be secured in this country.

National Education Association of the United States. Subcommittee on Industrial and Technical Education in the Secondary School "Report." In its *Journal of Proceedings and Addresses, 1910.* pp. 731-66.

National Society for the Promotion of Industrial Education. "[Report of the Meeting Held at Philadelphia, Pa., December 5, 6, and 7, 1912]." *Journal of Education* 76: 683-87, December 26, 1912.

See also Vocational Education, 2: 318-33, March 1913. Ably reviewed by William T. Bawden under the title of "Recent Progress in the Movement for Vocational Education."

"The most important piece of work," says Mrs. Bawden, "accomplished at this convention and perhaps the most important that has yet been accomplished in the movement as a whole, is the formulation of a 'statement of principles and policies that should underlie legislation for vocational education.' "

"National Vo-ed Council Urges Sweeping Reforms. *School Shop* 29 (Feb. 1970): 14, 18.
     A condensation of the first annual report of the U.S. National Advisory Council on Vocational Education. The report recommends major policy changes for the federal government in its approach to funding, the role of the U.S. Office of Education in vocational training, present and proposed manpower policies and legislation.

Nearing, Scott. "Industrial Education." In his *Biennial Report, 1909-11* [Lincoln, 1911]. pp. 113-313. illus.
     Conditions in Nebraska.

Neff, Monroe, C. "Adult Basic Education in North Carolina." *Adult Leadership* 13 (March 1965): 277-278, 305.
     Activities now under way in North Carolina for adult basic education under the Economic Opportunity Act of 1964. Describes also the teacher training institutes to prepare instructors for the basic education programs, and materials used in instruction.

Nelson, Richard S. "A Developmental Mode and Delivery System." *American Vocational Journal* 45(Mar. 1970) : 31-33, 36.
     How the state of California plans and evaluates its vocational education programs through a "systems approach", developed by three members of its State Department of Education staff. The author of this article is one of these staff members.

Newark, N. J. Board of Eduation. "Some Aspects of the Industrial Education Problem." In its *Annual Report, 1909-10*. pp. 93-98.
     The Warren Street Vocational school for boys, Newark, N. J., pp. 98-104.

"New Developments Under Vocational Educational Act — a Nationalwide Roundup." *School Shop* 25(April 1966) : 49-90.
     A group of 13 articles by leading vocational education personnel, each article describing a phase of the Vocational Education Act of 1963 and the goals attained through it.

Newell, A. C. "A Lesson Plan and Some Shop Lecture Outlines." *Manual Training Magazine* 13: 297-305, April 1912.
     The writer is convinced that class teaching is far better at the beginning of any course in shop work.

New Hampshire. Superintendent of Public Instruction. "The Influence of

Secondary Schools upon Movements of Population and upon Vocation." In his *Report* . . . Concord, 1908. pp. 261-70.
    Reprinted.

New Hampshire. Superintendent of Public Instruction. "Work in Secondary Schools Having Industrial Courses." In his *Report*. Concord, 1908. pp. 280-302. illus.

New York City. Department of Education. "Vocational School for Boys." In its *Annual Report*, July 31, 1912. pp. 354-62.

"New York City Trade School. "In *Ontario. Department of Education. Education for Industrial Purposes* . . . Toronto, 1911. pp. 203.
    Gives curriculum.

New York (State) Education Department. "Vocational School." In its *Annual Report, 1909*. Albany, N. Y., State Education Department, 1910. pp. 517-41.
    Reprinted.
    Schools organized under the law of 1908. pp. 535.

Nonell-Sayre, Adophe. "Girls' Technical High School of New York.' *School Journal* 69: 528-32, November 26, 1904.
    Name of the school changed to Washington Irving high school.

North Dakota Educational Association. Committee of Seven." On Adjustment of Educational Work in North Dakota with Reference to the Needs of the Times. Preliminary Report." In its *Proceedings, 1908-1909*. pp. 35-51.
    Chairman, C. C. Schmidt.
    Reprinted. The association[1908] 21 pp.
Rep Report. In its Proceedings, 1909. pp. 48-105.
    Discussion: pp. 10; 5-11.

Novak, B. J., and M. E. Sundheim. "Careers for Potential Dropouts." *Education* 85(December 1964) : 199-205.
    A review of existing programs which have been initiated to provide job training for potential school dropouts. Programs in Philadelphia, Pa., are among those discussed.

Noyes, William. "The Ethical Values of the Manual and Domestic Arts." *Manual Training Magazine* 11: 201-13, February 1910.

Noyes, William. "Overwork Idleness or Industrial Education?" In *National Child Labor Committee. Proceedings of Second Annual Meeting*. New York, 1906. pp. 84-95.
    "The alarming increase of neurotic diseases among school children, the crying need of facilities for play, and the social necessity for industrial education-all three facts point in the same direction namely, that the school

must assume the responsibility for a greater share of the child's time."

Nye, B. C., and W. B. Logan. "Courses for Upgrading the Vocational Skills of Adults." *Theory Into Practice* 3(December 1964): 179-182.
A discussion of the types of programs available under Federal sponsorship to train adults for a wider range of job opportunities.

Nye, L. B. "Rational Vocational Work in Smaller High Schools." *Pennsylvania School Journal* 59: 502-506, April 1911.
The vocational training of sixteen high schools, in reply to circulars of enquiry.

Ogden, Robert C. "Industrial Education from a Layman's Point of View." In *New York (State) University Convocation, 1905.* Albany, New York (State) Education Department, 1906. pp. 51-58. (Department Bulletin no. 3)
A plea for a broader and more scientific approach to the problem.

Ogilvie, W. K. "Occupational Education and the Community College." *Educational Leadership* 22 (January 1965): 244-246 +.
Examples of occupational training programs in the community colleges of various States.

O'Hara, Edward. "The First Step to Employability." *American Vocational Journal* 40 (October 1965): 14-15.
General information on the Job Corps, established by the Office of Economic Opportunity to give deprived youth basic training for employment.

"Ohio Education Association. OEA Special Report: an Analysis of the Report of the Governor's Task Force on Vocational and Technical Education." *Ohio Schools* 47 (Jan. 24, 1969): Insert 8 leaves.
A concise review of the report issued by a special Task Force appointed by Governor James A. Rhodes on July 19, 1968. The report deals with the shortcomings of vocational and technical education in Ohio and includes as a recommendation "a clear alliance and identification" between technical education and Ohio's state universities.

Ohio. State Commissioner of Common Schools. "Industrial Education." In his *Annual Report, 1909.* Springfield, Ohio. Springfield Publishing Company, State Printers, 1910. pp. 11-21.

Oleson, E. B. "Industrial-vocational Education for Needs of Youth and Adults." *South Dakota Educational Association Journal* 40(May 1965): 6-10.
The author is the State Director of Vocational Education in South Dakota. In this article he makes a distinction between "industrial arts" and "vocational education" by stating that "the former is a curriculum area while . . . the latter is to fit persons for useful employment in specific occupations."

Olive, C. Thomas. "A Leadership Training Breakthrough for the New

Vocational Training." *School Shop* 24 (April 1965): 54-55.
A description of New York State's program to train top-level administrators for vocational training programs. The author states ". . . the plan is feasible and practical to apply in other States."

Olson, J.C. "Pittsburgh's Bid to Blend Programs and Facilities: Great High Schools Project." *School Shop* 27 (May 1968): 31-34.
The accomplishments of the Occupational, Vocational and Technical Education Division of the Pittsburgh Public Schools. The twofold purpose of this Division is to initiate occupational training in existing academic high schools and design future projects to make vocational education more effective.

Olson, Jerry C. "The Marriageability of Vocational Education." *School Shop* 25 (October 1965): 39-42.

Description of a program initiated in the Pittsburgh, Pa., public high schools to "seek to end the separation of vocational schools and curriculums from the general academic programs."

"Operations Under National Apprenticeship Program." *Monthly Labor Review* 69 (August 1949): 126-130.
Brief review of the National Apprenticeship Program developed as an economic measure in the early 1930's, and its transfer to the U.S. Department of Labor in 1937. Statistics are given concerning the growth of this form of vocational training for the 1939-48 period.

Orr, Fred J. "Manual Arts in Rural Schools." In *Southern Educational Association. Journal of Proceedings and Addresses, 1905.* pp. 178-87.
Also in Southern Educational Review, 3: 882-92, April-May 1906.

Osgood, Clarence. "Raising the Standard of Efficiency in Work: Practical Training Given by the Manhattan Trade School for Girls." *Craftsman* 12: 634-41, September 1907.

Owens, C. J. "Secondary Industrial Education in Alabama." In *Alabama Educational Association. Official Proceedings, 1909.* pp. 138-46.
A course of study based on an elementary course of seven grades, p. 141-43.

"PCP: A Program to Rehabiliate Dropouts." *School Management* 9 (August 1965): 39-41.
A new program called Personalized Curriculum Project has been initiated in Oscoda, Mich., to give high school dropouts an opportunity for work and study.

Page, Walter H. "The Unfulfilled Ambition of the South." In *Conference for Education in the South. Proceedings, 1904.* New York, Issued by the Committee on Publication, 1904. pp. 98-110.

Passow, A. Harry. "Once Again: Reforming Secondary Education." *Teachers College Record* No. 77: 161-187, December, 1975.
  A review of five recent studies of the American high school and related institutions engaged in the education of adolescents and youth:
  (1) B. Frank Brown, The National Commission of the Reform of Secondary Education. The Reform of Secondary Education: A Report to the Public and the Profession (New York: McGraw-Hill, 1973): (2) James S. Coleman, Chairman, President's Science Advisory Committee. Youth: Transition to Adulthood (University of Chicago Press, 1974); (3) John H. Martin, Chairman, National Panel on High Schools and Adolescent Education. Report of the National Panel on High Schools and Adolescent Education (U. S. Office of Education, 1974); (4) NASSP. National Committee on Secondary Education. American Youth in the Mid-Seventies (Washington: National Association of Secondary School Principals, 1972); (5) Ruth Weinstock, ed. The Greening of the High School (New York: Educational Facilities Laboratories, 1973).

Pearse, Carroll G. "The City Trade School — An Important Instrumentality for Improving the Vocational Need of the City Child." In *National Education Association of the United States. Journal of Proceedings and Addresses, 1912.* pp. 411-16.
  Commends the American type of trade school. Shows the money value of the training in a good trade school.

Perry, Charles F. "The Milwaukee School of Trades." *American Academy of Political and Social Science. Annals* 33: 78-84, January 1909.
  The school was incorporated in the public school system, by act effective July 1, 1907.

Perry, Charles F. "The Public Trade School." In *North Central Association of Colleges and Secondary Schools. Proceedings, 1909.* Chicago, Published by the Association, 1909. pp. 89-100.
  "The influence of the trade school should be used in bridging the fatal gap between fourteen and sixteen years of age."

Perry, Charles F. "Trade Teaching in the Public Schools." In *Western Drawing and Manual Training Association. Proceedings, 1909.* [Normal, Ill., c1909] pp.131-142.
  Discussion: pp. 143-47.

Perry, Clarence Arthur. "Evening Schools." In his *Wider Use of the School Plant.* New York, Charities Publication Committee, 1910. pp. 19-114. illus.
  Evening schools abroad, pp. 55-78. The promotion of attendance at evening schools, pp. 81-114.

Person, Harlow Stafford. "Ideal Organization of a System of Secondary Schools to Provide Vocational Training." *School review* 17: 404-16, June 1909.

Phipps, Lloyd J. and Rupert N. Evans. "Curriculum Development." *Review of Educational Research* 38 (Oct. 1968): 367-381.

Curriculum development literature is reviewed here on a selected basis. Research topics include curriculum for students with special needs, the adaption of curriculum to change in educational technology and occupational areas.

Pittsburg University. "Co-operative Plan of Engineering Instruction." In its *Annual Catalogue, 1910.* pp. 123-25.

"The money consideration received for this practical work will be ordinarily sufficient to meet the tuition expenses for [the students'] entire course at the University.

"Place and Role of Vocational Education in the Total School Program." *American Vocational Journal* 40 (February 1965): 33-35.

Summary of discussion by State Directors of Vocational Education at the 58th annual convention of the American Vocational Association, 1964.

Plaisted, Laura L. "Educational Handwork." In her *The Early Education of Children.* Oxford, Clarendon Press, 1910. pp. 309-49. illus.

Portland, Oreg. Board of Education. "School of Trades." In its *Annual Report, 1909.* pp. 261-75. illus. 1910. pp. 263-75.illus.

Curriculum: pp. 263, 273-75.

Portland, Oreg. Board of Education. "School of Trades." In its *Annual Report, 1909.* pp. 261-75. illus. 1910. pp. 263-75. illus.

Curriculum: pp. 263, 273-75.

"Post-secondary Vocational Education." *American Vocational Journal* 44 (Feb. 1969): 68-69.

Summary of addresses given at the 62nd annual Vocational Education Convention in the Post-Secondary Department session.

Pragan, Otto. "Bridging the Vocational Gap." *American Federationist* 76 (Jul. 1969): 1-6.

Too many people are forced into on-the-job training, because of limited or nonexistent high school vocational training. The author points out the many changes that are needed in vocational education and enumerates the recommendations of the National Advisory Council, all of which advocate change in specific areas.

Pragan, Otto. "Labor's State in Vocational Education." *American Vocational Journal* 40 (March 1965): 13-14, 32.

Excerpts from an address delivered at the 1964 American Vocational Association convention by the assistant director of education, AFL-CIO.

Prescott, William B. "Trade Teaching Under the Auspices of the Typographical Union." *American Academy of Political and Social Science. Annals* 33: 178-84. January 1909.

Prescott, William B. "Trade Unions and Industrial Education." In *National Education Association of the United states. Department of Superintendence. Proceedings, 1910.* pp. 127-35.
    Also in School exchange, 1: 346-54, March 1910.
    Largely the work of the International Typographical Union; the correspondence course in printing.

Pritchett, Henry S. "The Place of Industrial and Technical Training in Popular Education." *Educational Review* 23: 281-303, March 1902.
    Discusses the growth of the higher technical education; demand for industrial training in elementary education; opportunities offered in Boston; solution of the problem in Berlin.

Probst, A. F. "The School Print Shop and its Possibilities." *Elementary School Teacher* 8: 265-70, January 1908.

Prosser, C.A. "Practical Arts and Vocational Guidance." *Manual Training Magazine* 14: 209-21, February 1913.
    An interesting presentation of the subject of vocational guidance. Shows the importance of the elementary school period. Discusses the problems that confront the teacher. If training in the practical arts is to assist boys "to find themselves in order that at 14 they may make an intelligent choice of their work for the future, it must be varied."

Prosser, Charles A. "Facilities for Industrial Education." *Vocational Education* 2: 189-203, January 1913.
    "Of immediate practical value to committees and boards of education considering the problems of ways and means."

Prosser, Charles A. "Massachusetts State-aided Vocational Schools." In *Massachusetts. Board of Education. 75th Annual Report . . . January 1912.* Boston, 1912. pp. 48-65. (Public document no. 2)
    The movement for vocational training has spread rapidly in Massachusetts since the first law giving state aid and encouragement to practical training was passed in 1906. Says the report: "In the year 1907-8, 6 schools gave, through day or evening classes, training in 4 occupations to about 1,400 persons. During the last school year there were 21 schools instructing about 6,000 persons through day, part-time, and evening classes, fitting for more than 50 occupations within more than 15 distinct industries. It is probably safe to say that for the present school year, 1911-12, there will be a total registration of more than 7,000 pupils in not less than 40 state-aided vocational schools."
    Give interesting statistical diagrams showing the growth of state-aided vocational schools; investment and expenditures of schools; and industries for which training is given, as follows: painting, stoneworking, textiles, agriculture, jewelry, bookbinding, printing, electrical working, high power machine work, millinery, dressmaking, household arts, motive power, metal working, and woodworking.

Prosser, Charles. A. "Organization and Administration of State-Aided

Vocational Schools. In *Massachusetts. Board of Education. 75th Annual Report . . . January 1912*. Boston, 1912. pp. 137-88. (Public document no. 2.)

Contents. — I. What is a state-aided vocational school. II. The establishment of state-aided vocational schools. III. The administration of vocational schools. IV. Courses of study and methods of instruction.

Appendices 1 and 2 contain data concerning legislation; Appendix 4, "Information regarding the approval of the qualifications of teachers in the state-aided vocational schools of Massachusetts," pp. 183-88.

Providence, R. I. School Committee. "Evening School Extension." In its *Report, 1905-6*. pp. 27-35.

Providence, R. I. School Committee. "Vocational Talks." In its *Report, 1909-1910*. pp. 59-64.

Subjects of talks given the pupils not going on into high school from 8th grade, in Providence. pp. 61-62.

Pucinski, Roman C. "Education in a Trillion Dollar Economy." *American Vocational Journal* 43 (Feb. 1968): 10-12.

An address given by Congressman Pucinski at the 61st annual convention. In it he describes the educational revolution now underway and what role vocational education can take in reconstructing the American Educational System for greater relevance.

Punke, H. H. "Outlook for Humanizing All Vocatinal Education." *American Vocational Journal* 43 (May 1968): 19-20, 32.

The author contends that "education must provide for both the general and vocational development of young Americans if they are to function constructively in a complex industrial economy."

Rapp, Eli. M. "Vocational Possibilities in Country Schools." *Pennsylvania School Journal* 57: 376-81, March 1909.

Reprinted.

Rathmann, C. G. "Vocational Training in Germany." *Educational Foundations* 23: 155-70, 228-39, November, December 1911.

A discussion of the continuation schools of Germany — commercial, agricultural, etc.

Ray, E. M. "Social and Philosophical Framework." *Review of Educational Research* 38 (Oct. 1968): 309-325.

A review of the literature published from January 1963-March 1968 on the social and philosophical justification for vocational education in our contemporary society.

Reading, Pa. Board of Education. "Report of Superintendent on Manual Training." In its *Minutes, March 23, 1909*. pp. 34-72. Also in its *Biennial Report, 1907-1909*, pp. 514-50.

Contains synopsis of detailed information secured by means of a questionnaire sent to one hundred cities.

"Recent Legislation Concerning Vocational Education." *Vocational Education (Peoria)* 1 : 43-50, September 1911.

Reed, H. J. "Educational Changes for Manpower Development." *Vocational Guidance Quarterly* 17 (Dec. 1968): 82-86.
An official of the U.S. Employment Service outlines the methods for mobilizing the training resources of the country, both in the public and private sector, in order to meet the educational needs of our citizens. He also suggests a regulatory educational body, created either voluntarily or by Federal action to implement such a mobilization.

Reynolds, J. H. "Higher Technical Instruction." In *Imperial Education Conference. Report, 1911.* London, Printed by Eyre and Spottiswood, 1911. pp. 133-48.
Deals chiefly with the German technical high schools.

Reynolds, John Hugh. "Relation of Education to Production." *Arkansas School Journal* 10 : 10-14, February 1906.
A strong plea for Arkansas to furnish proper training for the development of its industrial, resources by its own trained men.
Presidential address, Arkansas Teachers' Association.
Reprinted.

Rice, Oliver. "Some Observations on the Women's Job Corp." *Audiovisual Instruction* 13(Feb. 1968) : 130-137.
The accomplishments of the Clinton, Iowa, Job Corps Center for women, operated by the General Learning Corporation under contract with the U. S. Office of Economic Opportunity.

Richards, Charles R. "Progress in Industrial Education during the Year Education]." In his *Progress in Industrial Education During the Year 1910-11. U.S. Bureau of Education. Report of the Commissioner for the Year 1911.* pp. 299-311.

Richards, Charles R. "The Problem of Industrial Education." *Manual Training Magazine* 8 : 125-32, April 1907.
Brief analysis of the economic, social, and educational aspects of the problem, with a statement of the functions and limitations of the various existing agencies for industrial training.

Richards, Charles R. "Progress in Industrial Education During the Year 1910-11." In *U.S. Bureau of Education. Report of the Commissioner for the Year 1911:* 1. Washington, Government Printing Office, 1912. pp. 299-311.
Reviews legislation for the year 1910-11, and discusses recently developed tendencies.

Richards, Charles Russell. "Private Trade Schools for Boys." *Charities and The Commons* 19: 828-39, October 5, 1907.

Professor Richards divides these schools into two classes—the short-course trade school and the long-course trade school. The problem presented is the economic one of support. Describes six of the most prominent short-course trade schools of the country; their means of support, admission requirements, and results obtained by their students.

Richards, Charles Russell. "The Relation of Manual Training to Industrial Education." In *Eastern Art Teachers' Association, Eastern Manual Training Association, Western Drawing and Manual Training Association. Proceedings of Joint Meeting, 1907.* pp. 77-85.

Also in *Journal of Pedagogy,* 19: 240-50, June 1907; and in *Manual Training magazine* 9: 1-9, October 1907.

Richmond, Sada Foute. "The Vocational School." *Progressive Teacher* 18: 35-36, April 1912.

An account of the first vocational public school started in the South, at Memphis, Tenn.

Riger, Morris. "The Changing Priorities in National Manpower Policy: The Manpower Effort." *Economic and Business Bulletin* (Temple University) 21 (Spring 1969): 10-22.

A summary of training and employment activities in the U.S. during the decade of the 1960's.

Ristau, R. A. "Comprehensive High School Education for Occupations." *Wisconsin Journal of Education* 97(February 1965): 20-21.

General information on Wisconsin's implementation of the Vocational Act of 1963.

Rivlin, Alice M. "An Economist Looks at Vocational Education." *American Vocational Journal* 40 (December 1965): 9-10.

An economist in the Brookings Institute, Washington, D.C., examines these questions: "How much vocational education or training should the labor force have? . . . "Where should the training for work occur?" . . . "How should the costs of training be shared between the worker, the employer, and the taxpayer?"

Roberts, Arthur W. "The Basis of an Efficient Education—Culture or Vocation." *School Review* 15: 358-74, May 1907.

Argument against too early differentiation for vocational training.

Roberts, Elmer. "The Passing of the Unskilled in Germany." *Scribner's Magazine* 51: 199-204, February 1912.

A review of the status of continuation trade and commercial schools of Germany. According to the author "the processes at work tend to convert the whole population into the users of tools and machinery."

Robinson, James Harvey. "The Significance of History in Industrial Education." *Educational Bi-monthly* 4: 376-89, June 1910.

"Read before the superintendents of schools of the larger cities at the meeting of the National Education Association at Indianapolis, March 2, 1910."

Robinson, Theodore W. "The Need of Industrial Education in Our Public Schools." In *National Education Association of the United States. Journal of Proceedings and Addresses, 1910.* pp. 369-73.

"[Rochester, Minn., 'Job' Bureau]." *American School Board Journal* 42: 42, June 1911.

Roden, Carl and others. "A Bibliography of Vocational and Industrial Education and Vocational Guidance." *Educational Bi-monthly* (Pub. by Board of Education, City of Chicago) 7:270-79, February 1913.

Rogers, Howard J. "The Relation of Education to Industrial and Commercial Development." *Educational Review* 23: 490-502.

Discusses national development in material progress; the struggle for commercial and industrial supremacy, etc. Our system of public education. Contrasts American with foreign conditions in regard to the working classes.

Rogers, Virgil M. "What Kind of an Education in a World of Automation?" *National Association of Secondary-School Principals Bulletin* 48 (November 1964): 47-55.

Mr. Rogers, the director of the National Education Association sponsored project on the Educational Implications of Automation, lists 10 specific goals that must be accomplished in education if we are to improve its quality in an age of automation.

"The Role and Responsibility of Government toward Unemployed Youth." *The American Child* 43 (November 1961): 20 pp.

Issue devoted to the problems of the Nation's 800,000 unemployed, out-of-school youth. Contents: Government and the Problems of Youth by William Gomberg; Who's Afraid of Work by Buford Ellington; The Youth Employment Opportunities Act of 1961 by Carl D. Perkins; The Philadelphia Youth Conservation Corps by Randolph Wise; International Youth Employment by Mildred F. Woodbury.

"Role of Secondary Schools in Preparing Youth for Jobs." *National Association of Secondary School Principals Bulletin* 52 (Feb. 1968): 90-113.

The summary, conclusions and recommendations of the report written by Jacob J. Kaufman and others, and entitled "Role of the Secondary Schools in the Preparation of Youth for Employment". (See entry under Kaufman, Jacob J.) in Part I — Books and Monographs)

Rollins, Frank. "Industrial Education and Culture." *Educational Review* 34: 494-503, December 1907.

Address before Schoolmasters' Association of New York and vicinity, October 1907.

Roman, Frederick W. "Control of the Industrial Schools of Germany." *Elementary School Teacher* 13: 269-73, February 1913.

Owing to the dual school organization in Prussia, there has been a conflict of interests between the clerical party and those interested in industrial education. The clericals want "a guaranty that one hour per week shall be given over to their hands for religious instruction. The other party claims that religious teaching has no place in a trade school. As it is now, only the districts or communes can make attendance compulsory. The result is that for the most part Prussia has only voluntary trade-school attendance."

The author says that two public-school systems in the same city create jealousy. The interests of the people are divided; a feeling of class division in society exists, thus undermining democracy. Munich leads all German cities in its trade-school development, because it has a united school system. Describes conditions in the states of Wurttemberg and Baden, which were the first to develop industrial schools.

Roncovieri, Alfred. "The Relations of Organized Labor and Technical Education." *University of California Chronicle* 12: 368-80, October 1910.

Root, Martha L. "Carnegie Technical Schools." *World To-day* 20: 704-11, June 1911.

Routten, William W. "Industrial Education in Our Common Schools." In *Alabama Educational Association. Proceedings, 1911.* pp. 83-87.

Rumpf, E. L. "Planning Job Ahead." *American Vocational Journal* 44 (Apr. 1969): 24-26.

Implementing the 1968 Vocational Education Amendments will require more comprehensive planning for local, state and federal agencies engaged in vocational education programs.

Runkle, John D. "The Manual Element in Education." In (Massachusetts State Board of Education) *Forty-First Annual Report of the Board Together with the Annual Report of the Secretary of the Board* (Boston, 1878).

Influential plea for manual training which attracted national attention.

Russell, James Earl. "Discussion on How to Fit Industrial Training Into Our Course of Study." In *New York (State) University Convocation, 1906.* Albany, New York (State) Education Department, 1906. pp. 59-67. (Department bulletin no. 3)

Russell, James Earl. "The Point of View in Industrial Education." In *New York State Teacher's Association. Proceedings, 1909.* Albany, University of the State of New York, 1910. pp. 8-19. (Education Department. Bulletin no. 483, November 15, 1910)

Russell, James Earl. "The School and Industrial Life." *Educational Review* 38 : 433-50, December 1909.
A plea for industrial training. Regards it as "essential to the well-being of a democracy."

Russo, Michael. "14 Million Vocational Students by 1975." *American Education* 5 (Mar. 1969): 10-11.
Statistics on enrollments, local and state personnel, facilities and expenditures for fiscal years 1966-1968 and projections for 1970 and 1975.

Russo, Michael. "The What and Why of the Area Vocational School." *Industrial Arts and Vocational Education* 54 (November 1965): 28-32.
A special report prepared by an official of the U.S. Office of Education's Division of Vocational and Technical Education. It explains the provisions for planning and developing area vocational schools as authorized under the Vocational Education Act of 1963.

Rynearson, Edward. "Co-operation of the Business Men of Pittsburg with the Commercial Department of Its High School." *School Review* 18 : 333-38, May 1910.

"Saginaw (Mich.) High School. Employment Bureau." *Moderator Topics* 31: 543, March 16, 1911.

St. Louis, Mo. Board of Education. "Vocation Courses." In its *Annual Report, 1910.* pp. 116-32.

"[St. Louis, Mo. The David Ranken, Jr., School of Mechanical Trades]." *Manual Training Magazine* 11 : 289-90, February 1910. *Survey* 25 : 674-76, January 21, 1910. illus.
Endowment $3,000,000.

Santora, A. C. "Industry Takes STEP to Find Training Solutions." *American Vocational Journal* 42 (Sept. 1967): 22-23.
A description of a clearing house for information called STEP (Solutions to Employment Problems) initiated by the National Association of Manufacturers. Designed to bridge the "gap between learning and earning", STEP makes available hundreds of solutions to problems confronting the vocational educator.

Sargent, Walter. "The Place of Manual Arts in the Secondary Schools." *School Review* 18: 99-107, February 1910.

Schaefer, C. J. "Accountability; A Sobering Thought." *American Vocational Journal* 44 (Apr. 1969): 21-23.
Included in the 1968 Vocational Education Amendments are requirements never known before, thereby demanding a new concept of "accountability" for vocational educators. The author discusses the steps by

which such educators can prepare to render their reports later to the Congress and to the public.

Schaefer, Carl J. "The Old Stereotypes No Longer Apply to Job Training." *School Shop* 24(April 1965): 60-61, 118.

Reasons why the Vocational Education Act of 1963 may well serve as "the epitaph to vocational education as we have known it." The author predicts new organizational patterns and an increase of quality training under the new act.

Scheer, Meyer. "Industrial Work." *Philippine Education* 6: 22-23, November 1909.

Schmitt, Marshall L. "Opportunities for Industrial Arts Education." *Industrial Arts and Vocational Education* 54(June 1965): 16,43.

The specialist for industrial arts education, U. S. Office of Education, explains in this article how funds in the new Elementary and Secondary Education Act of 1965 may benefit industrial arts education.

Schneider, Herman. "Co-operative System of Technical Education." *Engineering Magazine* 34: 354, November 1907.

Details plan of co-operation existing between the University of Cincinnati and the manufacturers of the city. Students obtain shop practice in the different local industrial plants.

Schneider, Herman. "Growth of Co-operative System." In *National Metal Trades Association. Synopsis of Proceedings of 12th Annual Convention, 1910.* pp. 32-35.

Describes the St. Louis plan of co-operation with factories.

Schneider, Herman. "Partial Time Trade Schools." In *American Academy of Political and Social Science. Annals* 33: 50-55. January 1909.

Recommends a broad plan of co-operation between the public schools and the industries.

"Schooling Kids for Today's Jobs." *Changing Times* 19(September 1965): 41-45.

This article explains what is wrong about the present methods of vocational training in our schools when we turn out high school graduates with no job training for today's demands on the labor market. Optimistic predictions are made concerning the Vocational Education Act of 1963 and its programs to update vocational education which now is described as being "in the horse-and-buggy" days.

Schreiber, Daniel. "The Low Ability Group and the World of Automation." *National Association of Secondary-School Principals Bulletin* 48(November 1964): 73-82.

The problem of educating the slow learner is discussed in this article. Examples of school programs, combining work and instruction, are cited.

These are located in Tacoma-Pierce County, Washington (State), Champaign, Illinois, Community School District, and Iowa City, Iowa, High School.

Schuchat, Theodor. "The Vocational Education Amendments of 1968." *School Shop* 28(Jan. 1969): 25-27.
    A review of the 1968 amendments broken down into the component parts of each Title of the Act. Included also are three graphs giving statistics on Federal spending for vocational and technical education, student enrollments (1963-68), expenditures for the construction of area vocational schools under VEA 1963.

Schuler, Stanley. "Jobs for the Future." *Nation's Business* 51(June 1963): 31-41, 44-47, 55-56, 86-93.
    A special five-part report on meeting the challenge for job requirements in the future. Discusses the new skill requirements that will require new training, what the government can and cannot do in preparing workers for future employment, how automation will actually make more jobs available.

Scott, J. F. "Apprenticeship under the English Guild System." *Elementary School Teacher* 13: 180-88, December 1912.
    Describes apprenticeship during the Middle Ages and the period of the Renaissance.

Sears, William P., Jr. "Analytical Procedures for Scientific Research." *Research in Industrial Arts Education. Ninth Yearbook of the American Council on Industrial Arts Teacher Education.* Bloomington, Illinois: McKnight and McKnight Publishing Co., 1960, pp. 50-79.

Seefeld, Kermit A. "Vocational Education in the Liberal Education Continuum." *Industrial Arts and Vocational Education* 53 (November 1964): 20-21.
    A discussion of some sociological concepts affecting people's choice between liberal education and vocational-technical education. Includes brief bibliography.

Selden, Frank Henry. "Attitude of Pupils in Shop Work." *American School Board Journal* 39: 5, December 1909.

Selden, Frank Henry. "The Equipment of Manual Training Departments in the Public Schools." *American School Board Journal* 41: 4-5, 30, July 1910.

Selden, Frank Henry. [1]"Manual Training and Industry." [2]"Methods of Instruction in Manual Training." [3]"Our Duty toward the Manual Training Movement." *American School Board Journal* 40: 3, 28, January 1910; 3, 18, February 1910; 15-16, March 1910.

Selvidge, Robert W. "Industrial Education from the Viewpoint of Organized Labor." *American School Board Journal* 40: 6-7, 27, June 1910.

Selvidge, Robert W. "Study of Some Manual Training High Schools with Suggestions for an Intermediate Industrial School." *Manual Training Magazine* 10: 373-87, June 1909. diagrs.

Sheldon, E. E. "The Vocational School of the Lakeside Press, Chicago." *School Arts Book* 11: 922-32, May 1912.

Shields, Thomas Edward. "Survey of the Field." [Vocational Education.] *Catholic Educational Review* 5: 139-56, February 1913.

Discusses especially the report of Mr. Edwin G. Cooley, advocating a separate system of vocational schools. The author does not approve of adding a special tax to the heavy burden the people are now bearing in order that vocational schools may be built. He claims that "If industrial schools are to be erected and equipped, the financial burden of so doing should evidently be borne by the interests that would profit most by such a system of schools."

Shilt, Bernard A. "Some Facts about the Vocational Education Act of 1963." Past President's Report." *American Vocational Journal* 45 (Feb. 1970): 14-16.

The report of the out-going President of the AVA in 1969. In this report he discusses changes in vocational education in regard to federal support, recognition by educational administrators, programs for training the disadvantaged.

Shilt, Bernard A. "Some Facts About the Vocational Education Act of 1963." *Balance Sheet* 46(October 1964): 52-54.

"A history of the passage of the act and some suggestions for its application."

Shoemaker, B. R. "Preemployment Training for Out-of-school Youth and Adults." *Theory Into Practice* 3 (December 1964): 175-178.

The author of this article is the director of vocational education in the Ohio Department of Education. He reviews successful public vocational education programs of the past as the WPA and World War II training programs and lists the type of subjects now offered under title VIII of the National Defense Education Act and the Manpower Development and Training Act.

Shoemaker, B. R. and D. J. Fredericks. "Penta County Students Evaluate Their Joint Vocational School." *American Vocational Journal* 42 (Dec. 1967): 17-18.

A survey of the Penta County (Ohio) Joint Vocational School was conducted to determine the actual value of the school's programs.

Shoemaker, Byrl R. "National Need for Residential Schools." *American Vocational Journal* 43(Oct. 1968): 14-17.

The Director of Vocational Education for Ohio states that "the question is not whether we should or will have residential vocational schools for disadvantaged youth; the question is who can best operate these schools." A description of two residential centers for vocational education in Ohio is given.

Shoulders, Forest H. "Education and Retraining Programs for Employment." *Illinois School Board Journal* 32(March-April 1965):20-22.
    Report of a panel discussion held during the 1964 Convention of the Illinois Association of School Boards. Covers various programs in Cook County, Ill., and other areas engaged in rehabilitating and retraining welfare recipients.

Siepert, A. F. "Engineering and Industrial Problems as Factors in Seventh and Eighth Grade Manual Training." *Manual Training Magazine* 10: 193-99, February 1909.

Sigma. "The Bearing of Technical Education on Industrial Progress." *Journal of Education (London)* n.s. 30: 741-43, 816-19, November, December 1908.

Simeon, N. F. "Chicago's Vocational Guidance and Education Centers; A Program for Over-age Elementary School Youth." *Chicago School Journal* 45(October 1963): 15-21.
    A description of the seven centers initiated by the Chicago public school system in the effort to provide vocational training for youths 14 years and older, who had not yet graduated from elementary school.

Simpkins, Rupert R. "Legislation for the Last Three Years on Vocational Education." *School Review* 20: 407-16, June 1912.
    Cites the valuable work of the six commissions provided for by legislative enactment within the last three years.

Sing, Saint Nihal. "Learning by Doing at the Japanese Women's University." *Southern Workman* 37: 273-78, May 1908.

Sjogren, D. and D. Gutcher. "Current and Future Demands on Vocational Education." *High School Journal* 52(Feb. 1969): 219-228.
    A discussion of the American technological revolution and the resulting manpower problems that affect our vocational education system. Recommendations for future action are included.

Sledd, Andrew. "Rural Versus Urban Conditions in the Determination of Educational Policy." In *Association of American Agricultural Colleges and Experiment Stations. Proceedings, 1908.* Washington, Government Printing Office, 1909. pp. 53-59 (U.S. Department of Agriculture. Office of experiment stations. Bulletin 212.)

Sloan, Percy H. "The Organization of the Arts in the High Schools." *Educational Bi-monthly* 4: 182-90, February 1910.

Smith, G. W. "Vocational and Technical Education; A Survey of Current Programs in Illinois Public Junior Colleges." *Illinois Education* 53 (January 1965): 210-212 +
    A review of the current status of vocational and technical programs in the 18 public junior colleges of Illinois.

Smith, Robert M., and William J. Tisdall." Working with the Retarded Pupil in Industrial Arts and Vocational Education." *School Shop* 24(April 1965): 58-59, 114.

The applications of industrial education to prepare the mentally retarded for gainful occupation.

Smith, Wesley P. "Vocational Education in the High School." *California Education* 1(September 1963): 16-18.

California's State Director of Vocational Education presents "guidelines" for the further development and expansion of vocational education programs in the high schools of his State.

Snedden, David S. "The Combination of Liberal and Vocational Education." *Educational Review* 37: 231-42, March 1909.

Presents three methods of combining vocational with liberal education, and analyzes same.

Snedden, David S. "Debatable Issues in Vocational Education." *Vocational Education* 2: 1-12, September 1912.

Gives "a few of the problems of vocational education with reference to which there is now needed fuller analysis, discussion, and experimentation."

Snedden, David S. "Differentiated Programs of Study for Older Children in Elementary Schools." *Educational Review* 44: 128-39, September 1912.

In the estimation of the writer, "a complete scheme of secondary education should include not only one or more of the four-year programs as now commonly found but also flexible two-year programs of study, all containing English literature, English expression, general science, social science, and an option from one of the four great fields of practical arts study—namely, agriculture, industrial and practical arts, and commerce."

Snedden, David S. "The Practical Arts in Liberal Education." *Educational Review* 43: 378-86, April 1912.

States that "in practical arts teaching the place for drill, systematic approach, and approximation of journeyman's standards', is in the vocational school."

Snedden, David S. "Supplying Teachers of Vocational Education." *Journal of Education* 76: 687, December 26, 1912.

Suggests three ways of training teachers of vocational education, as follows: Evening classes may be organized in existing industrial schools for the specific purpose of training teachers. Short courses during the summer or dull season might attract suitably qualified workers to the training courses. Properly qualified workmen may be employed as assistants in vocational schools and by training and supervision may qualify as teachers.

Snedden, David S. "Vocations and Industrial Education . . . " In his *Administration and Educational Work of American Juvenile Reform Schools.* New York, Columbia University, Teachers College, 1907. pp. 69-118. Bibliography: pp. 117-18.

Snowden, Albert A. "Industrial Education in Public School Systems. With Special Reference to Grades below the High Schools." In *New Jersey State Teachers' Association. Proceedings, 1908.* pp. 19-25.

Snowden, Albert A. "The Industrial Improvement Schools of Wurttemberg, Together with a Brief Description of the Other Industrial Schools of the Kingdom . . . " *Teachers College Record* 8: 1-79, November 1907.
    Contains: 1. The place of vocational training in the kingdom, pp. 1-21. 2. The rise of vocational schools, pp. 23-34. 3. The reorganization of the industrial improvement schools, pp. 34-48. 4. The industrial school of Stuttgart, and the commercial schools, pp. 48-57. 5. Other industrial schools, and the Central bureau for industry and commerce, pp. 57-72.
    A resume of the economic conditions in Wurttemberg, one of the smaller kingdoms of the German empire. Records the development of the system of industrial schools and what they have done in up-building the state.

Snyder, Edwin Reagan. "Manual Training in Public Schools." *California Education* 1: 201-59, September 1906.
    A statistical study to ascertain loss of pupils' time through the central system, pp. 255-56.

Somers, Gerald G. "The Response of Vocational Education to Labor Market Changes."*Journal of Human Resources* 3(Supplement 1968): 32-59.
    An evaluation of the relationship of vocational education to the labor market from the view of: job-replacement results, cost-benefits, meeting the needs of the disadvantaged, changing composition of vocational school enrollments.

Somerville, Mass. School Committee. "Committee on Vocational Guidance." In its *Annual Report* 1910. pp. 23.

"Special Report: Vocational and Technical Education." *American School Board Journal* 150 (April 1965): 23-60.
    A group of 12 articles, including "New products in the field." Partial contents: Vocational education and Federal control by V. R. Cardozier; Vocational education, a community responsibility by Theodore Pearce; Community college for tomorrow by C. Thomas Dean; Case for vocational, technical training school by Arthur A. Dick.

Spence, William P. "Federal Funds for Industrial Arts." *Industrial Arts and Vocational Education* 54 (November 1965): 36, 78, 80.
    The ways in which industrial arts may qualify for Federal funds under the Elementary and Secondary Education Act of 1965.

Spence, William P. "The Summer Study on Occupational, Vocational and Technical Education." *Industrial Arts and Vocational Education* 56(Sept. 1967): 63-64 + .
    Highlights of study conducted at the Massachusetts Institute of Technology on the current practices of vocational education, with Dr. N. H.

Frank as the principle investigator. Among some of the objectives considered was the development of criteria for new instructional materials and learning aids, and the relationship between vocational schools and the comprehensive high school.

Spencer, Anna Garlin. "What Can the Grade School Do for Industrial Education." In *National Society for the Promotion of Industrial Education. Proceedings [1909].* pp. 148-56.

Springfield, Mass. School Board. "The Vocational School." In its *Report, 1909.* pp. 27-31.

Stahlecker, L. V. "Schoolwork Programs for the Slow Learners." *Clearing House* 38(January 1964): 299-301.
    An assessment of schoolwork programs in preparing slow-learning youths for suitable employment. General information is given in this article.

Starr, Harold. "Model for Evaluating State Programs." *American Vocational Journal* 42(Dec. 1967): 13-14.
    The project director of the Ohio Center for Vocational and Technical Education describes an evaluation system developed by the Center. This system is meant to provide the states with a model to assess their programs of vocational and technical education. The "testing ground" for the initial evaluation was the school system of three states, Colorado, Kentucky and New Jersey.

"State Action — Vocational Education and Community Colleges." *Compact* 4(Aug. 1970): 18-27.
    A brief summary of state action in regard to vocational education in the community college.

Stauffer, R. G. and R. L. Cramer. "Exploration in Pre-vocational Training for the Disadvantaged." *Journal of Reading* 12(Nov. 1968): 115-118, 171-176.
    Description of a pilot project in Newark, N. J. designed to connect occupational study and certain academic skills, as ability to read. A training program for vocational teachers for the disadvantaged is also discussed.

Stephens, George Asbury. "The New Apprenticeship." *Journal of Political Economy* 19: 17-35, January 1911.
    Co-operative system between factories and schools.
    Reprinted "Influence of trade education upon wages."

[Stephenson, George B.] "Scholars' Employment Bureau in Liverpool." In *North Carolina Association of City Public School Superintendents and Principals. Proceedings and Addresses, 1911.* Raleigh, Edwards & Broughton Printing Co., 1911. pp. 93.

Stevens, F. L. "How Can the High School Course Be Adapted to Meet the Needs of Pupils Living in an Agricultural Community?" In *North Carolina Teachers' Assembly. Proceedings and Addresses, 1910.* Raleigh, N. C., Edwards & Broughton Printing Company, 1910. pp. 169-76.

Stockbridge, E. P. "Half Time at School and Half Time at Work." *World's Work* 21: 14265-75, April 1911.

Describes the co-operative education plan of the University of Cincinnati, which is working with the industrial plants, the libraries, the schools, and other agencies.

Stone, Seymour H. "The Berkshire Industrial Farm." *Charities* 10: 138-41, February 7, 1903. illus.

Carpentry, printing, sloyd, and shoe repairing are taught the boys.

Story, M. L. "Vocational Education as Contemporary Slavery." *Intellect* 102: 370-372, March, 1974.

Straton, John Roach. "Will Education Solve the Race Problem?" *North American Review* 170: 785-801, June 1900.

Stratton, G. F. "Rising Industrial Problems: the New Apprenticeship." *Engineering Magazine* 34: 401-13, December 1907.

Indicates that the attitude of trade unions is hostile to attempts to recruit industrial workers through trade schools, but that they prefer and encourage shop training.

Strobel, J. R. "Resources Related to Objectives: the Key to the Vocational Education Act of 1963." *School Shop* 23 (April 1964): 35-39.

The assistant commissioner for vocational instructional services for New York outlines the specific implications of the Vocational Education Act of 1963 and how this new legislation will affect vocational training at different levels.

Sullivan, L. H. "Self-help and Motivation for the Underprivileged: Opportunities for Industrialization Center, Inc." *Adult Leadership* 16 (Feb. 1968): 282-284+.

The case history of a vocational training center for unemployed adults. In describing the scope and function of the Center, the author points out the particular training given to minority groups.

Summers, L. L. "Woodwork in the Lower Grades." *Manual Training Magazine* 14: 10-23, October 1912.

Gives an outline of a tentative plan of work for the first five grades. Copiously illustrated.

"Surveying the NDEA Institutes." *Industrial Arts and Vocational Education* 57 (Apr. 1968): 24, 92.

A condensation of the opinions of 29 directors of NDEA Institutes held in the summer of 1967, to improve instruction in the industrial arts.

Swanson, Gordon I. "Career Education: Barriers to Implementation." *American Vocational Journal* 47 (Mar. 1972): 81-82.

"The obstacles are difficult but not insuperable, says Professor Swanson. With strong leadership now emerging in federal, state and local agencies, career education (never a fragile concept) may survive its detractors."

Swanson, Gordon I. and others. "Vocational Curriculum: a Conceptual Framework." *American Vocational Journal* 44 (Mar. 1969): 22-24.

Elements to be considered in adopting a vocational education curriculum that will meet the needs of those who have left school as well as those who are still enrolled. Eight imperatives are listed, all considered as "crucial" in establishing a meaningful curriculum.

Swanson, J. Chester and Walter M. Arnold. "A New Look at Vocational-Technical Education." *State Government* 41 (Summer 1968): 181-186.

A review of the Federal legislation providing grants to the states for vocational education and a discussion of the recommendations made by the Advisory Council on Vocational Education.

"Symposium: The Place of Industries in Public Education." In *National Education Association of the United States. Journal of Proceedings and Addresses, 1908.* pp. 155-77.

Articles by J. E. Russell, E. C. Elliott, J. F. McElroy, etc. Dr. Elliott gives an interesting presentation of the philosophy underlying.public education. He says that until we possess "reliable data upon which to base a rational scheme of reorganization, the public schools cannot hope to become instruments for 'industrial determination'; neither will they cease to prevent the present positive misselection of individuals for their proper station of efficiency and happiness."

Mr. McElroy cites statistics of attendance in grammar schools of Albany, N.Y., to show a very rapid decrease in enrollment. Advocates industrial continuation schools.

Symposium: Secondary Education for Vocational Competence in a Changing Occupational World." *California Journal of Secondary Education* 33 (May 1958): 290-316.

A group of six articles by noted California educators in the field of vocational education.

Tausigg, Michael K. "An Economic Analysis of Vocational Education in the New York City High Schools." *Journal of Human Resources* 3 (Supplement 1968): 59-89.

The major finding of this analysis is: "Lack of apparent success of vocational training in increasing the market productivity of the graduates, despite the large incremental costs shown to be devoted to vocational training . . ."

Taylor, Graham Romeyne. "Industrial Education and National Prosperity." *Charities and The Commons* 19: 1579-84, February 8, 1908.

Discusses the work of the first annual meeting of the National Society for the Promotion of Industrial Education.

Taylor, John Madison. "Difficult Boys." *Popular Science Monthly* 69: 338-51, October 1906.

Tennyson, W. Wesley. "Career Development." *Review of Educational Research* 38 (Oct. 1968): 346-366.

Research completed since October 1962 on vocational development and behavior, including theories on work as it relates to "the life style of adults in the labor force."

Terman, Lewis M. "The Relation of the Manual Arts to Health." *Popular Science Monthly* 78: 602-9, June 1911.

Thomas, Wade F. "Reducing the Gap between Vocational and General Education." *Junior College Journal* 27 (March 1957): 367-374; (April 1957): 429-436.

In the first article the author points out the necessity for establishing relationships between vocational and general education programs and defines the criteria for use in ascertaining the effectiveness of such relationships.

In the second article he reports on practices as they exist in 10 public junior colleges of California and the extent of the relationship between vocational and general education in these institutions.

Thompson, F. V. "The Commercial High School and the Business Community." *School Review* 18: 1-11, January 1910.

The work of the Boston Business Men's Advisory Committee, organized 1906, in connection with the Boston High School of Commerce, and its traveling scholarships or students.

Thum, William. "Manufacturing-Works High School for Young Women." *Arena* 39: 303-307, March 1908.

Reprinted in his *A Forward Step,* pp. 77-88.

Tirrell, Winthrop. "Summer Apprenticeship in the Boston High School of Commerce." *School Review* 19: 34-41, January 1911.

The scheme devised by the Boston Business Men's Advisory Committee.

Toledo, O. Board of Education. "New Cosmopolitan High Schools." In its *Report, 1908-09.* pp. 71-79. illus. plans.

A complete system of differentiated courses, cultural and vocational, "offering all three lines of academic, manual and commercial training, and placing equal emphasis upon each."

Towson, Charles R. "The Industrial Outreach of the Y.M.C.A." *Survey* 29: 524-27, January 18, 1913.

Shows progress made in vocational training. Work among the immigrants, etc. Reports 30,000 industrial workers in night classes. In 1912, 1,500,000 attended shop meetings. Extension work done.

"Training Youth for Work." *The American Child* 44 (May 1962): 20 pp.

Entire issue devoted to ways and means of training unemployed youth for occupations in which shortages of workers exist.

"The Trouble with Training." *The American Child* 47 (January 1965): 23 pp.

Training is now the blanket term for a host of programs seeking to help youth gain confidence or improve reading, get work experience or learn technical skills. Five articles included in this issue discuss the forms of "training" now offered in various programs and the probable success and failure of these programs.

Troxwell, Margaret. "Adequate Manpower in the 1960's—a New Challenge for Vo-ed! *American Vocational Journal* 35 (April 1960): 14-15.

The author is informational specialist, Bureau of Apprenticeship and Training, Department of Labor. The "new challenge" to vocational education in the 1960's is the large growth in job opportunities for the skilled worker, while opportunities for the farmworker and unskilled worker decline.

Turner, Kate E. "What Shall I Do after High School?" *Ladies' Home Journal* 29: 10, 76, April 1912.

Describes the various professional and industrial channels open for girls, and their requirements.

United States. Bureau of Education. "Commercial Education in Switzerland." In *Report of the Commissioner for the Year 1902*. Washington, Government Printing Office, 1903. pp. 837-55.

Gives historical review; status of existing status of commercial schools, with curricula, etc. Illustrated.

United States. Bureau of Education. "Industrial Education in the United States." In its *Annual Report of the Commissioner for the Year 1910*. v.1. Washington, Government Printing Office, 1910. pp. 223-53.

General review. Statistics of schools in this country which offer training for specific vocations in the industries. For reviews of manual and industrial training in the United States see previous reports of the Bureau, from 1898 to 1909.

United States. Bureau of Education. "Juvenile Labor Bureaus and Vocational Guidance in Great Britain." In its *Bulletin No. 11, 1912*. Washington, 1912. pp. 13-17.

Shows what is being done in Birmingham, London, and Edinburgh. "In London, where poverty exists in its greatest extent and complications, the public school is rapidly becoming the chief center of the movement for social and industrial reform."

United States. Bureau of Education. "The Prussian System of Vocational Schools from 1884 to 1909." In *Report of the Commissioner for the Year 1910*. Washington, Government Printing Office, 1910. v. 1. pp. 301-43.

A resume of the third report of the Royal Prussian state industrial office, 1909. (Verwaltungsbericht des Koniglich Preussischen Landesgewerbeamts. Berlin, Carl Heymanns, 1910. 436 pp. tables)

Gives an historical review, followed by detailed accounts, statistical and textual, of the various classes of schools which constitute the system considered.

United States. Bureau of Labor. "Attitude of Employers, Graduates of Trade and Technical Schools, and Labor Unions . . . toward Trade and Technical Education." In *Report of the Commissioner of Labor, 1902.* Washington, Government Printing Office, 1902.
Includes: United States, pp. 367-424; Austria, pp. 560-63; Belgium, pp. 672-84; France, pp. 853-68; Great Britain, pp. 1129-52; Switzerland, pp. 1303-05.

United States. Bureau of Labor. "[Industrial Schools]." In *25th Annual Report of the Commissioner, 1910.* Washington, Government Printing Office, 1911. pp. 35-360.
Describes representative schools of different types.

United States. Bureau of Labor. "Laws Relating to Industrial Education." In its *Twenty-fifth Annual Report of the Commissioner, 1910.* pp. 501-18.

United States. Bureau of Labor. Vocational Guidance. In its *Twenty-fifth Annual Report, 1910.* pp. 410-97.
Contains history of the movement. Work in New York City and Boston. Statistics of principal opportunities for industrial education in Boston, etc., compiled by the educational department of the Women's Municipal League, April 1910. Gives forms, blanks, and records used.

United States. Commissioner of Labor. "Trade and Technical Education in Italy." In his *17th Annual Report, 1902.* Washington, 1902. pp. 1169-1212.

Upton, R. R. "High School Attendance as Influenced by Commercial and Technical Training." In *Illinois State Teachers' Association. Journal of Proceedings, 1902.* Springfield, Ill., Phillips Bros., State Printers, 1903. pp. 127-33.

Ury, Claude M. "Recent Developments in Vocational Education." *Catholic School Journal* 69 (Sept. 1969): 51-53.
Brief summaries of successful experimental programs in vocational education, particularly work-study projects, all made possible by the 1968 Amendments of the Vocational Education Act.

Usherwood, T.S. "The Place of Manual Training in the Curriculum of the Secondary School." *Manual Training (London)* 9: 136-39, 158-64, March, April 1912.
A discussion of the necessity for manual training in the curriculum of the secondary school, and the value of a proper co-ordination with literary, mathematical, and experimental work as a basis for a liberal education.

Utah Educational Assocation. Committee on Industrial Education in Public Schools. "Report." *Utah Educational Review* 4: 34-36, February 1911.
Chairman, John A. Widstoe.

Van Cleve, C. L. "The Ohio State Reformatory—A Study in Modern Pedagogy." *Journal of Pedagogy* 20: 90-100, September-December 1907.

Vanderlip, F. A. "Trade Schools and Labor Unions." In his *Business and Education.* pp. 56-81.

Great emphasis is laid upon the need for continuation trade schools to train, not the captains of industry, but the rank and file of the American industrial army. The German schools of this sort are cited as good examples.

Venn, Grant. "Eye on Tomorrow's Jobs." *American Education* 5 (Mar. 1969): 12-15.

A discussion of the major issues involved in the transition of the student from school to work and the importance of cooperation between the school system and industry.

Venn, Grant. "Learning beyond the Classroom." *American Vocational Journal* 42 (Sept. 1967): 14-16.

The role of vocational education in responding to the manpower needs of an industrial society, while assisting the student in learning to live as an individual in that society.

Venn, Grant. "Needed: a New Relationship between Education and Work." *School Shop* 24 (April 1965): 42-45, 106.

This noted educator believes that an entirely new set of standards and values must be used in training workers for present day needs and for future needs. A new concept of vocational education must be evolved, combining training for saleable skills with cultivation of civic and personal understanding of others.

Venn, Grant. "Occupational Education for Everyone." *National Association of Secondary School Principals Bulletin* 52 (Dec. 1968): 112-122.

"Occupational education is fundamental to every individual's well being." Using this as a premise, the author discusses such factors as the relationship of status and work in our society, the new role of the school in meeting manpower requirements and the educational level of the nation's adults.

Venn, Grant. "Title I HR 15066: a Better Answer?" *Journal of Industrial Arts Education* 27 (May 1968): 16-19.

Implications for industrial arts as found in the 1968 Amendments of the Vocational Education Act of 1963.

Venn, Grant. "The Vocational Education Amendments of 1968. *American Education* 5 (Dec. 1968-Jan. 1969): 8-9.

A summary of the Amendments including information on the eligibility requirements for the basic state vocational education programs, and appropriations authorized through 1974.

Venn, Grant. "Vocational Education in a Dynamic Labor Market." *Manpower* 1(Oct. 1969): 25-27.

A review of the revived interest in vocational education since the passage of the Vocational Education Act of 1963 and how the 1968 Amendments to this law can bring about the needed changes in this field.

Vickroy, W. R. "Manual Training as an Entrance Requirement." *Southern Educational Review* 3: 828-34, March 1906.

Virginia Vocational Association. Public Information Committee. "Vocational Education in Virginia." *Virginia Journal of Education* 57(March 1964): 13-15 +.

The present status and organization of vocational education programs in the public high schools of Virginia and needed changes for future developments are discussed.

"Vocational and Technical Education; Reviews the Literature for the 6-year Period since October 1950." *Review of Educational Research* 26(October 1956): 349-410.

Partial contents: Vocational selection; industrial education; technical education; work experience.

"Vocational Education." *High School Journal* 52(Feb. 1969): 219-69.

Entire issue of six articles devoted to vocational education. Of special interest are: "Current and future demands on vocational education" by D. Sjogren and D. Gutcher and "A total and interdisciplinary program of vocational education" by R. J. Agan.

"The Vocational Education Act of 1963." *School Life* 46(March-April 1964): 3-12.

This is a detailed presentation of the provisions of this act and some background information pointing out the necessity for its passage.

"Vocational Education Act of 1963 and Suggested Lines of Action Relating to Vocational Education for Business and Office Occupations." *Business Education Forum* 18(January 1964): 29-32.

A special report prepared by the Legislative Action Committee of the National Business Education Association.

"Vocational Education Challenged." *American Vocational Journal* 44(Feb., 1969): 19-20.

Summary of the remarks made by Senators Wayne Morse and Ralph Yarborough at the general session of the 62nd annual vocational education convention.

"Vocational Education; the New Approach." *Nation's Schools* 80(Aug. 1967): 36-43.

The new movement underway in vocational education is briefly described. A "round-up" of case studies in various schools serve as examples of current vocational education activity.

"Vocational Education; Time for Decision." *National Association of Secondary School Principals Bulletin* 49(May 1965): 3-153.

Entire issue devoted to vocational education. Contents: The needs and possibilities; vocational education at work in diverse situations; patterns of organization of vocational education; curriculum development and guidance.

"Vocational, Technical, and Practical Arts Education." *Review of Educational Research* 38: 305-442, October, 1968.

A critical review of the literature since 1962, keyed to extensive bibliographies. See also, *Ibid.,* vol. 32 (October, 1962); and *Ibid.,* vol. 26 (October, 1956).

"Vocational, Technical and Practical Arts Education; Reviews the Literature for the Six Year Period since October 1962; with Summary by J. Moss, Jr." *Review of Educational Research* 38(Oct. 1968): 309-440.

Entire issue devoted to research in nine different phases of vocational education. Partial contents: Manpower supply and demand, organization and administration, program evaluation.

"Vocational Training Lags; Needs More Federal Aid and Community Cooperation; School Administrators Opinion Poll Findings." *Nation's Schools* 71(April 1963): 61+.

Pertinent facts from an opinion poll conducted by the editors of *Nation's Schools* from which this majority opinion was gained: "Public schools today need to update greatly their vocational training curriculums."

Voorhes, O. P. "The Inception and Development of an Industrial Elementary School." *Elementary School Teacher* 12: 383-387, April 1912.

Describes work at the Oyler school, Cincinnati, Ohio. Development of manual and industrial training.

Wahlstrom, Leonard W. "The Place of Typical Industries in the Elementary School." In *Eastern Art Teachers' Association and Eastern Manual Training Association. Proceedings of the Joint Convention, 1906.* [Asbury Park, New Jersey, Kinmonth Art Press] pp. 89-105.

Wahlstrom, Leonard W. "A School Print Shop." *Manual Training Magazine* 10: 134-47, December 1908. illus.

Walker, Eric A. "Automation and Education." *Junior College Journal* 25(May 1956): 498-503.

This article states the implications of automation for education, suggests the types of content needed for education in this light, outlines the tasks of the junior colleges in providing this training.

Walker, Hugh, "Are the Brains behind the Labour Revolt All Wrong?" *Hibbert Journal 11:* 348-65, January 1913.

Incidently discusses industrial education as a remedial agency for many of the social ills. Explains how the state by a system of industrial training, prolonging the period of instruction to about 18 years, would solve the baffling problem of "blind-alley employments." Says: "The breeding of men who can not earn their own living is as costly as it is morally disastrous; and the present system, which, at the close of the school period, turns thousands of children on to the streets, there to make a precarious living for a few years, inevitably produces that result." Shows the wonderful results accomplished in Munich, Germany, by industrial education.

Walker, J. P. "Industrial Training." *American Annals of the Deaf* 50: 98-103, January 1905.
    Discussion: p. 103-15.
    Industrial education of deaf girls.

Wanamaker, John. "The John Wanamaker Commercial Institute — a Store School." *American Academy of Political and Social Science. Annals* 33: 151-54, January 1909.
    Under the name of the American university of applied commerce and trade, the school applied for charter, September 1908.

Ware, Allison. "Life and the Elementary Curriculum." *Sierra Educational News* 5: 10-20, May 1909.

Warfield, Benjamin B. "The 90th Congress and Vocational Education." *National Association of Secondary School Principals Bulletin* 53(Feb. 1969): 57-66.
    An informative assessment of the 1968 Amendments of the Vocational Education Act of 1963. The author states that "this Act provides little comfort to those who hope for a policy of block grants or tax refunds delivered directly to the States with no strings attached."

Warmbrod, J. R. "New Design in Vocational and Practical Arts Education." *American Vocational Journal* 42(Dec. 1967): 53-57.
    A report on vocational and technical education developments in 13 central states, and the influence of the Vocational Education Act of 1963 in this growth.

Warner, Charles F. "Education for the Trades in America. What Can the Technical High Schools Do for It? "In *National Education Association of the United States. Journal of Proceedings and Addresses, 1901.* pp. 665-73.
    Discussion: p. 673-82.

Warner, Charles F. "Public Evening Schools of Trades." In *American Academy of Political and Social Science. Annals* 33: 56-67, January 1909.
    Describes schools of Springfield and Cambridge, Mass.; and Cleveland, Ohio. Gives course of study in the first-named school.
    See also paper by Mr. Warner in *National Education Association of the United States. Journal of Proceedings and Addresses, 1905.* pp. 570-76.

Warner, W. R. "The Apprenticeship Question of To-day." *Iron Age* 81: 1786-87, June 4, 1908.

Warriner, E. C. "Industrial and Vocational Training in the Public Schools." In *Michigan. Superintendent of Public Instruction. Annual Report, 1909-10.* Lansing, Michigan, Wynkoop Hallenbeck Crawford Co., State Printers, 1910. pp. 14-21.
> Reprinted. 10 p. 8°. (Bulletin no. 2, 1909)

Washington, Booker T. "Relation of Industrial Education to National Progress." *American Academy of Political and Social Science. Annals* 33: 1-12, January 1909.
> Lays particular emphasis on industrial education of the Negro. Describes "demonstration farms." In regard to manual training author says: "It is now pretty generally recognized that manual training does not meet the needs of the situation. Any form of schooling that merely provides discipline and culture is not sufficient." Advocates the fitting of young men and women for some definite vocation.

Washington, Booker T. "Successful Training of the Negro." *World's Work* 6: 3731-51, August 1903. illus.
> Tuskegee Institute.

Webster, W. F. "Our Present Needs." In *Minnesota Educational Association. Journal of Proceedings and Addresses, 1909.* [Minneapolis, Minn., Press of Syndicate Printing Company] pp. 30-38.
> President's address. Reprinted.

Weeks, Arland D. "The Training of the Industrial Teacher." *Education* 33: 375-78, February 1913.
> Advocates broad professional training for the industrial teacher. He should be well equipped "on the side of professional and liberal culture . . . He should especially be conversant with the bearings of industrial teaching upon the social order."

Wendt, Erhard F. "Brief History of Industrial Arts and Vocational Education." *Industrial Arts and Vocational Education* 35: 151-154, April, 1946.
> Useful outlines of history of vocational education with notices of leading figures. Also, *Ibid.,* vol. 35 (May, 1946), pp. 202-203.

Wenrich, R. C., *et al.* "Vocational, Technical, and Practical Arts Education: History of Vocational Education." *Review of Educational Research* 32: 370-, October 1962.
> Developments since World War I, with some notices of major figures and federal roles.

West, Earle H. "Editorial Comment: Education and Jobs." *Journal of Negro Education* 37(Fall 1968): 359-363.

"Drastic and rapid changes are needed in American education with reference to its vocational function." To support his argument, the author lists and discusses five propositions to indicate into which directions change must go to be effective.

Western Drawing and Manual Training Association. Committee on Investigation of Art and Manual Training in Normal Schools. "Report." In its *Proceedings, 1909* pp. 77-86.
   Chairman, E. E. Meyers.

Whitcher, George B. "Children Differ in Vocational Aims — a Discussion." *School Exchange* 4: 358-63, March 1910.

White, Frank M. "Business Men in the Making." *Outlook* 98: 989-97, August 26, 1911. illus.
   Student aid and vocational advice.

White, Frank R. "Industrial Education in the Philippine Islands." *Vocational Education* 2: 265-77, March 1913.
   To be continued. The Philippine Bureau of Education has aimed "to turn the pupils directly and normally from the public schools into an industrial life which would-enable them to more adequately meet their growing needs." Illustrated.

White, R. E. "Junior Colleges, a Technical Education Role." *Minnesota Journal of Education* 45(February 1965): 12-14.
   The role of the American junior college in furnishing post-high school programs in vocational training, how the junior colleges of Minnesota measure up to this role.

Whiteford, John A. "Means of Extending and Improving the Teaching of Manual Arts in Small Towns and Rural Communities." *Western Journal of Education (Ypsilanti)* 2: 312-19, September 1909.

Whitney, F. P. "Differentiation of Courses in the Seventh and Eighth Grades." *Educational Review* 41: 127-34, February 1911.

Wickliffe, Mary Frances. "Some Results from Manual and Industrial Training." In *Southern Educational Association. Journal of Proceedings and Addresses, 1906.* pp. 188-97.
   Students in textile schools, p. 195-96.

Wiener, Rose. "Finishing Schools for Workers." *Manpower* 2(Mar. 1970): 2-7.
   The growth of the junior colleges during the decade of the 60's is reviewed. Their role in providing technical education and semiprofessional studies is also discussed.

Wightman, H. J. "Technical Courses in High Schools." *School Journal* 74: 248-51, March 9, 1907.

"In the type of course which I am advocating, the value of each thing made lies in the fact that it has a definite purpose in the later work and life of the pupil."

Wilcox, Glade. "The Challenge of Automation to Technical Education."- *School Shop* 16(June 1957): 9-11.

The various aspects of automation and the implications for technical education. Reports also on company studies involving automation installations and the relationship to vocational training of workers.

Wild, Laura H. "Training for Social Efficiency: the Relation of Art, Industry and Education." *Education* 32: 226-33, 343-53, 494-504, 624-35, December 1911; February, April and June 1912; 33: 91-99, 159-65, 208-22, October November and December 1912.

A plea for efficiency, not based upon skill in producing "the largest output, in making the biggest and most brilliant showing, but as ability to do something which the world wants in a superior way."

Williams, A. S. "Technical School in Naples." *School Review* 13: 398-410, May 1905.

Williams, Joan. "Schools Study Job Corps Lessons." *Manpower* 2(Mar. 1970): 22-25.

With its inception in 1965, the Job Corps initiated "a new mode of education" that increased the employability of a large number of deprived youth. This article describes how the Job Corp system is being adopted in many youth training programs, including those in the public schools.

Williams, S. Horace. "The Educative Value of Manual Training." I, II, III. *Manual Training Magazine* 11: 36-45, 158-67, 252-60, October, December 1909, February 1910.

Williams, W. T. B. "Fort Valley High and Industrial School." *Southern Workman* 39: 627-31, November 1910.

Williamson, E. G. "Historical Perspectives of the Vocational Guidance Movement." *Personal and Guidance Journal* 42: 854-859, May, 1964.

Useful historical outlines and educational backgrounds.

Willis, Benjamin C. "The Changing Story of Vocational Education and What's Needed Now." *Nation's Schools* 71(February 1963): 57-60.

Mr. Willis presents the recommendations of the Panel of Consultants of Vocational Education and lists categories of persons to whom vocational education should be made available.

Wilson, Harry Bruce. "The Motivation of the Children's Work in the Elemen-

tary Schools." In *National Education Association of the United States. Journal of Proceedings and Addresses, 1910.* pp. 418-20.
Discussion: p. 427-29.
Also in *School and Home Education,* 30: 57-64, October 1910.

Wilson, Lewis A. "The Rochester Shop School; a School Whose Graduates Make Good Every Time." *School Arts Book* 11: 481-93, January 1912.

Winch, W. H. "Some Measurements of Mental Fatigue in Adolescent Pupils in Evening Schools." *Journal of Educational Psychology* 1: 13-23, 83-100, January, February 1910. tables. statistics.
"Evening work is comparatively unprofitable, and a short time in class in the evening is sufficient, plus the labors of the day, to induce a very low condition of mental energy.

Winston, George T. "Industrial Education and the New South." In *U.S. Bureau of Education. Report of the Commissioner for the Year 1901.* v. 1, pp. 509-13.
An address delivered at the tenth annual meeting of the Southern Education Association, Richmond, Va., December 27-29, 1900.

Wirth, A. G. "Charles A. Prosser and the Smith-Hughes Act." *Educational Forum* 36: 365-371, March 1972.
Backgrounds of the Act, and the role of the profession in its enactment.

Woerdehoff, Frank J., and Ralph R. Bentley. "A Study of the Viewpoints Held by School Administrators Regarding Vocational Education in the Secondary School." *Journal of Experimental Education* 27(June 1959): 297-309.
Report of a study conducted by Purdue University faculty members to secure the viewpoints of Indiana school administrators on vocational education, because they believe that ". . . their viewpoints regarding vocational education contribute much toward the degree of acceptance or rejection of this phase of secondary education and the way in which the program is carried out.

Wolfbein, Seymour L. "Employing the Next Generation." *School Shop* 24(February 1965): 25-26+.
The author is the Duputy Manpower Administrator, U. S. Department of Labor. He discusses the necessary changes that must come in our training programs if we are to win "in our war on unemployment and poverty."

Wolfson, H. E. "Vocational Education in the Urban Setting." *American Vocational Journal* 44(Apr. 1969): 52-53.
The reasons why occupational education should be combined with academic subjects to help the inner-city youngster achieve self-identity and establish a relationship with the world outside of his ghetto surroundings.

Wood, Eugene. "School for Boys." *Everybody's Magazine* 13: 435-45, October 1905. illus.

Ohio boys' industrial school.

Wood-Simons, May. "Industrial Education in Chicago." *Pedagogical Seminary* 17: 398-418. September 1910.
Bibliography: p. 417-18.

Woodward, Calvin Milton. "Education." *Harper's Weekly* 44: 1129-30, December 1, 1900.
Mainly a record of growth of manual training in the nineteenth century.

Woodward, Calvin Milton. "The Logic and Method of Industrial Education." In *North Central Association of Colleges and Secondary Schools. Proceedings, 1910.* Chicago, Published by the Association, 1910. pp. 3-23.

Woodward, Calvin Milton. "Manual, Industrial, and Technical Education in the United States." In *U.S. Bureau of Education. Report of the Commissioner for the Year 1903.* v. 1. pp. 1019-46.

Wooley, Helen T. "Child Labor and Vocational Guidance." *Child Labor Bulletin* 1: 24-37, June 1912.
Gives some interesting schedules of the industrial history of children.

Woolman, Mary Schenck. "Private Trade Schools for Girls." *Charities and The Commons* 19: 839-48, October 5, 1907.
Describes the work of the Manhattan trade school for girls, New York City. Illustrated.

Woolman, Mary Schenck. "The Relative Value and Cost of Various Trades in a Girls' Trade School." *American Academy of Political and Social Science. Annals* 33: 127-40, January 1909.
Gives curriculum of the Manhattan trade school for girls, New York City. Reviews status of various trade schools in this country—equipment, budget, courses of study, etc. Gives the wages of those who have been placed in trade, after a course in the Manhattan trade school, showing first, "the tendency of each worker to rise to better positions, and second, the increasing wage at entering the market owing to improved methods of training the workers."

Woolman, Mary Schenck. "Trade Schools—An Educational and Industrial Necessity." *Social Education Quarterly* 1: 74-79, March 1907.
Also in *Southern Educational Review,* 4: 161-66, October-November 1907.

Zack, Jacob B. and others. "The Best Place for Vocational Education." *N.E.A. Journal* 55(December 1965): 48-52.
Four educators, Jacob B. Zack, Burr D. Col, Ted Urich and Joe Mauch discuss the best place for vocational education considering the high school, the special school, and the community college.

Zeller, John W. "The Problem of Industrial Education in Rural Schools." *Ohio Educational Monthly* 59: 353-57, July 1910.
  Discussion. 357-60.

III. UNPUBLISHED DOCTORAL DISSERTATIONS

Adams, Arlon E. "Career Education: A Study of Socioeconomic Status, Race, Community of Residence and Self-concept as Determinants of Prestige Level of Occupational Aspirations." Unpublished doctoral dissertation, Northwestern State University of Louisiana, 1974. 104 pp.

Alger, Leon J. "A Rationale for the Establishment of Area Vocational Programs in Michigan," Unpublished doctoral dissertation, Michigan State University, 1967. 242 pp.

Allen, David. "The History of Professional Industrial Education Organizations in California." University of California at Los Angeles, 1962.

Almen, Roy E. "The Evaluation of a Vocational Program for Dropout-prone Junior High School Students." Unpublished doctoral dissertation, University of Minnesota, 1971. 156 pp.

Amberson, Max L. "Variables and Situational Factors Associated with High School Vocational Education Programs." Unpublished doctoral dissertation, Ohio State University, 1968. 236 pp.

Anthony, William P. "A Study of the Effectiveness of Public Post Secondary Vocational-technical Education in Preparing Graduates for the Labor Force." Unpublished doctoral dissertation, Ohio State University, 1971. 218 pp.

Arnold, Walter M. "Federal-State Cooperative Activities in Vocational Education," Oklahoma Agricultural nd Mechanical College, 1957.

Ashbrook, William D. "The Development of Industrial Education in the Schools of Pennsylvania." University of Pittsburgh, 1943.

Baily, Athol R. "Envolving Concepts of Industrial Education in the Thinking of Organized Industrial Management. University of Missouri, 1949.

Barlow, Melvin Lewis. "A History of Trade and Industrial Education in California." University of California at Los Angeles, 1949. 373 pp.

Bass, Wilbur A. "A Study of the Impact of the Vocational Education Act of 1963 on Selected Texas Public Junior Colleges." Unpublished doctoral dissertation, University of Texas, 1967. 134 pp.

Bettina, Albert A. "The Development of Vocational-industrial Education in New Mexico." Bradley University, 1953.

Bikkie, James A. "The Meanings of Selected Vocational Education Concepts to Vocational Education Leaders." Unpublished doctoral dissertation, University of Minnesota, 1973. 454 pp.

Blauch, Lloyd E. "Federal Cooperation in Vocational Education." University of Chicago, 1923.

Blume, Paul R. "An Evaluation of Institutional Vocational Training Received by American Indians through the Muskogee, Oklahoma Area Office of the Bureau of Indian Affairs." Unpublished doctoral dissertation, Oklahoma State University 1968. 264 pp.

Briggs, Lloyd D. "Basic Competencies Necessary for Administration of Vocational and Technical Education." Unpublished doctoral dissertation, Oklahoma State University, 1971. 115 pp.

Carr, Harold L. "A Program Review Paradigm for Ohio Vocational Education." Unpublished doctoral dissertation, Ohio State University, 1970. 449 pp.

Chapline, Allen W. "The NAM and Its Efforts to Influence Education." Columbia University, 1948.

Chavous, Arthur M. "Industrial Education for Negroes in Ohio." University of Ohio, 1946.

Cooper, William M. "Industrial Arts in the Public Secondary Schools of Alabama." Auburn University, 1961.

Corazzini, Arthur J. "Vocational Education: An Analysis of Costs and Benefits. (A case study of Worcester, Mass.)" Unpublished doctoral dissertation, Princeton University, 1967. 131 pp.

Cotton, George R. "Collegiate Technical Education for Negroes in Missouri with Proposed Plans for Development." University of Ohio, 1944.

Covey, James W. "The Testing of Four Major Dimensions of Professional Preparation Models for the Development of Vocational-technical Educators." Unpublished doctoral dissertation, University of Wisconsin, 1973. 183 pp.

Crawford, Bryant, Jr. "Industrial Arts Programs for Adults: A Study to Develop Procedures and Practices with References to Industrial Arts Programs with Implications for Adult Living." Ohio State University, 1961.

Crawford, Harold Wakeling. "Organizational Patterns for Industrial Education Programs in Selected Land-grant Colleges." Wayne University, 1960.

Davenport, Joe U. "An Analysis of the Status of and Suggestions for Improving Industrial Arts Education in the Public Secondary Schools of Arkansas." University of Arkansas, 1959.

Dilts, Harold E. "The Status of Vocational Trades and Industries Programs in Iowa Secondary Schools." Iowa University, 1961.

Douglas, Paul H. "American Apprenticeship and Industrial Education." Columbia University, 1921.

Dutro, Kenneth R. "A History of Vocational Rehabilitation within the Veterans Administration since World War II." Unpublished doctoral dissertation, University of Northern Colorado, 1973. 206 pp.

Dutton, Bernard. "A Study of Television for Instruction in Industrial Arts Education." Unpublished doctoral dissertation, University of California, Los Angeles, 1966.

Dykhouse, Jay. "Dualism in American Public Education since 1906 with Special References to the Vocational Education Movement." University of Michigan, 1950.

Edmonds, William S. "A Study of the Technological Curricula of the Separate Southern Land-grant Colleges, 1941-51." Columbia University, 1954.

Espinoza-Bravo, Arsenio. "Organizational Needs for Organization Development for the Kentucky System of Vocational Education." Unpublished doctorial dissertation, University of Kentucky, 1971. 195 pp.

Farmer, Joe T. "The Teaching of Industrial Arts in the Secondary Schools of Texas." University of New York, 1951.

Fike, Iris L. "Historical Development of Vocational Industrial Education Programs of Secondary Grade Level in Public Schools of Pennsylvania from 1900 to 1954." University of Pittsburgh, 1956.

Fisher, Richard E. "Status and Need for Terminal Vocational Technical Curricula in Senior Colleges and Universities." University of Missouri, 1956.

Fowler, Harmon R., Jr. "Selected Variables Related to Differential Costs of Programs in Community Colleges." Unpublished doctoral dissertation, University of Florida, 1970. 142 pp.

Frederick, Lawrence M. "Origin and Development of Industrial Education in New Mexico." University of Missouri, 1955.

Fringer, Harry A. "A Century of Vocational Education Concepts. 1848-1948." Rutgers University, 1949.

Fryer, Douglas H. "Intelligence and Interest in Vocational Adjustment; A Statistical Study." Clark University, 1923.

Gibson, Charles H. "The Development of a Model for Utilizing the Techniques of Cost-benefit Analysis in the Evaluation of Vocational Programs." Unpublished doctoral dissertation, University of Kentucky 1968. 154 pp.

Gilliland, Hugh R. "Attitude of Slum Versus Suburban Dwellers toward Manual Occupations and Vocational Education." Unpublished doctoral dissertation, University of Missouri, 1967.

Grover, Jerry D. "The Status of Industrial Arts in the Secondary Schools of Hawaii, 1967-1968." Unpublished doctoral dissertation, Brigham Young University, 1968. 234 pp.

Gruber, Herbert H. "A State Plan for Subsidizing Vocational Education in Pennsylvania." Pennsylvania State University, 1942.

Grywalski, Stanley. "A History of Technical-vocational Education in the Secondary Schools of Alberta, 1900-1969." Unpublished doctoral dissertation, University of Oregon, 1973. 482 pp.

Hackett,. Donald F. "The Status and Needs for Industrial Education in Georgia." University of Missouri, 1953.

Hall, Clyde W. "A Survey of Industrial Education for Negroes in the United States." Bradley University, 1953.

Hampton, Thomas E. "A Survey of Technical Occupations in Louisiana with Implications for Technical Education." Cornell University, 1951.

Hathaway, Jesse E. "The Organization and Administration of Trade and Industrial Education in California Secondary Schools." University of Southern California, 1948.

Hayes, Glenn E. "Work Experience Education Programs in California: Status and Appraisals." Unpublished doctoral dissertation, University of California at Los Angeles, 1971. 278 pp.

Heinsohn, Marvin E. "Equalization of Local Tax Rates Required to Finance Vocational Education." Unpublished doctoral dissertation, University of California (Los Angeles), 1973. 119 pp.

Hendrix, William F. "Construction of an Instrument for Use in Designing High School Programs of Vocational Education." Unpublished doctoral dissertation, University of Arizona, 1967. 238 pp.

Hill, Charles R. "A Study of the Status and Need for Industrial Education in Missouri." University of Missouri, 1950.

Hill, James L. A Study of the Various Aspects of Industrial Arts as Influenced portunities." Unpublished doctoral dissertation, Brigham Young University, 1950." University of Pennsylvania, 1953.

Hinrichs, Roy S. "The Need for Technical Education in the New Orleans Area, with Implications for the Delgade Technical Institute." University of Missouri, 1963.

Hirschi, Harvey C. "A Study of the Economic Value of Technical Education." Unpublished doctoral dissertation, University of Utah, 1969.

Howard, William J. "Vocational Decision-making Ability and Its Relationship to a Theory of Thinking." Unpublished doctoral dissertation, University of Rochester, 1973. 185 pp.

Howe, Trever G. "Pilot Study of Vocational-technical Education in 12 North Iowa Counties." Iowa State University, 1963.

James, Calvin. "Industrial Arts Education in Arizona." University of Arizona, 1963.

Jochen, Albert E. "The History and Development of State and Federally Aided Trade and Industrial Schools in New Jersey, from Their Inception to 1943." Rutgers University, 1947.

Johnston, Richard E. "The History of Trade and Industrial Education in Ohio." Unpublished doctoral dissertation, Ohio State University, 1971. 312 pp.

Jones, Darrell G. "An Evaluation of the Socio-psychological and Socio-economic Effects of MDTA Training on Trainees in Selected Michigan Programs." Unpublished doctoral dissertation, Michigan State University, 1967.

Judd, William P. "The Status of Present and Projected Vocational-technical Training Programs in the State of Utah and Related Occupational Opportunities." Unpublished doctoral dissertation, Brigham Young University, 1971. 467 pp.

Karnes, Morris R. "Evolving Concepts of Industrial Education in the Thinking of Organized Labor." University of Missouri, 1948.

Keener, Clyde. "A Study of the General Education Contributions of Industrial Arts." University of California at Los Angeles, 1959.

Keller, Louise, J. "Principles for Vocational Education-Validation of

Statements of Belief Selected from the Literature and Research." Unpublished doctoral dissertation, Montana State University, 1969. 189 pp.

King, Thomas G. "Fundamental Procedures of Research for Industrial Education." Wayne University, 1959.

Klingensmith, Ralph E. "A Study of the In-school Work Projects of the National Youth Administration in West Virginia." New York University, 1943.

Kohrman, George E. "An Analysis of the Activities, Training and Opinions of Coordinators of Cooperative Vocational Education." University of Missouri, 1952. 214 pp.

Leavitt, Murray P. "A Proposed Model for the Vertical Extension of Technical Education in the Community College." Unpublished doctoral dissertation, University of California, Berkeley, 1970. 220 pp.

Linton. Thomas E. "A Historical Examination of the Purposes and Practices of the Education Program of the United Automobile Workers of America, 1936-59," University of Michigan, 1961.

Luy, Jack Andrew. "Backgrounds, Occupational Aspirations and Attitudes of Unemployed Youth in a MDTA Program in St. Louis, Mo." University of Missouri, 1964.

Lynn, William L. "Resident Taxpayer and Industrial Attitude and Support and Student Attitude, Support and Interest in a Vocational Education Facility in Butte, Lawrence and Meade Counties of Western South Dakota." Unpublished doctoral dissertation, University of South Dakota, 1968. 226 pp.

McBryde, Neal M. "The Role of Industry in Public Secondary Vocational Education in Medium-sized School Systems." Unpublished doctoral dissertation, Texas A&M University, 1973. 160 pp.

McCullough, Lloyd M. "Attitudes of Selected Black Students toward Secondary-level Vocational Education." Unpublished doctoral dissertation, University of California (Los Angeles) , 1974. 156 pp.

McElheny, John R. "Industrial Education in Puerto Rico: An Evaluation of the Program in 'Operation Bootstrap' from 1948 to 1958." Ohio State University, 1960.

McGrath, William J. "History of Vocational Education." Unpublished doctoral dissertation, New York University, 1913. 154 pp.

MacLeech, Bert. "Workers' Education in the United States." Harvard University, 1951.

McNeil, Jackson M. "A Study of Vocational Education as Perceived by Principals in Thirty-two High Schools." Unpublished doctoral dissertation, Auburn University, 1968. 424 pp.

Magisos, Joel H. "An Analysis of Factors Associated with Perception of Role by State Supervisors of Vocational Education." Unpublished doctoral dissertation, Ohio State University, 1968. 241 pp.

Mahoney, William. "Industrial Art in General Education." Columbia University, 1956.

Marshall, Charles R. "Criteria for the Development of Guidelines for an Information-decision Model for Vocational Education." Unpublished doctoral dissertation, Washington State University, 1971. 142 pp.

Martin, Waldo D. "The Identification of Occupational Areas of Emphasis in Vocational Education Program Planning." Unpublished doctoral dissertation, University of Illinois at Urbana-Champaign, 1970. 149 pp.

Massie, Jean E. "The Identification of the Processes of Vocational Education Administration." Unpublished doctoral dissertation, Oregon State University,. 1973. 219 pp.

Mayer, Herbert C. "Democratic Vocational Education." Harvard University, 1941.

Melendez, Juan R. "A Study of the Puerto Rican Technical Cooperation Program in Selected Vocational Schools." University of Tennessee, 1961.

Menengat, Paul A. "History of Trade and Industrial Education in Oregon." Oregon State University, 1953.

Messana, Joseph. "The In-school Youth Work Training Program in the Detroit Public Schools: an Evaluation." Unpublished doctoral dissertation, Wayne State University, 1967.

Meyers, Larry D. "A Skilled Needs Survey with Implications for Vocational-technical Education within the Iowa Western Community College District Area XIII Including Douglas and Sarpy Counties of Metropolitan Omaha, Nebraska." Unpublished doctoral dissertation, Iowa State University, 1968. 262 pp.

Milam, Thomas R. "Vocational Education in Selected High Schools." Unpublished doctoral dissertation, Auburn University, 1968. 444 pp.

Miller, Murray L. "Development of Factors Relating to Industrial Arts Education in School Surveys." University of Pittsburgh, 1947.

Morgan Jack Ward. "Factors Influencing the Passage of Federal Legislation for Vocational Education." University of Missouri, 1951.

Murbach, Nelson J. "Development of Area Vocational School Programs in New York State." New York University, 1949.

Navara, James L. "Analysis of Opinions of Teacher-coordinators, Administrators, and Guidance Counselors Concerning Cooperative Vocational Education." Unpublished doctoral dissertation, Oregon State University, 1974. 174 pp.

Neasham, Ernest R. "Faculty Acceptance of Organizational Values in the Junior College as Indicated by Disposition toward Vocational Education." Unpublished doctoral dissertation, University of California, Berkeley, 1968. 297 pp.

Neff, William L. "A Study of Federally Reimbursed Vocational Education in the State of North Dakota." Stanford University, 1942.

Nicholson, Davis. "Why Adults Attend School: An Analysis of Motivating Factors." University of Missouri, 1948.

Ogle, Robert L. "The Status of Industrial Arts in the Public Junior and Senior High Schools of West Tennessee." University of Tennessee, 1962.

Olsen, Fred Alfred. "Industrial Arts in the Public Secondary Schools of the State of Washington." Ohio State University, 1962.

Parks, Darrell L. "Attitudes and Principles Regarding Vocational Education in Ohio." Unpublished doctoral dissertation, Ohio State University, 1968. 176 pp.

Penny, Forest L. "Origin and Development of Industrial Education in Kansas." University of Missouri, 1960.

Phillips, Augustus C. "Industrial Education for Negroes in the South Atlantic Region — Development of a Program Based on Population and Occupational Changes." University of Ohio, 1942.

Pitale, Anthony J. "An Analysis and Comparison of Selected Roles for State Advisory Councils on Vocational Education." Unpublished doctoral dissertation, University of California (Los Angeles), 1973. 129 pp.

Polk, Harold J. "Characteristics of Directors of Area Vocational-technical Schools." Unpublished doctoral dissertation, University of Missouri, 1969 110 pp.

Pratt, Arden L. "An Appraisal of the Impact of Federal Funds Granted Under Section 4(a) of the Vocational Education Act of 1963 on the Occupational Programs Offered by the Public Two-year Colleges in New York State." Unpublished doctoral dissertation, State University of New York at Buffalo, 1968. 470 pp.

Price, Carroll S. "Instructional Innovations in Public Junior College Occupational Programs." Unpublished doctoral dissertation, University of California, Los Angeles, 1968. 235 pp.

Quinton, Johnny D. "The Effectiveness of an Industrial Education Program." University of Houston, 1961.

Rabenstein, John Earl, Jr. "A Study of the Employably Handicapped and Vocational Rehabilitation in an Economically Depressed Area." University of Pittsburgh, 1964.

Raichle, Henry F. "A Cost-utility Analysis of a Selected Post-secondary Vocational-technical Education Program." Unpublished doctoral dissertation, Florida State University, 1969. 137 pp.

Reed, Howard O. "Evaluation of Industrial Arts in Secondary Schools of Illinois. University of Illinois, 1948.

Robinson, Walter J. "Origin and Development of Industrial Education in Louisiana." University of Missouri, 1950.

Romano, Louis A. "Manual and Industrial Education at Girard College, 1831-1965: an Era in American Educational Experimentation." Unpublished doctoral dissertation, New York University, 1975. 414 pp.

Ross, Herbert J. "Guidelines for Serving Youth with Special Needs in Vocational Education Programs." Unpublished doctoral dissertation, Temple University, 1971. 153 pp.

Russell, Harvey R. "Patterns of Cooperation Between Industry and Education." Columbia University, Teachers College. 1956.

Sams, Denver. "Implications of Automation for Industrial Education." University of Indiana, 1961.

Schmitt, Victor. "Employee Education in the Nation's Basic Industries." Cornell University, 1953.

Seidel, John Jacob. "A Plan for Studying Vocational-industrial and Vocational-technical Education Programs." University of Maryland, 1951.

Sewell, David O. "Training the Poor: A Benefit-cost Analysis of Vocational Instruction in the United States Anti-poverty Program." Unpublished doctoral dissertation, Duke University, 1971. 310 pp.

Shank, Bruce C. "The Role of Vocational Education in the Secondary Schools of the United States." University of Denver, 1956.

Shibata, Kenneth E. "A Program to Determine Educational Needs in the Field of Vocational Education in Local School Districts." University of Nebraska Teachers College, 1965.

Shibler, Herman L. "Cooperative Vocational Education and the Public High School." University of Ohio, 1942.

Silvey, Wray D. "Ability and Scholastic Success in High School and College of Diversified Occupations Students Versus Nondiversified Occupations Students." University of Missouri, 1950.

Slattery, Raymond A. "Economic and Social Variables Associated with Vocational-technical Education." Unpublished doctoral dissertation, University of California at Berkeley, 1969. 136 pp.

Spinti, Robert J. "The Development of Trade and Industrial Education in Wisconsin." Unpublished doctoral dissertation, University of Missouri, Columbia, 1968. 399 pp.

Stahl, Edgar E. "The Scope, Organization, and Principles of Vocational-technical Training in Industry." University of Indiana, 1960.

Stuart, Chipman G. "Industrial Arts and Vocational Education: Their History and Present Position in Texas." Unpublished doctoral dissertation, University of Texas, Austin, 1968. 232 pp.

Svendsen, Ethan A. T. "The Matrix of a Philosophy for Industrial Arts Education." University of Minnesota, 1961.

Taylor, Cyrus B. "Mechanic Arts Programs in Land-grant Colleges Established for Negroes. A Study of the Type and Status of the Programs Operating and an Analysis of Selected Factors that Influenced the Development of these Programs." University of Minnesota, 1955.

Thomas, Wilbert R. "Career Education: a Process Evaluation." Unpublished doctoral dissertation, University of Minnesota, 1974. 306 pp.

Thompson, James Joseph. "Concepts of Automation with Implications for Public Education." University of Florida, 1964.

Thrower, Robert G. " The Status and Adequacy of Industrial Arts Programs in the Public Secondary Schools of North Carolina." Ohio State University, 1963.

Tunkel, Leon S. "Policies and Procedures in Adult Vocational-industrial Education in New York State Based on a Consideration of the History and Development of the Program, 1917 to the Present." New York University, 1961.

Urgell, Francisca C. "The Development and Contemporary Problems of Vocational Education in Puerto Rico." Pennsylvania State University, 1942.

vander Linde, Albert. "Emerging Models for Financing Area Vocational Technical Schools." Unpublished doctoral dissertation, Colorado State University, 1971. 190 pp.

Wasden, Jed W. "A Study of Trade and Industrial Education in Utah." Unpublished doctoral dissertation, Brigham Young University, 1968. 164. pp.

Wockenfuss, William A. "Sociological Bases of Industrial Arts for Secondary Schools." University of Florida, 1960.

Wooden, Ralph L. "Industrial Arts in the Public Secondary School Programs for Negroes in North Carolina." Ohio University, 1956."

Zweilbe, Malcolm C. "A Proposal for Developing and Financing Junior College Vocational-technical Centers in Rhode Island." Unpublished doctoral dissertation, Columbia University, 1968. 226 pp.

IV. RETROSPECTIVE AND CURRENT JOURNALS

American Vocational Journal. (1925 —)
Issued monthly, September through May.

Apprenticeship Bulletin. Published by School of Printing, North End Union, Boston, Mass. Printed by the Pupils of the School. (Monthly)
Contains abstracts and current items on trade teaching and trade schools.

College and University Personnel Association. Journal. (1949)
Issued quarterly, in winter, spring, summer, and fall.

College Board Review. (1947 —)
Issued quarterly.

College Student Journal. 1966 —)
Issued quarterly.

Counselor Education and Supervision. (1961 —)
Issued quarterly, in September, December, March, and June.

Die Arbeitschule. Edited by Dr. Alwin Pabst. Leipzig, Germany. Published by Messrs. Quelle & Meyer, 14 Krenzstrasse, Leipzig, Germany. (Monthly)

Educational Handwork. Edited by George F. Johnson, Liverpool, England.
Official organ of the Educational Handwork Association. Published by Messrs. Percy Lund Humphries & Co., Ltd., Bradford, England. (Monthly)

Elementary School Guidance and Couseling. (1965 —)
Issued quarterly, in October, December, March, and May.

Engineering Education. (Formerly *Journal of Engineering Education.*)
(1894 —)
Issued eight times each year, October through May.

Guidance Exchange. (1960 —)
Issued annually, in February.

Industrial Education. (Formerly *Industrial Arts and Vocational Education.*) (1914 —)
Issued nine times each year, September through May/June.

Journal of Aerospace Education. (1974 —)
Issued 10 times each year, September through June.

Journal of Architectural Education. (1912 —)
Issued quarterly, in August, November, March, and June.

Journal of College Placement. (1940 —)
Issued four times each year, in October-November, December-January, February-March, and April-May.

Journal of College Student Personnel. (1959 —)
Issued six times each year, in January, March, May, July, September, and November.

Journal of Counseling and Values. (1955 —)
Issued quarterly, in October, January, April, and July.

Journal of Employment Counseling. (1964 —)
Issued quarterly, in March, June, September, and December.

Journal of Environmental Education. (1969 —)
Issued quarterly.

Journal of Industrial Teacher Education. (1962 —)
Issued quarterly, in fall, winter, spring, and summer.

Man/Society/Technology. (1940 —)
Issued eight times each year, in September-October, November, December, January, February, March, April, and May-June.

Manual Training. Edited by John Arrowsmith, Halifax, N. S.
Official Organ National Association of Manual Training Teachers. Published at Byron House, 85 Fleet Street, London, E. C., England. (Monthly)

Manual Training Magazine. Edited by Charles A. Bennett. Published by The Manual Arts Press, Peoria, Ill. (Bimonthly)

Measurement and Evaluation in Guidance. (1968 —)
Issued quarterly, in April, July, October, January.

National Association for Women Deans, Administrators, and Counselors. Journal. (Formerly *National Association of Women Deans and Counselors. Journal.*) (1916 —)
Issued quarterly, in fall, winter, spring, and summer.

National Association of College Admissions Counselors. Journal. (Formerly *Association of College Admissions Counselors. Journal.*) (1937 —)
    Issued quarterly.

National Association of Colleges and Teachers of Agriculture. Journal. (1957 —)
    Issued four times each year, in March, June, September, and December.

Personnel and Guidance Journal. (1922 —)
    Issued 10 times each year, except July and August.

Revista de Educacion. Published by the Sociedad General de Publicaciones, Diputacion, 211, Barcelona, Spain.

School Counselor. (1942 —)
    Issued five times each year, in September, November, January, March, and May.

School Shop. (1941 —)
    Issued monthly, September through June.

Schoolcraft. Edited by W. A. Milton, "Bryghte Holme," Berea, Johannesburg, South Africa. Published by Messrs. J. C. Juta & Co., P. O. Box 1010, Johannesburg, South Africa.

Student Personnel Association for Teacher Education. Journal. (1961 —)
    Issued quarterly, in fall, winter, spring, and summer.

Technical Education News. (1941 —)
    Issued periodically during the shool year.

Vocational Education. Edited by Charles A. Bennett, Peoria, Ill. Published by The Manual Arts Press, German Fire Insurance Building, Peoria, Ill. (Bi-monthly)

Vocational Guidance Quarterly. (1952 —)
    Issued four times each year, in September, December, March, and June.

AUTHOR INDEX

SUBJECT INDEX